DATE DUE

THE AMERICAN MANUFACTORY

THE AMERICAN MANUFACTORY

Art, Labor, and the World of Things
in the Early Republic

LAURA RIGAL

PRINCETON UNIVERSITY PRESS
PRINCETON, NEW JERSEY

Library of Congress Cataloging-in-Publication Data
Rigal, Laura, 1958–
The American manufactory : art, labor, and the world of things
in the early republic / Laura Rigal.
p. cm.
Includes bibliographical references and index.
ISBN 0-691-01558-9 (CL : alk. paper)
1. Philadelphia (Pa.)—Intellectual life—18th century.
2. Philadelphia (Pa.)—Intellectual life—19th century.
3. Artisans—Pennsylvania—Philadelphia—History—18th century.
4. Artisans—Pennsylvania—Philadelphia—History—19th century.
5. Industrialization—Social aspects—Pennsylvania—Philadelphia—
History. 6. Art, American—Pennsylvania—Philadelphia—
Themes, motives. 7. Art, Modern—18th century—Pennsylvania—
Philadelphia—Themes, motives. 8. Art, Modern—19th century—
Pennsylvania—Philadelphia—Themes, motives.
9. Enlightenment—United States—Case studies. I. Title
F158.44.R55 1998
973.4—dc21   98-7152

For Trish, Jacob, and Zofia

CONTENTS

ILLUSTRATIONS

ACKNOWLEDGMENTS

I FIRST began to think about the early industrial Delaware Valley while in California, at Stanford, where Sam Edwards, Jr., Jay Fliegelman, George Dekker, Mary Louise Pratt, and David C. Miller all supported my erratic growth with a generosity I will never forget. I was equally fortunate to be associated with the graduate students of the Departments of English and Modern Thought and Literature at Stanford and with the Stanford Humanities Center, where I received a fellowship in 1989 for which I remain grateful. It was in the company of, among others, Doree Allen, Lydia Fillingham, Nancy Glazener, Deidre Lynch, Paula McDowell, Trudy Palmer, and Katie Trumpener that I began to read Marcuse, Benjamin, Arendt, Foucault, Baudrillard, and Barthes, during the years of Reagan's presidency, a time, like now, of profound political retrenchment, institutional cynicism, and rampant technological change. Most of us arrived in Palo Alto with typewriters in tow and proceeded to swim out into a backwash of utopia, a tide of critical and political commitments that were much older and far more complicated than the mere legacy of '67 or '68—though that was there too. I came from a canal town in Ohio and, after that, from Oberlin, near Kent, and so I was somewhat equipped for the swim back and out—and for resistance to the curious scenery of the South Bay. This book is the fruit of that time.

In the 1990s, at the University of Chicago, I began to explicitly frame the labor-making, art-producing world of the American Enlightenment as an affair of visual and graphic art, as well as of writing, rhetoric, and social and political history. I am deeply indebted to the Department of English, to the American Studies Workshop at Chicago, and, in particular, to the observations and advice of Lauren Berlant, James Chandler, Gerald Graff, Beth Helsinger, Curtis Marez, Richard Strier, Tom Mitchell, Joshua Scodel, and Jay Schleusener. I am grateful as well to the graduate students in my seminars and in the American Studies, Feminist Theory, and Early American Cultures Workshops for the ways their insight and criticism inspired, and often redirected, me; to Loren Kruger for her unforgettable example of learning, intelligence, and commitment; and to William Veeder for his remarkable care and insight as a reader. This book would simply not have been written at all without the friendship and help of Bill Brown, Zofia Burr, Janice Knight, Christopher Looby, Trish Loughran, Lisa Ruddick, and Alok Yadov. It would not have been written, furthermore, without the work and many kindnesses of Anna-Maria Alvarado and her children Adam and Selene; without the care, time, and skill of Caryle Perlman;

nor without the child care, the gifts of books, food, paper, potting soil, conversation, and affection provided variously by Charlie (Beatrice) Gibbons, Rahul and Anya Chatterjee, Paula McQuade, James Navarre, Cherie Coleman, Tony Hill, Kyle Greenwald, Marie Nguyen, Tim Cook, and Alexia Hultman.

I have relied continuously since 1990 upon the conversation and support of Fredrika Teute at the Institute for Early American History and Culture; lately, here in Iowa City, the fine friendship and beautiful books of Richard Horwitz and Eduardo Cadava have helped to sustain and integrate my thinking. It has been deeply satisfying to work with Deborah Malmud and Victoria Wilson-Schwartz at Princeton University Press, while, over the years, research and editorial assistants Nina Marks, Jon Sachs, and Russell Peterson have been resourceful, imaginative, and tolerant beyond anything I could have expected. My extended family, my parents Joan and R. Daniel, my brothers Dan and Ted, and my grandmother Edna Rigal have all taught me practices of intellectual engagement, memory making, and hopeful improvisation upon which I continue to rely. My son Jacob Rigal (now eight years old) is a continual joy; his interests and concerns mark these pages at every turn. Above all, though, it is to Trish Loughran, the most lovely writer, rhetorician, and editor I have ever encountered, that I owe the greatest debt. Her companionship and her work with me on this manuscript—her repeated instructions, in particular, on the art of transition—are now inseparable from the useful and radically critical book that you are about to read.

THE AMERICAN MANUFACTORY

The Extended Republic in
the Age of Manufactures

W HAT MIGHT an American farmer say at the end of the American Revolution when asked to explain how he came by fame, fortune, and celebrity? In St. John de Crèvecoeur's semifictional letter "A Visit to Mr. Bertram, the Celebrated Pennsylvania Botanist" (1784), the character Bertram traces it all back to a sudden, inexplicable insight into the structure of a daisy, which as a farmer he had not previously regarded as useful, enjoyable, or productive of value: "[O]ne day," Bertram recounts,

> I was very busy in holding my plough (for thee see'st that I am but a ploughman), and being weary, I ran under the shade of a tree to repose myself. I cast my eyes on a daisy; I plucked it mechanically and viewed it with more curiosity than common country farmers are wont to do, and observed therein very many distinct parts, some perpendicular, some horizontal. "What a shame," said my mind, or something that inspired my mind, "that thee shouldest have employed so many years in tilling the earth and destroying so many flowers and plants without being acquainted with their structures and their uses!" . . . I hired a man to plough for me and went to Philadelphia.[1]

Crèvecoeur's Bertram is a portrait of the famous Pennsylvania botanist and traveler John Bartram (1699–1777), who lived just outside Philadelphia, and was a cofounder of the American Philosophical Society, a friend of Benjamin Franklin, and "Botanist Royal" to King George III.[2] In this passage, as throughout his *Letters from an American Farmer,* Crèvecoeur is preoccupied with probing and parodying the economically invested, curiously knowing quality of successfully self-made Americans like Bertram/ Bartram who present themselves as rural innocents, inspired ploughmen, and disinterested informants. Crèvecoeur's "Visit to Mr. Bertram" subtly parodies the uncertain origin of the Quaker botanist's transition from labor to visual literacy: is Bertram's initial relationship to the daisy randomly mechanical or the product of an already informed interest ("I plucked it mechanically and viewed it with more curiosity than common country farmers are wont to do . . .")? What is the origin of the voice that speaks to him and seems to partake at once of his mind and his body (or "brain"), of divine inspiration, desire, and ambition (". . . said my mind, or something that inspired my mind . . .")? And where does a simple ploughman suddenly find the economic resources to "hire a man to plough" for him and to venture to Philadelphia, the home of the American Philosophical Society and the privileged scene of the American Enlightenment?

Whatever the cause, Bertram leaves his plough and goes to Philadelphia. There he visits a bookseller and, though he claims that he "[knows] not what book to call for," buys a Latin grammar. With the help of a neighbor, the ploughman quickly learns "Latin enough to understand Linnaeus" and obtains a copy of the *Systema Naturae* (1735), Carl Linnaeus's system of botanical classification. He then begins "to botanize all over [his] farm" and, gradually, throughout Pennsylvania and Maryland, until, remarkably, within several years, he has "acquired a pretty general knowledge of every plant and tree to be found in our continent." Now, after decades of traveling and posting letters, plants, and seeds to Europe, Bertram is "made easy," and, having "ceased to labour," spends his time primarily in "see[ing] and convers[ing] with . . . friends."[3]

It is the reference to Linnaeus that explains the "many distinct parts, some perpendicular, some horizontal" emerging from—or discovered in—Bertram's daisy. These "parts" refer to the horizontal white petals on the one hand and on the other to the daisy's yellow center, which, jutting up "perpendicularly" from the petals, contains the sexual parts of the plant.[4] Sexual dimorphism was one aspect of the Linnaean system, according to which the entire universe of plants could be categorized by genus and species and introduced into representation through their organic structure or, rather, the "parts" that simultaneously articulated structure and identity.

Foucault has argued that what made plant rather than animal structure the founding object of Linnaean science was that plants resembled lines. Contrasted with animals, plants had no anatomical "insides" and thereby constituted pure extension; their parts appeared virtually skeletal. Moreover, the empirical, written descriptions of plants prescribed by Linnaean science were designed to be graphic in their capacity to transmute organic parts into words. As Foucault points out, according to "the botanical calligrams dreamed of by Linnaeus," when "the four variables of extension (number, form, proportion, and situation) were applied to the five parts of any plant (roots, stem, leaves, flowers, fruits), the plant could be considered as having passed completely into language." In short, Linnaean science offered a remarkable new kind of access to nature; its technologies promised the possibility of actual representation whereby word and image, writing and drawing, were transparently one with nature's works in the "herbarium of the world."[5] Or, as the Philadelphia museum proprietor

Charles Willson Peale so often repeated, the "Book of Nature" lay open to any reader, viewer, and would-be naturalist who possessed the "Ariadne thread" of classification that allowed him to read it systematically, or "leaf by leaf."[6]

As a key to natural language, then, Linnaean science generated a sudden, explosive division and proliferation in the knowable forms of organic life. By the mid-eighteenth century, the empirical practices of collection, description, illustration, classification, publication, and display had helped bring into being whole new fields of knowledge, radically expanding the field of visibility to embrace what was previously obscure—from Pennsylvania daisies to American farmers. With the *Systema Naturae* in hand, any provincial farmer or mechanic had access to a global organizational system through which all plants (and, eventually, insects, birds, and quadrupeds) emerged into visibility and knowability, precisely as if, at the moment of their creation, they had been stamped with a species identity by some original Author of all being. The subjects and the objects of new fields emerged together wherever provincial naturalists used the Linnaean system to make themselves the founders and framers of, among other things, American ornithology, paleontology, conchology, mineralogy, ichthyology, entomology, and so on.[7]

However, Crèvecoeur's "Visit to Mr. Bertram" also articulates a series of disjunctions in the farmer's fantasy of transparent, or actual, representation. Despite farmer Bertram's claim to spontaneous insight, "A Visit to Mr. Bertram" asks, Who is "the true" or original Bertram/Bartram? What is the relationship between the inner and outer man? And can Quaker "friendliness" sometimes be just another face of social climbing and economic calculation? Such questions suggest that when a laborer turns curious, his emergence into literary life cannot be separated from social ambition. This sketch of Linnaean character is just one of Crèvecoeur's many ironic and skeptical inquiries into the possibility of natural literacy, or the self-evident truth and virtue of American "farmers."[8] These inquiries extend to questions of political and national virtue wherever Bertram/Bartram admonishes his reader that the self-representations of the American Revolution, and of the American Enlightenment in general, were never simple, innocent, or natural.

But there are other meanings here which go well beyond Crèvecoeur's ironic, even reactionary, limning of ambiguous character. These meanings lie in the relationship of Linnaean representational practices to the cultural creation and division of labor. The most revelatory aspect of Crèvecoeur's "Visit" is the connection it makes and displays between labor and looking. Bertram's first glimpse into the Book of Nature, for example, begins when he is at rest from ploughing. It is furthered when he "hire[s] a man to plough" for him and sets forth to buy books in Philadelphia. And it comes to fruition when he ceases from labor entirely, to become an American character in his own right: a celebrated specimen, accessible to any literary visitor/viewer who might stumble across him, by accident or design.[9] What Bartram saw in the daisy, then, was not just the story of his own making as a botanist but a representational mechanism that divided labor and constituted class. It is, in fact, as a sketch of productive labor itself emerging as the (reproductive) ground of multiple representational technologies (collection, classification, publication, exhibition, illustration) that Bertram's encounter with the daisy is so articulate, and Crève-coeur's "Visit to Mr. Bertram" so much more than a gently parodic portrait of an American farmer.

Like Crèvecoeur's "Visit," this book connects the emergence of visual and literary culture in the late-eighteenth-century United States with the creation and division of labor. And—like Bertram—this book turns to Philadelphia, the home of the American Philosophical Society, the nation's political capital from 1791 to 1801, the center of the American Enlightenment and of Revolutionary and Constitutional nation building as it emerged together with the division of labor. Historians as diverse as Thomas Cochran, Richard S. Dunn, and Sharon Salinger have traced the origins of industrialism in the United States to institutional, technological, and demographic transformations in late-eighteenth-century Philadelphia. Cochran, in particular, notes the institutional diversity of these changes. Long before the American Revolution, Cochran observes, Philadelphia was a center of banking and financial innovation. The largest city in British North America, Philadelphia was the commercial hub of a geographically central agricultural state. The development of banking and finance in the city was a response to this geography, as well as to the expansion and concentration of capital in the Delaware Valley during the Seven Years War (1754–63) and the American and French Revolutions. It was in these years that Philadelphia's merchants and financial leaders created the financial institutions that would be essential to industrial development in the nineteenth century: the Bank of North America (founded in 1781), the Bank of the United States (1791), the Philadelphia stock exchange (1792), the Bank of Pennsylvania (1794), and various mutual fire and maritime insurance companies.[10] With the institution of reforms in laws regarding bankruptcy and incorporation after the American Revolution, capital was pooled and invested with increasing ease; the improved efficiency and "liquidity" of exchange led the French traveler de Chastellux to observe as early as 1782 that "Philadelphia is so to speak, the great sink wherein all the speculation of America terminates and mingles."[11]

Similarly, both Richard Dunn and Sharon Salinger have argued that the employment of "free" or temporary and itinerant wage laborers (many of whom were also recent immigrants) distinguished the rise of American industry in Philadelphia from early industrialization in New England, where factories such as the Lowell Mills drew their laborers from local, largely rural populations (the sons and daughters of New England farmers).[12] In the Middle Colonies, and especially in Philadelphia, Dunn observes, "both immigrant and native-born, unskilled and semi-skilled workers were thrown onto the free wage market"—in marked contrast with other regional labor systems ("family labor" in New England; slave plantations in the Caribbean; mixed chattel slavery and family labor in the Chesapeake). But, if a distinctive wage labor system originated in the Middle Colonies, it did not remain there. The long-term significance of "the Philadelphia system" lay, in part, in its extension to western cities, such as Pittsburgh. As Dunn puts it, "The Philadelphia method, with its increasing reliance upon underpaid wage labor supplied by a pool of un-skilled and semi-skilled casual workers, was exploitative and inhumane, but it too was a functional method that capitalist entrepreneurs would utilize as they built new western cities and recruited factory workers after the Revolution."[13]

Social and labor historians such as Salinger have provided us with the details of the system of temporary and wage labor that emerged in the Delaware Valley—while reminding us that the years between the Revolution's end and Andrew Jackson's election (1828) saw uneven but intensifying industrialization and increasingly visible class division throughout the urban northeast. John Commons, Philip Foner, Eric Foner, David Montgomery, Sean Wilentz, Alfred Young, Gary Nash, Bruce Laurie, Billy Smith, Stephen Rosswurm, Cynthia Shelton, and Ronald Schultz, among others, all remind scholars that the "making" of an American working class was visible and legible already in 1776, if not well before.[14] But, while these historians put labor and class at the center of the American Revolution and the Constitutional period, students of literature and art history rarely integrate this scholarship directly into their accounts of early national texts and objects.[15] The reasons for this are many but, insofar as social and labor historians demonstrate (inarguably) that the late eighteenth century was a period of industrialization in the United States, they place a demand on students of culture. Cultural studies of federalism must offer some account of the visibly emerging phenomenon that labor history calls class formation but that might also be called the postwar, early industrial reorganization of property and privilege, coming unevenly but vividly into view in the years immediately after the American Revolution (that is, well before Jackson's presidency—or the publication of Emerson's *Nature*).

On their side, of course, social, labor, and economic historians have not been particularly concerned to pursue an observation they themselves often make—that the growing division, rationalization, and (even) mechanization of labor in the early national period was a phenomenon of culture.[16] One reason for this lack of concern is, no doubt, the real difficulty of keeping in view the mutually constitutive relationship of labor and culture. The cultural constitution of labor only really becomes clear, for example, when one considers the remarkable range of sites in which it occurred. The making of American labor was not simply caused by the exploitation of real, or actual, producers in factories; it emerged as the artifact of myriad representational structures, or, as this book argues, via a dense, multiply mediated "cultural production of production." This book, therefore, traces the uneven emergence of labor and class in the early industrial Northeast by considering episodes of cultural production and display that brought multiple (verbal and visual) media into play— and into contradiction with each other: Philadelphia's massive craft procession in honor of the Constitution's ratification (the Grand Federal Procession of 1788); the autobiographical writing of steamboat inventor John Fitch (1744–98); the exhumation and exhibition of "the first American mastodon" skeleton during Jefferson's presidency (1801–9); the publication of the *Port Folio*, the nation's first long-running magazine of print miscellany; the assembly of the first *American Ornithology* (9 vols.; 1807–14) by a Scots dialect poet named Alexander Wilson; and, finally, the arrest of the Philadelphia locksmith Pat Lyon for bank robbery and his eventual transformation in John Neagle's portrait *Pat Lyon at the Forge* (1825, 1829) into an icon of the American workingman (and of the steam-engine and railroad industries of Philadelphia). With the significant exception of chapter 4 ("The American Lounger"), which serves largely as a counter-example, each chapter is concerned with the productions, performances, and exhibitions of people who belonged at one time or another to the rank of urban artisan rather than American farmer. These mechanical artists struggled to emerge from obscurity and "rise" in the world via the Enlightenment frameworks of visibility and legibility—or the new representational structures of Independence—emerging around (and through) them.

As demonstrated by John Bertram's journey from his farm to the bookstore in Philadelphia, the making and the management of labor as a collective resource could be found at many sites of production and distribution in federalizing America—in places other than the particular weaving establishments or machine shops where craft production was also being centralized, divided, and mechanized. As the home of the American Philosophical Society and innumerable other learned or improvement societies, Philadelphia was not only the scene of the Continental Congress and the Constitutional Convention; it was the institutional home of what has been called the American Enlightenment.[17] It is in the corporations and professions, the learned organizations and changing trades, the sciences as well as the arts of the Delaware Valley that one finds the cultural constitution and division of labor in the early industrial, or "founding," period. And it is to these sites, therefore, that one looks to find federalism itself.

In 1788, the writing and ratification of the American Constitution was routinely characterized (as it sometimes is today) by metaphors of manufacturing: as a collective forging, framing, or fabricating of a thing called the United States. In fact, these metaphors were not coincidental; they indicate the deep structure of American federalism. While technologies of writing were certainly one form of federalist self-production, federalism must not be reduced to the text and textuality of a written constitution.[18] Rather, federalism was both artifact and agent of the changing technologies of American manufacturing itself, a fabric or frame "raised" not by a single founding document—nor, in turn, by the scattered forms of mechanized production that we associate with late-eighteenth-century industrialization (spinning jennies, steam engines, printing presses)—but, more complexly, by the dense intersections of technologies of representation, technologies that made and displayed production itself as the founding principle of union.[19]

The structuring principle of American federalism is commonly explained as a dynamic equilibrium established by dividing and balancing power in a variety of ways. Within the national government, for example, power is said to be divided between three branches of government, each of which "checks" and "balances" the other so that, among other things, no single branch can fully dominate the rest. The Constitution further institutes balance by separating state and local powers from those of the national government; this distinction between a local and a centralized and nationalized point of view is characterized in the neoclassical republican theory of James Madison, Alexander Hamilton, and James Wilson, among others, as a necessary dominance of an elevated (but knowing) mind over the passions of the body, or of the public good over myriad local interests and investments. Like the raised center of a pyramid, the comparatively higher and wider perspective of the new national government (and within its legislature, of the Senate, as opposed to the House of Representatives) was supposed to balance and focus the seemingly endless diversity of local interests. It was this dynamic, pyramidal structure that marked the emerging oversized republic as a new "species" of confederation within the world of nations. It was in keeping with its expanded spatial dimensions (extended, that is, both horizontally and perpendicularly) that the taxonomists of government dubbed the new nation an "extended republic."[20]

But the extended republic was not merely a species of government; it was a spatial architecture, an extended sphere of visibility, a complex of representational sites outside of (but including) the institutions of government that constituted collectivity through the division, balance, and elevation of power. Critic Tony Bennett has coined the phrase "exhibitionary complex" to describe such an array of cultural technologies. In the great exhibitionary spaces of the nineteenth century (from the Crystal Palace of the 1850s to the Paris Exposition of 1889 and the Chicago Columbian Exposition of 1893), the question of discipline, Bennett argues, becomes "a question of culture," of winning hearts rather than merely disciplining bodies. In the open exhibition of objects arranged and exhibited for public view (and the public good), the populace is invited to see how power works. By touring displays of new inventions, national manufactures, or great works of art, the viewer assumes the point of view of the maker—the founder, framer, organizer, and exhibitor—of the whole. Here, Bennett argues, the viewer receives "object lessons in power—the power to command and arrange things and bodies for public display." The architectural forms of the exhibitionary complex invite people "to become, in seeing themselves from the side of power, both the subjects and the objects of knowledge, knowing power and what power knows, and knowing themselves as (ideally) known by power, interiorizing its gaze as a principle of self-surveillance, and hence, self-regulation."[21]

As the chapters of this book will demonstrate, the exhibitionary "organization of spectacle for large, undifferentiated publics" emerged in the United States in the eighteenth century—together with an increased demand for expertise: the sheer size of the extended republic demanded both an elevated point of view and a representational apparatus for the production of knowledge, whereby bodies and objects might be observed, counted, arranged, classified, displayed, and "diffused" as information. In the early republic, as today, scientific and technological expertise was generated and justified on the grounds of "the public good." In a geographically sprawling confederation, the empirical techniques of collection, classification, and publication in particular appeared as essential representational mechanisms through which innumerable local particulars could, presumably, be brought under collective view so that disinterested decisions could be made by representative bodies at state and national levels. In the early republic, the bureaucratic assembly of useful information was epitomized by (though of course not reducible to) Linnaean science, itself one of the most efficient early industrial technologies for the organization of detail into a newly visible and legible world of things. This book looks, therefore, to precisely such intermediate fields of visibility and legibility in order to argue that, as forums and formats of federalism, the arts and sciences of Philadelphia constituted the extended republic as a set of stages for the performance of production itself. In the exhibitionary spaces and texts of the extended republic, in other words, the crucial term was (to quote a motto of the Peale Museum): "Explore the wondrous *work.*"

It would seem that in early industrial Philadelphia, federalism's curious reliance upon the production and display of works constituted the "stamen and pistil" of social order. At the same time, however, the collections, texts, and exhibitions—the labor-making "organic conceptions" that are the concern of this book—eventuated without the full knowledge or control of the collectors, authors, artists, and actors who produced them. In fact, what most marked the early industrial culture of production was its repetitive and compulsive attributions of agency and originality to anything and everything as a way of licensing itself and multiplying its investments—even while the compulsion testified to its own lack of control. As a study of such structures of self-assembly, this book, therefore, offers itself as a counterassembly—in which details continually resist narrative framing, in which the structure becomes multidimensional, and at times disproportionate, and where parts do not always fit contiguously or neatly into wholes. It is as counterassembly, then, that *The American Manufactory* makes its argument that it was not actual artisan producers—nor labor itself—that produced the extended republic but, rather, a partial, disunified, and multiply mediated culture of production. The works and workers assembled here both raised but also exceeded and resisted the culture of representative self-production that called them to produce—a culture that manufactured "nation" together with "work" and "labor" by joining citizenship to the "abstract concrete labor" of commodity production and by repeatedly repressing that articulation.[22]

It is impossible to comprehend the meaning of the word "art" apart from the long industrialization of the crafts in the United States. In late-eighteenth-century Anglo-America, an artist was a skilled producer of commodities, essentially indistinguishable from a "mechanic," an "artisan," or a "mechanical artist."[23] "Art," in turn, was synonymous with craft, or technical skill, and was typically coupled with "manufactures" or assimilated to "useful knowledge" (as in phrases like "arts and manufactures"). This way of using the words "art" and "artist" does not mean that Philadelphia was without poets or painters. It does mean that poems and paintings were being created, and construed as creations, in the midst of early industrial awareness of (and ambivalence about) the inseparability of "art" from "craft"—where "art" meant the new forms of experience that some Europeans called the aesthetic or, in more popularizing contexts, the fine arts.[24]

But, in order to define the meaning of "art" in federal Philadelphia, it is necessary to frame it in relation to "culture." Understood in the eighteenth-century context of its emergence, "culture" is used here and throughout this book in a double sense, to indicate the emergence together during the European Enlightenment of the disciplines of both aesthetics and the social sciences. Used in this way, "culture" insists that the forms of representation categorized as aesthetic were inseparable from the emergence of the fields of ethnography, political economy, and history—inseparable, that is, from "culture" meaning all human systems: the secular or humanist disciplines organized around the study of Man.[25] It is particularly necessary to keep this double meaning of culture in mind when discussing the late eighteenth century, which (as a period of both industrialization and Enlightenment) saw the emergence of new institutions and professions of culture in both the arts and sciences. Most importantly for this book, the double use of "culture" (to embrace both the arts and the sciences) keeps in view—and under criticism—the inseparability of cultural forms from their own "making." This double use of the word culture, in other words, simply emphasizes the circularity at work in the cultural production of production—in an early-industrial state in which the constitution and division of productive labor through the exhibition and performance of production was a central fact(um) of nation building.

When literary criticism has focused on texts and textuality apart from visual technologies, it has been more likely to forget both labor and class and to follow Jefferson and Crèvecoeur by implicitly reinstating the "husbandman" as the author of national culture. But, in fact, it is the mechanical artist, the artisan producer of the early industrial manufactory, who shows us that federalism is inherently a subject for students of the arts. The early industrial mechanic reveals that art cannot be confined to the disciplinary professions of painting or poetry, but that the arts, in fact, embrace the history of technology. Only when arts and sciences are considered together as structures of representation under the rubric of technology does the significance of the cultural productions of early industrial Philadelphia come into view—together with the deep structure of American federalism. Conversely, it becomes particularly crucial to attend to the instances when a mechanic turns writer. In this book the (peculiarly technographic) writing of mechanics like John Fitch or Patrick Lyon stand in troubled, even counterproductive and nonfederal, relation to the ethics of cultivation traditionally identified with "husbandry" and celebrated by Jeffersonians such as Peale.

As skilled producers, urban artisans in North America bridged what a production-based political economy depended upon breaking apart: skill, or knowledge (sometimes called the "secrets" or "mysteries" of a craft), and labor, or the body's productive activity under the management of the mind.[26] In her study of science, scientific education, and class formation in Britain, Julia Wrigley identifies a "cross-class conviction" during the late eighteenth and early nineteenth centuries "that artisans were the legitimate bearers of technical and . . . scientific knowledge," a conviction that grew "from the reality of employer dependence on artisan skills." It was, Wrigley argues, simply impossible to ignore the relationship between craft skills and technological innovation.[27] As the devisers of new machines that were, at first, impossible to standardize, skilled English machinists (particularly in the metalworking trades) could retain a monopoly on the autonomy and prestige of "the master craftsman" long after industrialization had deprived other tradesmen of traditional forms of economic and social security.[28] At the end of the eighteenth century, Wrigley concludes, advanced technology "was thought to inhere in the persons and knowledge of the artisans themselves, even as capitalists competed to develop new machinery that would reduce their reliance on artisan skills."[29] Here, the figure of the artisan is divided into "knowledge" and "person"; advanced technology is seen to lie both in the mind and in a visibly functional working body.[30] Or, as John Rule has argued, artisans were represented as possessing a "property of skill" that was simultaneously mental and material, a capacity to see into and then change the order of things that both the unskilled laborer and the "idle aristocrat" supposedly lacked.[31] As an ideological projection, the divided figure of the late-eighteenth-century mechanical artist constellates, in his peculiarly divided person(hood), both labor itself *and* labor's (intellectual, cultural, and representational) management.

The word "manufactory" in the title of this book is meant to articulate precisely this division and transformation of the culturally constitutive figure of the mechanical artist by the nation-making devices of representation that constitute (and, in this book, define) federalism as a republic extended gradually, unevenly, and via diverse genres of representation.[32] In *Capital*, Marx uses the word "manufactory" somewhat differently, as Adam Smith does in *The Wealth of Nations*, to mean the division of labor prior to mechanization, as in Smith's example of the pin factory. In this book, the term "manufactory" is used both more broadly and more specifically, to denote, among other things, the uneven, multiform, and variously mediated quality of industrialization in early national Philadelphia—where partial or experimental mechanization frequently accompanied the rationalization of labor and where such changes assumed a remarkable variety of forms across more than fifty crafts or "trades."[33] Mechanical artists in Philadelphia ranged from highly skilled craftsmen (clockmakers, silversmiths, gunsmiths, blacksmiths) to tradesmen with fewer skills (sailmakers, brickmakers, nailers, bread and biscuit bakers). Their arts included the production of light consumer goods—by glovers, shoemakers, tailors, whip and cane manufacturers—as well as more heavily capitalized industries, such as coachmaking, sugar refining, brewing, shipbuilding, carpentry, and their associated crafts.[34] By contrast with the artisan shop, American manufactories were "early factories," in which the production of commodities (hats, books, beer, soap, carriages) had moved beyond the deferential customs, patriarchal households, and preindustrial work patterns of the apprentice system but without, by any means, leaving artisanal forms of social and labor organization behind.[35] A manufactory differed from an artisan shop by gathering artists into a centralized production site (rather than a shop or yard adjacent to a master's household) and by gradually introducing machinery—for grinding, turning, boring, stamping, spinning, weaving, and so on—into the production process. An intermediate, quintessentially mixed mode of production, manufactory production was craft manufacturing in the midst of the gradual, uneven processes of rationalization and mechanization that define mass production.

Some of the first and largest manufactories in the United States were organized in Philadelphia with the aid of PSEMUA, the Pennsylvania Society for the Encouragement of Manufactures and the Useful Arts. Founded in 1787 by Tench Coxe, John Nicholson, and other investors, PSEMUA was a semiprivate, voluntary organization whose mixture of concern for the public good with for-profit enterprise was typical of federalist-era experiments in "improved" commodity production. In 1787, the year of the Constitutional Convention, PSEMUA opened a textile manufactory at the corner of Ninth and Market Streets. When it burned down in 1790 (arson was suspected but never proved), the Guardians of the Poor organized another weaving manufactory at the Philadelphia almshouse that, until 1812, employed dependent paupers and the city's working poor. Both of these establishments assembled weavers under a single roof, so that their work could be observed and, if necessary, reorganized—an arrangement that transformed the relationship of craftsmen not only to their work but also to the men who were (or would have been) their masters. In the early national manufactory, then, craft producers who had served traditional apprenticeships were increasingly more likely to find themselves permanent wage laborers and increasingly less likely to achieve economic "competence" (self-sufficiency) or the status of "master," as would have been expected under a traditional craft apprenticeship, according to which a journeyman begins as an apprentice and ends as a master of his craft. In turn, the position of master of the craft was itself becoming less easy to define, since it had begun to mingle ownership with managerial functions—and with humanitarian concerns about both public order and the welfare of "the industrious poor."[36]

In his report on the growth of manufacturing in the United States between 1787 and 1804, Tench Coxe provided a highly particularized list of the new machinery recently introduced into production. His report illustrates the diversity of this gradual move to manufactory production across many crafts. In Coxe's encomium, improvements center upon, but also go well beyond, the mechanization and rationalization of weaving and spinning that is often taken to signal the origins of industrial production:[37]

> We have also invented or acquired the machinery for freeing cotton wool from the seed, the spinning jenny, the spinning mule, the roving, twisting and carding machinery, the perpetual carding and spinning water mill, the fly-shuttle with its appropriate loom, the machinery for coining or stamping metals, leather, &c. that for cutting cardwire and nails, for reducing old woolen cloths or rags to the state of wool, for boring cannon which have been solidly cast, for pressing, packing and lading cotton, for spinning flax, hemp and combed wool, for various operations in the staining and printing of cotton and linen cloths, for rolling the finer metals, for plating the coarser metals with silver, for steam-engines, for grinding, in quantities, optical lenses, for fine turning in wood, metal, stone and other substances. . . . We have also obtained . . . improved and increased knowledge of mixing and preparing metals, colors and dye-stuffs, in dying, bleaching and dressing goods, in the manufactory of printing types and printing blocks for linen, cotton and paper hangings, and other manufacturing implements, processes and secrets.[38]

Coxe's list of improvements amply illustrates that early industrialization was a polymorphous phenomenon, occurring across many crafts. In its multiplicity of reference (from the grinding of optical lenses to the staining of cloth and other "secrets"), his catalogue also suggests that manufactory-era technologies of production engaged and even depended upon visual frameworks of exhibition that lay behind the new machinery celebrated in such reports. As a way of advertising and displaying the mechanisms of productive power, Coxe's catalogue anticipates an audience of spectators, reading and viewing subjects who, if they did not produce, were at least called to view (and, eventually, to buy) the dyed and printed products of American manufacturing.

This book reiterates the word "manufactory," then, to indicate this early industrial context of changing modes of production as they were mediated by an array of visual and legible representational technologies: the word "manufactory" denotes, in other words, both an historically specific mode of production and the historical specificity of early national cultural "productions" in general. It is now acknowledged by most historians of work and labor that, in England, France, and the United States, the institutional and representational forms of industrialization were in place long before the establishment of a full-blown factory system.[39] As self-evident as such an assertion might seem, it has yet to fully reverberate in American cultural studies, where many scholars still implicitly view the early national period in general, and federalist Philadelphia in particular, as a kind of prehistory, a "seed-time" prior to the flowering of American industrial and cultural forms in mid-nineteenth-century New England and New York. In American studies, furthermore, the connection that was once often made between a gradual fading of religious faith (especially in New England) and the rise of a national aesthetic culture (American literature, sculpture, painting), while no doubt accurate, has also, to some degree, discouraged sustained analysis of the early national "machinoculture" of the Delaware Valley.[40]

In the disciplines of history and political science, likewise, the extended debate over the relative importance of "liberal" versus "republican" ideals in American political formation has encouraged disengagement from specificities that are not merely effects of language (oratory, sermons, writing, and print) but also the effects of an American culture articulated along other lines—in drawing, design, demonstration, display, collection, street performance, painting, carving, sewing, weaving, and the graphic arts of commodity production generally.[41] And, what is almost invariably overlooked in studies of the liberal versus republican traditions is that the line between economic liberalism and the political culture of republicanism—or, conversely, between the antimarket poses of republicanism and the economic investments of liberal political ideals—is always a mediated one, made and unmade at the point of culture, between and among heterogeneous representational structures.[42]

Lastly, and perhaps most obviously, for many students the always already quaint spectacle of Philadelphia's cultural importance would seem to have ended, more or less forever, in 1800, when the federal capital moved to Washington, D.C. and the state capital to Lancaster (and, later, Harrisburg). By 1810, New York and Baltimore had also become major commercial ports, while Philadelphia was in relative "decline" as an "entrepôt" of international trade.[43] Art museums collect late-eighteenth-century portraits and miniatures, busts, and furniture; but federal Philadelphia is equally if not better known through souvenir Liberty Bells, tours of Independence Hall, bicentennial parades, family vacations, and framed copies of the Declaration of Independence, offered for sale alongside books titled *The Miracle at Philadelphia*.[44] One might think, at first, that such mass-produced artifacts violate the faith in origins, founding, and framing upon which Independence depends. But, in fact, the mechanics of a mass-mediated culture were a way of life in Philadelphia from its first days as a federal city. The arts of spectatorship, commemoration, collection, and display were structural to the political economy of nation-making at a place and time crisscrossed by economic, political, and cultural innovations that were restructuring the mechanical arts and constituting a domestic or "home" economy in the United States. (It is not an insignificant coincidence, in other words, that both Benjamin Franklin and Andy Warhol, at some point in their lives, called Philadelphia home.)

Histories of federalism and republicanism which center on linguistic evidence alone leave largely untouched the framing role of visual culture that is so evident in the multidisciplinary artworks of the early national period. As performances of production, the practices described by this book bridged technology and aesthetics, in the forms of engraving, carving, drafting, trompe l'oeil and sign painting, engineering and surveying, magazine production and book illustration, tourism, travel, and museum display. To be sure, the empirical, specifically "Lockean," epistemological tradition of late-eighteenth-century intellectual and political life has been fully documented from the perspective of intellectual history: the empirical models of mind, the educational projects, the bureaucratic data-collecting practices, and the anxious faith in environmental influence.[45] But what is still wanting is a post-Lockean study of visual culture in the federalist era. Until late-Enlightenment visual culture and its relationships to the scenes or sites of the making of commodity production are brought more fully into view, the history of federalism will remain structured by a collectivist Linnaean and Lockean paradigm; it will continue to replay, without seeing, what Alan Liu calls an ongoing "bureaucratization of the Lockean aggregate" wherein words transparently mirror, collect, and redisplay (the sense impressions of) a world of things.[46]

Finally, although this book views the artworks of the early national period as creations of the culture of production, it does not argue that early national culture in the United States was somehow hostile to the "real" arts of poetry or painting because of some necessary commitment, characteristic of any developing country, to economic or technological growth.[47] Nor, on the other hand, does this study employ "manufactory" in the spirit of material culture studies, as a way of celebrating the democratizing functionalism of popular, folk, vernacular, utilitarian, or technological forms of early American culture, as opposed to "European" literary and visual genres.[48] Isolating neither the aesthetic nor the mechanic side of the emergent, culturally productive distinction between "art" and "craft," the following chapters look instead to American social and labor history as a way of insisting anew upon "production" as the repressed, operative term in American art and culture after the Revolution.[49] As cultural history, in other words, this book finds a mode of analysis as well as a mode of production in the uneven, multiform, quintessentially intermediate processes signified by the American manufactory.

PART I

Federal Mechanics

Figure 1. William Russell Birch, "Preparation for War to Defend Commerce: The Swedish Church Southwark with the building of the frigate *Philadelphia*," in *The City of Philadelphia in the State of Pennsylvania North America as it appeared in the Year 1800* (Springfield Cot, Pennsylvania: William Birch, 1800), plate 29. (Courtesy of the Library Company of Philadelphia.)

Raising the Roof: Authors, Architects, and Artisans in the Grand Federal Procession of 1788

[A]ll European processions . . . yield, in the effect of pleasure, to our hasty exhibition. . . . The whole of this vast body was formed, and the entertainment of the day conducted with a regularity and decorum far beyond all reasonable expectation. The footways, the windows, and roofs of the houses were crowded with spectators, exhibiting a spectacle truly magnificent and irresistibly animating. But what was more pleasing, . . . universal love and harmony prevailed and every countenance appeared to be the index of a heart glowing with urbanity and rational joy. . . . Such is the difference between the effects of a republican and monarchical government on the minds of men.

Benjamin Rush, *The American Museum and Repository*, July 1788

IN THE spring and summer of 1788, a series of Federal Processions were held in North American seaports from Charleston and Baltimore to New York, Boston, and Portsmouth, New Hampshire. As the Constitution of 1787 was ratified in state after state, triumphant federalists in each capital city celebrated with toasts, dinners, rounds of gunfire, and a street parade. By the early summer of 1788, as it became clear that the Constitution would be ratified by ten of the thirteen states, Philadelphia began to plan a national celebration. Drawing on diverse European and Euro-American processional traditions, including the recent state processions, Philadelphia federalists put the city's craftsmen, or mechanical artists, at the center of a parade that performed the making of the new federal state by analogizing republican nation building to the myriad productive processes of American manufacturing. More than forty-five crafts or trades marched in the city's "Grand" Federal Procession, arranged "promiscuously" ("equality being the basis of the constitution"[1]) and divided by "troops of light cavalry, infantry and militia" from each other and from other "ranks" ahead of or behind them (government officials, city merchants, ministers, university teachers, and students). Organized into "companies" or "corps," and making up the procession's largest contingent, the artisans wore the costumes and carried the emblems, flags, and implements of their respective trades. Journeymen and apprentice ropemakers walked behind their masters with "spinning clouts" in hand and "hemp around their waist." Coach painters carried their "pallettes and pencils," while house, ship, and sign painters held "gilded brushes" and "gold hammers" and an heraldic standard displaying "three shields in a field azure" with "a hand holding a brush, proper," and the motto "Virtue alone is true nobility."[2] The city's bricklayers marched with trowels, "plumrules," and a flag representing "the Federal city rising" beneath a rising sun. The flag displayed the following motto: "both buildings and rulers are the works of our hands."[3] Three hundred cordwainers (shoemakers) marched six abreast, "each wearing a white leather apron, embellished with the company's arms . . . above the arms, [St.] CRISPIN, holding a laurel branch in his right hand, and a scroll of parchment in his left." They followed a "carriage drawn by four horses, representing a cordwainer's shop, in which six men were actually at work . . . the shop hung round with shoes, boots, etc."[4]

As the cordwainers did, virtually all of the larger or more heavily capitalized industries in the procession actually performed their crafts on rolling platforms, or stages, drawn by horses past the huge streetside crowd perched "on fences, scaffolds, and roofs of houses."[5] Sailmakers manufactured sails on a stage "representing the inside view of a sail-loft with masters and men at work," while boatbuilders built a boat thirteen feet long, "which was . . . nearly completed during the procession." A company of gunsmiths wearing "green baize aprons with green strings" accompanied a rolling platform bearing the sign "FEDERAL ARMORY," with a "number of hands thereon at work," performing the production of military hardware. A model blacksmith's shop followed as the peacetime counterpart to gunsmithing: more than two hundred "brother blacksmiths, whitesmiths and nailers" walked behind "a machine drawn by nine horses" representing a "federal blacksmith, whitesmith, and nailer's manufactory" with a "real chimney . . . furnished for use." The motto on their standard read: "by hammer and hand, all arts do stand." This "manufactory was in full employ during the procession": the "blacksmiths completed a set of plough-irons out of old swords, worked a sword into a sickle," and "turned several horseshoes," while a whitesmith "finished a complete pair of plyers, a knife, and some machinery" and the nailers "finished and sold a considerable number of spikes, nails, and broadtacks."[6] On a stage representing a miniature coachmakers' shop (sixteen feet by eight by nine), "a master-workman" performed his tasks alongside "a body and carriage-maker, a wheelwright, a trimmer, and a harness-maker . . . and a painter ornamenting a body." The saddlemakers rode in a model saddler's shop, where "Mr. Stephen Burrows and a number of hands at work . . . complet[ed] a neat saddle during the procession." One hundred journeymen and apprentice cabinet- and chairmakers, followed "a workshop on a carriage" whose wall bore the sign "federal cabinet and chair-shop." Wearing "linen aprons and buck's tails in their hats," the apprentice and journeymen cabinet- and chairmakers marched behind the float while, in one of countless displays of the deferential hierarchy that coexisted with the parade's demonstration of equality under the Constitution, "their masters marched six abreast in front of the stage."[7]

In its linking of nation building with commodity production, Philadelphia's civic celebration was descended, in part, from the European ceremonial tradition of "the Triumph" and, more immediately, from the organizational forms, emblematic devices, and mechanical wonders of British craft processions and Lord Mayor's Day celebrations. As a late-eighteenth-century festival, however, it was also inflected with the principles and practices of republican festivity of the European Enlightenment more generally. In this it both differed from and expanded upon military or monarchical triumphs and craft ceremonial.[8] Within this Enlightenment tradition of republican festivity, for example, the Grand Federal Procession aspired to a feeling state that Montesquieu, among others, had classified as peculiar to republics: namely, civic love, or the virtuous love of the state for itself that arises when a republic sees itself assembled. In his *Letter to D'Alembert*, Jean-Jacques Rousseau called this collective and exhibitionary self-love the "sweet sentiment" of republicanism. It is within the tradition of republican assembly referenced by Montesquieu and Rousseau, and exemplified in republican theory by ancient and modern city-states (Sparta, Athens, Geneva), that the Philadelphia Procession aimed to raise its own kind of federal feeling—a decorous, essentially orderly sentiment—of "[u]niversal love and harmony . . . a heart glowing with urbanity and rational joy."[9]

But the United States was not a city-state. The representational machinery of production in early industrial Philadelphia necessarily articulated republican sentiment through a demographically and geographically extended, and still expanding, sphere of representation. In the reconfigured confederation, in other words, civic love could never be the affair of one city, or even of a single state or former colony. Likewise, in the extended republic, the transparent, face to face form of assembly imagined by Rousseau (in which a small republic appears as united in its attachment to itself) was an imaginary concept, projected by multiple, radically diverse representational forms. Under federalism, no single art alone—not even the craft of authorship—could dominate the innumerable acts of collective self-making that constituted the federal republic by linking individuals, through countless, intermediate sites of incorporation, to a phantasmic whole. Philadelphia's procession therefore assembled an array of

arts, crafts, and professions in a celebration that raised into view the principle of production itself as the common ground of Union-through-representation. In other words, within the expanded sphere of republican assembly under federalism, the principle of productive labor united
innumerable little acts of self-creation, bringing together diverse arts,
fields, institutions, and disciplines—from shipbuilding, shoemaking, and
textile production to civic parades, oratory, medicine, magazines, and museums.[10] On the grounds of the shared fact/um of work itself, then, Philadelphia's republican festival became an extended pun on political representation as craft production and on the newly ratified Constitution as
a well-constructed "fabric," "frame," or "edifice." In turn, contemporary
published accounts, such as those in Matthew Carey's *American Museum
and Repository*, reiterated the meaning of the parade's display of productive
procedures: on the pattern of American manufacturing anything and everything could be made federal, and a universe of things—and persons—
assembled together under a newly "raised" federal roof.

In its representational/productive ambition, the Federal Procession
also distinguished itself from Revolutionary-era street genres of colonial
protest and crowd action. The organizers of the Philadelphia procession
believed that the size and orderliness of their federal spectacle supplanted
the local ad hoc activism that had characterized urban political expression
in the 1760s and 70s. Street parades, marches, rituals, and spontaneous
crowd actions had been staples of political practice during the Revolution.
As in Europe, this tradition of extralegal street activity had not infre-
quently resulted in riots and assaults on buildings or persons.[11] Such riots
had involved far fewer participants, however, than Carey's *Museum* estimated as assembled by the procession: "five thousand in the line of the
Procession and seventeen thousand" awaiting the feast (a "cold collation")
on the "Union Green" at parade's end.[12] Of equal importance to federalist
observers, the huge procession managed to eliminate "spirituous liquors"
together with disorderly conduct, in an assembly of spectators who experienced (or performed) "political joy" in awestruck silence—or so Benjamin
Rush claimed. "The order of the procession was regular," Rush declared,
"and begat correspondent order in all classes of spectators. A solemn silence reigned both in the streets and at the windows of the houses."[13]

Our single most important source for the events of the procession is
Matthew Carey's Philadelphia magazine, the *American Museum and Repository of Ancient and Modern Fugitive Pieces, &c* for July of 1788. Prefaced with
testimonials by leading federalists such as Rush, the entire July issue of
Carey's *Museum* was dedicated to George Washington and displayed, in a
miniature replay of ratification, a list of the *Museum*'s four hundred or
more subscribers. This special issue also printed accounts of earlier processions in Baltimore and New Hampshire, along with Francis Hopkinson's

official "Account of the Grand Federal Procession" and such literary artifacts of the day as Hopkinson's poem "The raising: a song for federal mechanics"; his satire of antifederalism, "The New Roof"; and physician Benjamin Rush's "Observations," in which he noted the physiological and psychological effect of the day's events on spectators and partici- pants alike.

Chaired by federalist poet (and justice of the admiralty) Hopkinson, the city's "Committee of Arrangement" devised a festival that, like the new republic it celebrated, relied upon a spectacular conjunction of fellow feel- ing with productive work. "Productive work" is the key phrase here, be- cause—as the emblems and mottoes, the texts and productive procedures of the procession demonstrate—it was the performance of commodity production that displayed openly, for all assembled, a new basis on which to organize relations, not only between individuals and the state, but be- tween words and things as well. Where representational forms themselves were understood as modes of production, the procession did not rely on any one, single exemplary art or genre. Rather, like a living "museum and repository" itself, it embraced a vast representational field of arts, sciences, and emerging professional groups, from the crafts of commodity produc- tion to doctoring, teaching, architectural design, civic engineering, writ- ing, painting, and museum display.[14] Or, as Rush wrote in his report on the parade and its effects: "The remarks of every man partook more or less of his profession, and the constitution received nearly as many new names, as there were occupations in the procession."[15] Considered, then, as a multiply mediated event, occurring between and among arts, crafts, fields, and professions—which were potentially as numerous as there were classifiable objects of representation in the world—the Philadelphia pro- cession asks us to redefine the writing and ratification of the Constitution itself as simply one more political "occasion" in an exhibitionary reper- toire, as one more artifact in an expanding American Museum of republi- can self-assembly that *they*, the arts of production, raised into view.

THE NEW ROOF AND ITS ASSEMBLY-MEN

> [R]eaders may require to be informed that the NEW ROOF is alle- gorical of the new federal constitution; the thirteen rafters of the thirteen states.
>
>   Hopkinson, *American Museum*, 1788

Although Carey's *Museum* reports that the order of the mechanical arts in the procession was decided randomly and democratically "by lot," the pa- rade in fact privileged housebuilding and shipbuilding over the rest of the crafts.[16] In the commercial seaport of Philadelphia, carpentry and shipbuilding encompassed and employed many different craft companies and required particularly large pools of investment capital. By incorporating many diverse craft skills, the enterprises of constructing ships and mansions epitomized the procession's construction-based conception of *E pluribus unum*—and a hoped-for union of merchant capital with artisan interests under the new Constitution. As the "kings" of the crafts, then, carpentry and shipbuilding were represented near the head of the parade by two particularly spectacular floats: "The Grand Federal Edifice or *The New Roof*" and "The Federal Ship *Union*." Distinguished from the other crafts in the line of march, the building trades were given pride of place, together with floats representing the more grand and abstract "interests and alliances" united under the Constitution, such as "Agriculture," "Manufacturing," "Foreign Alliances," and "The Constitution."[17]

"Manufacturing," for example, was represented by the "managers, subscribers, and committee for managing the manufacturing fund." The accompanying float epitomized the manufactory-stage mode of production in the textile industry: ten bay horses pulled a "carriage" that displayed "a carding machine worked by two persons and carding cotton at the rate of fifty pounds weight per day . . . and a spinning machine of eighty spindles worked by a woman (a native of and instructed in this city)."[18] "The Constitution" itself was represented by a "lofty, ornamental car," in the form of a large bald eagle, drawn by six horses. "Thirteen feet high, from head to tail, thirteen feet long; the breast emblazoned with thirteen silver stars, in a sky-blue field," the "dexter talon" of this eagle "embraced an olive branch; the sinister grasped thirteen arrows." "Fixed on springs," it wore a banner that read "THE CONSTITUTION." Three men—two judges and a chief justice—rode within it, dressed "in their robes of office," while "ten gentlemen marched behind, arm in arm," representing each of the ratifying states.[19]

Both the Grand Federal Edifice and the Federal Ship *Union* accompanied "The Constitution" as privileged craft metonyms for the Union; but it was the "Grand Federal Edifice or *The New Roof*" that was the day's symbolic center. The New Roof was "an elegant edifice mounted "on a carriage drawn by ten white horses, . . . [I]ts dome [was] supported by thirteen Corinthian columns raised on pedestals proper to that order . . . with ten columns complete and three left unfinished" (in honor of the ten ratifying states and three who had yet to comply) and "a frieze decorated with thirteen stars." Atop the dome, a cupola supported the goddess Plenty with her cornucopia. Ten citizens, "representative of the citizens at large," rode beneath its roof, seated in ten chairs representing the ten ratifying states. Behind the Edifice walked some 450 "architects and house carpenters" beneath their standard, and behind them the saw cutters and filemakers, led by their masters and "carrying a flag with a hand saw and a mill saw, gilt on a pink field."[20] At the procession's end, the New Roof was brought to a halt at the center of a huge circle of tables on "the Union Green," the lawn of Bush Hill, William Hamilton's estate. There it served as the stage from which Pennsylvania federalist James Wilson delivered the speech of the day.

A city merchant and key participant in the Constitutional Convention, Wilson was also a longtime opponent of Pennsylvania's radical state constitution. Since the end of the Revolution, the state constitution had been at the center of political warfare between Painite mechanics and militiamen in the city (the "Constitutionalists"), who supported it, and federalist merchants and city leaders (the "Republicans") such as Wilson, who opposed it.[21] Opponents argued that Pennsylvania's constitution violated the principles of balanced government by allowing for a relatively "weak" executive branch (with the governorship divided between several men) and a unicameral, or single-house, as opposed to a bicameral, or divided, legislature. In his arguments before the Convention of 1787, Wilson had summarized his support for the federal Constitution by comparing it to a pyramid, declaring that he was for "raising the federal pyramid to a considerable altitude, and for that reason wished to give it as broad a base as possible."[22] By contrast with this raised, extended, and balanced "pyramid," Pennsylvania's constitution appeared radically unstable to Wilson and his allies, because it lacked the proverbial "division and balance" of powers thought necessary to civic virtue and social stability.

Within two years of the federal Constitution's ratification, the Pennsylvania state constitution was officially repealed and a new state constitution was drafted—largely by Wilson—on the pattern of the federal Constitution. By 4 July 1788, then, Wilson's position had prevailed, along with the pyramidal principles of federalism—and the merchant was an acceptable enough figure of Union to deliver the day's address. As he spoke from the "Grand Federal Edifice," Wilson declined to refer to the fissures of struggle and compromise represented by the long debate over the state constitution and the artisan radicalism of Philadelphia that had given it birth. He focused, instead, upon the living spectacle of "the people" assembled:

> You have heard of Sparta, of Athens and of Rome; you have heard of their admired constitutions, and of their high-prized freedom. In fancied right of these, they conceived themselves to be elevated above the rest of the human race, whom they marked with the degrading title of *Barbarians*. But did they, in all their pomp and pride of liberty, ever furnish, to the astonished world, an exhibition similar to that which we now contemplate? Were their constitutions framed by those, who were appointed for that purpose, by the people? . . . Were they to *stand* or *fall* by the people's *approving* or *rejecting* vote?[23]

In the visual tropes of Wilson's speech, the American republic is "an exhibition," furnished "to an astonished world." In an extension of Rousseau's fantasy of republican assembly, the new state becomes identical with the people literally assembled as spectators before Wilson: a nation's emergence under a new Constitution is not a text applied to institutions of government but "a spectacle which we are assembled to celebrate . . . the most dignified one that has yet appeared on our globe."[24]

Samuel Beer has argued that of all federalists at the Constitutional Convention, it was James Wilson who, as an early democrat and ardent centralizer, most accurately anticipated "modern American nationalism."[25] Wilson was a close friend of Benjamin Rush's and, like Rush, he justified his federalism by way of Scottish Common Sense philosophy. When Wilson argued for "raising the federal pyramid to a considerable altitude, and for that reason [giving] it as broad a base as possible," he described a structure raised vertically to a very high pinnacle (the national government) and extended horizontally upon a broad demographic and territorial base (the voting public in thirteen states). Wilson hoped to broaden the "base" of the federal pyramid by extending white male suffrage, and he justified this "expansion" by way of the mingled psychology, physiology, and philosophy of common sense. Like Rush, he believed that in every well-ordered human being, a native and inborn "sixth sense"—a moral sense or "common sense"—could be trusted to steady and center human choice.[26] The right to vote could be safely democratized, in other words, on the basis of this sixth sense, for an internalized pinnacle of moral and republican "elevation" had been diffused or "implanted" in every political participant as part of his organic makeup. As the framework for modern American nationalism, Wilson's design did not merely depend, however, upon the fact or fiction of common sense philosophy; his pyramid was, in fact, already constituted by a spectatorial and exhibitionary framework engaging a wide range of arts and professions. In its construction of an "astonished" audience of witnesses to the spectacle of nation making, this federal frame went well beyond the principle of voting rights *per se* to constitute "the people" as what, in fact, it already was: an incomprehensible crowd that included both republican citizen-workers and noncitizens, such as enslaved and unskilled laborers, women, children, and speakers of languages other than English.[27]

Jay Fliegelman has argued that, as an orator imbued with the principles of common sense philosophy, Wilson participated in an early national "elocutionary revolution." According to Fliegelman, Wilson's oratorical practice was a form of "soft compulsion," articulating cultural authority through and in spite of the performative paradoxes of late-eighteenth-century oratorical practice.[28] As a manufactory-era phenomenon, however, federalist elocutionary culture depended outright upon the principles and practice of commodity production: the orator's performance, emerging as it did via multiple arts, crafts, sciences, technologies, and professions, was itself a class-constituting mode of production. When Wilson stood up to speak from the Grand Federal Edifice on the Union Green in 1788, his praise for the exhibition before him participated in, and was the product of, a cultural creation and division of labor through the exhibitionary—as well as oratorical—technologies of representative self-production.

Consider, by extension, another version of this same edifice as it is described by Francis Hopkinson's poem "The raising: a song for federal mechanics." In this *Museum* artifact, the extended republic is constellated by an array of representational frameworks articulated around the body of the mechanical artist, the very juncture where artisans were being made into workers.[29] In "The raising," the performative and rhetorical paradoxes not only of oratory but of writing and authorship as well are made federal by virtue of their identification with the mechanical processes of construction. Displaying the cultural construction of construction as the deep, daily structure of federal power, Hopkinson's "song for federal mechanics" reiterates the central analogy of the procession, while explicitly extending the conceit of federal mechanics to republican authorship itself:

The raising: A song for federal mechanics

Come muster, my lads, your mechanical tools.
Your saws and your axes, your hammers and rules:
Bring your mallets and planes, your level and line,
And plenty of pins of American pine;
    For our roof we will raise, and our song still shall be—
    A government firm, and our citizens free.

Come, up with the plates, lay them firm on the wall,
Like the people at large, they're the ground-work of all;
Examine them well, and see that they're sound;
Let no rotten part in our building be found;
    For our roof we will raise, and our song still shall be—
    Our government firm, and our citizens free.

Now hand up the girders, lay each in its place,
Between them the joints must divide all the space;
Like assembly-men, these should lie level along,
Like girders, our senate prove loyal and strong:
    For our roof we will raise, and our song still shall be—
    A government firm, over citizens free.

The rafters now frame—your king-posts and braces,
And drive your pins home, to keep all in their places;
Let wisdom and strength in the fabric combine,
And your pins be all made of American pine;

> For our roof we will raise, and our song still shall be—
> A government firm, over citizens free.

> Our king-posts are judges—how upright they stand,
> Supporting the braces, the laws of the land!
> The laws of the land, which divide right from wrong,
> And strengthen the weak, by weak'ning the strong;
>> For our roof we will raise, and our song still shall be—
>> Laws equal and just, for a people that's free.

> Up! up with the rafters—each frame is a state!
> How nobly they rise! their span, too, how great!
> From the north to the south, o'er the whole they extend,
> And rest on the walls, while the walls they defend!
>> For our roof we will raise, and our song still shall be—
>> Combined in strength, yet as citizens free.

> Now enter the purlins, and drive your pins through,
> And see that your joints are drawn home, and all true;
> The purlins will bind all the rafters together,
> The strength of the whole shall defy wind and weather:
>> For our roof we will raise, and our song still shall be—
>> United as states, but as citizens free.

> Come raise up the turret—our glory and pride—
> In the centre it stands, o'er the whole to preside;
> The sons of Columbia shall view with delight
> It's pillars, and arches, and towering height;
>> Our roof is now rais'd, and our song still shall be—
>> A federal head, o'er a people still free.

> Huzza! my brave boys, our work is complete,
> The world shall admire Columbia's fair seat;
> It's strength against tempests and time shall be proof,
> And thousands shall come to dwell under our ROOF.
>> Whilst we drain the deep bowl, our toast still shall be—
>> Our government firm, and our citizens free.[30]

Francis Hopkinson, 4 July 1788

Clearly, in Hopkinson's poem the analogy between roof raising and the writing and ratification of a constitution is accomplished primarily by an attempt to identify the author/speaker of the poem with the woodworkers who raise the roof into place. The poet opens the poem by hailing the craftsmen as "my lads," while his almost encyclopedic display of craft jargon and his account of wood-frame construction imply that he is himself a practicing mechanic or, perhaps, a manager of mechanics. The impression of shared mechanical know-how is accomplished rhetorically by the do-it-yourself sequence of operations that structures the poem and by the poet's display of words peculiar to house carpentry: level and line, plates and girders, king posts, braces, pins, rafters and purlins.

The mechanical steps of roof raising, which are the poem's narrative frame, turn the poet's "song" itself into work and worksite, demonstrating the degree to which, as a federal mechanism, federalist authorship simulated a mechanical realism. Having "mustered" their tools (as militiamen muster with guns), the actual mechanics or carpenters of the poem perform the following operations. First, the horizontal pieces (plates and girders) are put into place upon and across the tops of the walls. ("Plates" are the horizontal "caps" on the vertical beams of the walls, while girders cross the ceiling space.) The "plates" hold and support the rafters—which are separately constructed (in stanzas four and five) out of "king-posts and braces." Each rafter is a triangle, made by "pinning" three braces to a king post so that each king post extends vertically from one of the crossbeams to the apex of the triangular truss. The rafters are then raised up onto the plates and fastened together via "purlins," horizontal supports, so that their apexes meet at the peak of the roof. Finally, a martial-sounding "turret" (a decorative tower) is added to the front of the building as a virtual crown on the "federal head."

However, the federal poet's display of carpentry know-how is also obviously a mimic structure, or float, the seams of which are its elisions of the differences between authors and mechanics, writing and roof raising. Riven with contradictions, the poem actually articulates an emerging class distinction. Doubt and uncertainty over union are manifest in several places, perhaps most obviously in the overinsistent repetition of the word "still" in each refrain ("and our song *still* shall be"), which strikes a note of doubt, verging almost on nostalgia, in the poem's otherwise celebratory tone. This note becomes insistent after stanza three, as it becomes increasingly clear that the "roof" is being raised above and finally out of—or "over" and "o'er"—the hands of the workmen who are raising it. The roof is first positioned "over" the mechanics in stanza three, at precisely the place where "actual" wood-frame construction is analogized to political representation and, specifically, to "assembly-men." At this juncture, the pun on "assembly-men" epitomizes the conundrum of union-through-representation that structures the poem: on the one hand, as the raisers of the new roof, the mechanical "lads" in the poem are its "assembly-men"; but as its builders, the craftsmen who assemble or raise the roof are *not* identifiable with the political representatives—the state "assembly-men" or federal Congressmen—who supposedly represent them, any more than they are identical with the beams they raise into place or with the "architects" of the Constitution. Here, the gridlike "joists" divide "all the space" in a spatial trope for order that anticipates an even more explicit material-ization of "fixity" and stability in stanza four: "And drive your pins home to keep all in their places."

It was fully in keeping with federalist political theory that local and state "assembly-men" rather than federal representatives must be kept straight, or made to "lie level along." It was precisely the local levels of representa-tion in city and state assemblies that federalists claimed to fear as a source of corruption (the "rotten parts") in the collective frame. According to constitutional theory, only a divided federal government and, within it, the Senate, could achieve the extended and extensive view that was said to be identical with the public good. As an outcome of sheer distance from local particulars, the elevated, national view accomplished by a "raised" central government was supposed to offset merely "mechanical" or "ma-chine-style" politics, which was said to be (and often was) more typical of local governments and smaller states.[31] Here, then, is the structural contra-diction: precisely where the poem connects political representation to "ac-tual" mechanics, its artisanal, woodworking mechanics are also identified negatively (as "assembly-men") with the local interests of city and state assemblies—even while the roof is jointly raised by poets, congressmen, assembly-men, and mechanics.

In federalist political theory, the newly constituted Senate was the quint-essentially federalist creation and, likewise, explicitly opposed to merely mechanical assembly-men. Because of their distanced and detached view, senators were supposed to be an overseeing force for order in the ex-tended republic. The distinction within a national Congress between the House of Representatives and the Senate was based largely upon the com-paratively raised situation of the Senate. Divorcing the number of senators (two from each state) from consideration of population, while granting them a six-year term that released them from frequent campaigning, the Constitution aimed to put the Senate at a greater distance from the direct influences or mechanical "instructions" of the actual people who had elected them—apart, in other words, from those citizens (and nonciti-zens) of the states, towns, and households of the Union to whom the House of Representatives might be too closely connected by kinship or by the everyday, face-to-face relationships of local life. In contrast to local assemblies and the federal House of Representatives, it was the federal Senate that was, in theory, less likely to become the "tool" of any particular interest or "mechanical" influence. By virtue of sheer distance, the Sen-ate's view was to be relatively untainted by locale and particularity; it was expected to maintain an "elevated" view of the public or common good, while remaining dynamically balanced by the negative pull of local attach-ments or state and city interests. Like federal poets, then, federal senators epitomized the principle of distanced and virtual, as opposed to actual, representation; like "the turret" in Hopkinson's "song for federal mechanics," the upper house of the national legislature was an artifact of the class-constituting, federalist faith in the elevated view—and in the technologies that raise it.[32]

To summarize: throughout Hopkinson's poem, the conceit of "federal mechanics" collapses the difference between the author/architects of the Constitution and Philadelphia's actual mechanics. By identifying the "authors" of the Constitution with the social rank of the skilled craftsmen (to which virtually no leading federalist belonged), it displays the founding structure of American constitutionalism as class division, and class division as that line at which words themselves become objects when construction frames the state. Preserved in the *American Museum*, the poem is framed and displayed itself by the artifactual logic it frames, wherein words become works and writing another mode of producing and collecting things. Conflating writing with the mechanic dream of "actual" political representation, the poem's performance of house construction is a device suturing multiple representational frameworks, from oratory and poetry and to carpentry and architecture.

The contradiction in the phrase "federal mechanics" is most explicit in the last two stanzas of Hopkinson's "song for federal mechanics" when its "federal head" (the turret) is raised "o'er" the people who raise it. It is at this moment, when the work of construction is done and the Edifice transformed into an object of spectatorship, that the mechanics become truly detached from "their" federal structure as its viewers rather than its owners: "The sons of Columbia shall view with delight/It's pillars, and arches, and towering height." Here, the transformation of craftsmen into spectators is linked to the control of "spirits." As the worksite becomes an object of visual display and spectatorship, the "brave boys" withdraw from their work completely, into a very different kind of public house, a "pub," where they "drink the deep bowl." Hopkinson's subtitle, "a song for federal mechanics," implicitly associates the poem with a worker's song, as well as with a drinking song of the kind that might accompany the raising of "the deep bowl." This is a bowl of federal spirits, however. When the work of authoring and constructing is complete, it is spectatorship that, as a form of "rational amusement," will replace "spirits" as the accompaniment to work discipline.[33]

Certainly, the effort to separate working from drinking was a familiar aspect of early industrial reforms of workshops, and a sign of their transformation into manufactories. As Herbert Gutman and others have pointed out, drinking at work could in fact become a form of protest against the new work disciplines of industrial reform.[34] "Spirituous liquors" were also associated with the Anglo-American customs of crowd activity or riots (of the sort most fully described by E. P. Thompson) that found wide expression in America during the Revolution.[35] In fact, some ten years before he mounted the Edifice as federalism's representative, James Wilson himself had been the target of a reportedly drunken riot over food reserves and wartime price controls. In 1778, hostility to Wilson and his merchant allies had emerged around the issue of merchant opposition to Pennsylvania's State Constitution but also, more immediately, around price controls instituted by the city's governing Committee of Trade. Artisans and militiamen in the city suspected that Wilson and other merchants were hoarding goods in order to inflate prices, and their anger culminated in the "Fort Wilson Riot," an attack on Wilson's house by a crowd of angry and supposedly drunk militiamen.[36] Foreshadowing the alliance of merchants and craftsmen presumed by the Federal Procession, it was the militia officers and artisan members of the Committee of Trade itself who finally dispersed the crowd at "Fort Wilson."[37]

It was this kind of disorderly struggle over prices and power that the procession claimed to transform into the sober decorum of lawful union, wherein Revolutionary spirits were both memorialized and buried. As they had in Baltimore, Boston, New York, and Charleston, Philadelphia federalists observed that American "Freemen" require "no soldiers to make them behave with propriety."[38] In the federal state, crowd activity, drunkenness, and shows of military power had reportedly evaporated, together with social division; or, as Rush put it, "rank for a while forgot all its claims . . . [and] every tradesman's boy in the procession seemed to consider himself as a principal in the business."[39]

FACTION VERSUS ASSEMBLY IN THE AMERICAN MANUFACTORY

In his *Letter to M. D'Alembert,* Rousseau recommended "republican entertainments" appropriate to a small republic such as Geneva. Held in the open air, ancient republican spectacle had preserved rather than degraded moral, political, and economic virtue: for Rousseau, the "coarse feasts . . . modest festivals and games" of Sparta, in particular, were the moral and political antithesis to the European theater, where (as if in an "Oriental" boudoir) virtuous citizens became enervated and feminized. The Spartans, he writes, assembled "constantly" in "laborious idleness," consecrating "the whole of life to amusements which were the great business of the state and to games from which they relaxed only for war."[40] In addition to their physical rigor, open-air assemblies were quintessentially republican, because they promoted love for the state by renewing the love of the citizens for each other. According to Rousseau, this civic love was the heart blood of the virtuous republic, distinguishing the open-air festivals of republicanism from the theaters of degenerate states, where citizens were not brought together but deprived of one another by a confining idleness and false display.[41]

Rousseau's own *Letter* is crisscrossed by contradiction, however. While he praised the face-to-face intimacy and virtue of the republican city, Rousseau himself wrote his *Letter to M. D'Alembert* far from Geneva.[42] And, despite his skepticism about theatricality, it is the performative appearance of citizens in an open visual field that guarantees virtue and stability in Rousseau's ideal small republic: the people must see themselves collected in order to love themselves collectively. In small republics such as Geneva or the Greek city-states, Rousseau writes, the people "assembled often," in order to see one another and thereby renew "the sweet bonds of pleasure and joy." For only a republican people could "have so many reasons to like one another and remain forever united"[43]: "Plant a stake crowned with flowers in the middle of a square; gather the people together there, and you will have a festival. Do better yet; let the spectators become an entertainment to themselves; make them actors themselves; do it so that each sees and loves himself in the others so that all will be better united."[44]

In Rousseau's *Letter*, the small republic serves as the exemplary site of republican virtue in ways that, after the American Revolution, it could not serve the American federalists. In their legislative and print debates of 1787, the author-architects of American constitutionalism substituted their design of a large "extended republic" for that of the small republican city-state, even while acknowledging the small city-states of Athens, Sparta, and early Rome as original theaters of civic virtue.[45] On their side, antifederalists read Montesquieu more literally than the federalists, arguing that the extended republic of federalist design was virtually imperial in its enormous size and that its federal "head" would prove too distant to guarantee liberty or happiness.[46] Federalists responded that, on the contrary, the crucial check to degeneracy in the federal republic would be its spatial extension. In defending their plan for an extended republic of thirteen growing states, Hamilton, Madison, and Jay returned continually in the *Federalist* papers to the legendary tendency of small republics to devolve into luxury and faction. As exemplified by ancient Athens in particular, geographically and demographically small republics resembled unmixed or pure democracies in their tendency to degenerate into social splintering, tyranny, and, eventually, military empire. But this tendency, "Publius" (the pseudonymous author of *The Federalist*) told his readers, would be offset by the sheer size of the new nation. So wide a territory—from Georgia to New Hampshire, from Boston to western Virginia—could be united under a central government without any loss of either civic feeling or virtue. As Madison wrote in *Federalist* no. 10, it was precisely the gigantic size of the union that would prevent the tyranny of collusive minorities over the republican majority, through a combination of its elevated and detached national legislature (and within it a senate) with an expanded territorial and demographic field. Again, in this extended republic, the warmth of attachment, desire, and interests would be offset by distance in two directions, horizontal and perpendicular, making impossible the concentrations of power that led to demagoguery or tyranny.[47] By both extending and raising the representational field of republican union, civic "feelings" could be safely diffused, and never kindle into "the fire" of faction.[48] In short, where Rousseau declared, "let the spectators become . . . actors themselves," Philadelphia federalists Hopkinson and Wilson would say, in effect, "Let the spectators become silent monuments to the productive power of American manufacturing, and let them see themselves displayed in its monumental assembly of a virtual world of commodities."[49]

If the danger of the theater was foremost in Rousseau's mind, it was not the center of federalist concerns in 1788. Instead, the exhibitionary frameworks of federalism were, more immediately, a reaction to postwar violence and economic localism—categories that were increasingly identified with one another as "faction." In the *Museum*'s accounts of the procession, the fear of faction is manifested by ambivalence over the legacy of the American Revolution: the passions raised, the blood spilled, and the local militia called forth by the war. The Revolution evoked contradictory responses in the *Museum*: on the one hand, federalist observers represent the war as the lifeblood of union, while, on the other, they argue that the powerful but dangerous energies of the Revolution must now be channeled into productive labor.

This ambivalence is particularly manifest, of course, where the procession celebrated the army, navy, and militia. Benjamin Rush, in particular, regretted the procession's mixture of military parading with peacetime productivity. Contemplating the Federal Ship *Union*, for example, Rush observes, "She was a ship of war." "I wish," he complains, "the procession could have been conducted without blending the emblems of Peace and War together."[50] Writing in the persona of an anonymous gentleman in his "Observations, . . . in a letter from a gentleman of this city to his friend in a neighbouring state," Rush elevates the peacetime products of American manufacturing over the military readiness required by international commerce. He declares that American cotton rather than military dress will soon clothe "every citizen of the United States," and that, "cultivated in the southern and manufactured in the eastern and middle states," cotton cloth will ultimately prove "a bond of union . . . more powerful than any article of the New Constitution."[51] This statement starkly exhibits federalism's repeated erasure of the coerced labor of slaves, here represented by cotton production in "the southern states." Where the bond of union was productive labor, and citizenship a performance of production, the production of commodities through enslaved labor was the face of union most deeply buried, or most emphatically excluded, by the exhibitionary Edifice of 1788.

The refusal to acknowledge or display the facts of ongoing enforced labor, or the uses of force generally, certainly explains Rush's antipathy to military show. It also probably explains why the procession put the Grand Federal Edifice rather than the more martial ship *Union* at the center of its celebration. Not only Rush but federalist authors in general declared that violence had been overcome in the raising of the new state—a state with the power to translate the factional spirits of Revolutionary memory, local interests, and antifederal sentiment into nation building. Among its other artifacts, the *Museum* preserves the following ode, composed for the ratifying celebration in Portsmouth, New Hampshire. In this fantasy of monument building, the blood of the Revolution is transformed (via masonry rather than carpentry) into both the cornerstone and the "top stone" of a monument that is also an enormous grave.

> I made each hardy son,
> Who in war's purple tide
> First laid the corner stone,
> His utmost energy employ
> To bring the top stone forth with joy.
>
> Tis done! the glorious fabric's rear'd!
> Still be New-Hampshire's sons rever'd
> Who fix'd its base in blood and scars,
> And stretch'd its turrets to the stars![52]

Here, the relationship between "base" and "turret" reiterates the trope of the new roof to figure a harmonious integration of the Revolutionary war with the new nation where war itself is represented as having planted and watered the nation with blood. Philadelphia's procession would reiterate the translation of the spirit of 1776 into the producer-state of 1788. Among other things, the often repeated "name of [ex-]general Washington," Rush reports, "was happily calculated to unite the most remarkable transports of the mind which were felt during the war, with the great event of the day."[53] And the procession reportedly linked the name of Washington with that of Franklin as a way of uniting the military with the peacetime political leader, the republican farmer with the urban artisan, the federalist writer with the federal mechanic: "I need not suggest to you," Rush writes,"how much this mixture of the mechanical and learned professions in a public exhibition is calculated to render trades of all kinds respectable in our country. . . . It would seem as if heaven stamped a peculiar value upon agriculture and mechanical arts in America, by selecting

Washington and Franklin to be two of the principal agents in the late revolution."[54]

Rush does observe one exception to the harmony between the learned and mechanical professions when he reports that, "Mr. P—— who walked with the farmers, just behind a man who was sowing grain, upon passing by the lawyers, said, 'we sow, gentlemen, but you reap the fruits of our labours.' "[55] However, in the *Museum*, such animus between ranks is limited to words or jokes, and shows of violence are overcome by federal productivity on all levels. As one "worthy citizen who served in several battles" told Dr. Rush, "the numerous collection of boys of every size and age" marching with "the instructors of youth" drew "tears from his eyes."[56] And, after the parade, a "worthy German who carried the standard of one of the trades . . . desired his wife to take care of the flag till the next time he should be called upon to carry it, 'and if I die, (said he) before I can have that honour again, I desire that you would place it in my coffin, and bury it with me.' "[57]

With these anecdotes the *Museum* not only declares that "the reign of violence" is over but that no one is "intoxicated" here, where federalism employs the Revolution itself to dominate the spirit of faction. Physician Rush, for one, would have readers believe that no one in the crowd was drunk on the day of the procession. He rejoiced that federal "spirits"— beer and cider—had replaced intoxicating "liquors" on the federal green. Rush, in fact, proposed a federal monument of his own to commemorate the republic's capacity to transform dangerous spirits into an orderly feeling state. Offering his design for a "Memorial to American Beer and Cyder" in the pages of the *Museum*, Rush proposed that his memorial be raised on the Union Green to commemorate the spectacle of thousands assembled in peace and good behavior (fig. 2).[58]

As Rush's *Museum* memorial demonstrates, the sober joys of the federal crowd were, in part, the artifacts of print production. But the conviction that writing-in-print is the keystone of American constitutionalism is itself another artifact of federalist self-production. In the procession, printing was just one more craft among the others (although perhaps one of the more spectacularly performed). Marching behind "the tallow chandlers" and "victuallers," the city's "printers, book binders, and stationers" accompanied a printing press on a stage drawn by four grey horses: "Mercury, the god of intelligence, was personated by [M]r. Durant, who was dressed in character, having wings affixed to his head and feet, a garland of flowers round his temples, and a caduceus in his hand. He distributed among the spectators some thousand copies of the following ode, written for the occasion by the hon F. Hopkinson, esq. and printed before and during the procession at the Federal Press."[59] In the course of the parade, copies of this ode were periodically wrapped up in ten small packages together

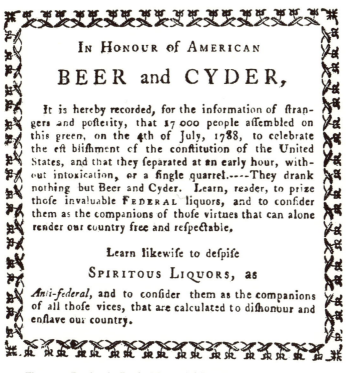

Figure 2. Benjamin Rush, Memorial "In Honour of American
Beer and Cyder." *American Museum and Repository of Ancient and
Modern Fugitive Pieces, &c.*, July 1788, 78.

with the list of toasts for the day. Having been addressed to the ten states
in the union, these were then "tied to pidgeons, which at intervals rose
from Mercury's cap, and flew off, with the acclamations of an admiring
multitude."[60] Hopkinson's ode—thrown to the crowd during the procession and sent skyward on the wings of pigeons—was finally reproduced
entire in the pages of Carey's *Museum*:[61]

> Oh for a muse of fire! to mount the skies
> And to a list'ning world proclaim—
>
> Behold! behold! an empire rise!
> An era new, Time as he flies
> Hath enter'd in the book of Fame.
> On Alleghany's tow'ring head
> Echo shall stand—the tidings spread,
> And o'er the lakes, and misty floods around,
> An era new resound . . . [62]

As artifacts of the printers' float, these lines proclaiming federal elevation and peace are literalized in the "dove-like" flights of print: here, print
production and distribution perform the part of "Echo," reproducing and
spreading "the tidings" of "an empire" from multiple (elevated) points.

Elevation was the emotional corollary to roof raising. And, as Rush's
memorial to beer and cider demonstrates, "elevation" was closely associated with intoxication. What federalism's self-representations also articulate, however, though somewhat less explicitly, is that elevation was an economic metaphor too. Ronald Schultz points out in his history of
Philadelphia artisan politics that an economic depression followed the
American Revolution, during which shopkeepers, merchants, and "servants" alike suffered under a postwar "torpidity" of trade.[63] The Grand
Federal Procession aimed explicitly to support the federal project of producing a cure for what was diagnosed as the laxness of economic life under
the Articles of Confederation. Or, as Rush put it in his "Observations":
" 'Tis done! We have become a nation. . . . The torpid resources of our
country already discover signs of life and motion."[64] For Rush, this healthy
economic/physiological stimulation is a product of the totality of the spectacle—"the sublimity of the sight, and the pleasure it excited in every
mind."[65] But in fact the stimulus lay centrally in the "exciting" proliferation
of free particulars,[66] in the enumeration of details that constituted the
extended republic of American-made products. For example, the *Massachusetts Centinel* articulated the message of diversity united under the banner of detail when it proposed that, in honor of the new Constitution, the
term "federal" should be applied to anything made in America: nails and
paper, cloth buttons, "leather breeches, Hare's porter, New Jersey and
Connecticut Cheeses, Massachusetts women's shoes . . . and all other
things manufactured in the United States."

As the exhibitionary domain of the textile industry, the descriptive discourse of fashion proliferated detail with as much abandon as a natural
history text. Consider the little flag raised by "the calico printers" in the
Philadelphia Procession: "in the centre [were] thirteen stars in a blue
field, and thirteen red stripes in a white field; round the edges of the flag
were printed thirty-seven different prints of various colors (one of them a
very elegant bed furniture chintz of six colours) as specimens of printing
done at Philadelphia."[67] Under the New Roof, however, the diffuse proliferation of collective detail was always offset by elevation—as when the
Grand Federal Edifice itself was reimagined as "patriotic millinery" by a
Boston paper that advised American women to wear a federal hat: "pretty,
neat and genteel, . . . the rim . . . should be formed of 13 concentric rings;
the crown should represent the Grand Federal Edifice itself; while ribbons
and streamers, 'with stars interspersed,' might signify the United States'
tie with France, Sweden, Morocco, and other kingdoms with which the

nation was allied."[68] On the one hand, the thirteen concentric circles of this commodified crown recapitulate the structure of federalist self-making as a pyramidal system, broader at the bottom than at the top, but united around a single center. On the other hand, the "federal hat" is simply one more instance of union multiplied, individuated, and reproduced in even the smallest detail.

For Benjamin Rush, these artifacts of the state—their proliferation and containment, rise and fall, elevation and descent—were also physiological in origin and effect. The New Roof extended, in his view, to its subjects' inner lives, which were, like little extended republics, brought into a state of union where all variety, even emotional variety, was encompassed, contained, and recomposed. "Perhaps," Rush exclaims, "a greater number or a greater combination of passions never seized, at the same time, upon every faculty of the soul":

> The patriot enjoyed a complete triumph, . . . [in] the security of liberty, the establishment of law, the protection of manufactures, or the extension of science. . . . The benevolent man saw a precedent established for forming free governments in every part of the world. The man of humanity contemplated the end of the distresses of his fellow-citizens in the revival of commerce . . . . Even the selfish passions were not idle—The ambitious man beheld, with pleasure, the honours that were to be disposed of by the new government, and the man of wealth realized once more the safety of his bonds and rents, against the inroads of paper money and tender laws.[69]

Every spectator, Rush continues, "felt one of these passions; many more than one, and some all of them during the procession." Presumably anyone who could feel, contain, and recognize all passions would be the most elevated and cultivated—or "museumized"—of all spectators: the most federal federalist of all.

However, such an emotionally varied and elevated federal subject must also be economically centered enough to desire "the safety of his bonds and rents." Eric Foner traces the debate over specie versus paper money that divided artisan interests in Philadelphia during the early 1780s. Economic nationalists, including Thomas Paine, supported a national bank and a far more centralized economic monetary system; they preferred an economics of federal "specie" to a supposedly inflationary, localist, and Revolutionary economic practice of democratizing growth and investment by printing "paper money."[70] These federalists argued in an economic register that the proliferation of local diversity must be controlled and managed, that the federal head must be raised above the otherwise torpid, idle, exhausted, or ill body of the state under the old Articles of Confederation. Here, as a formula for balance, the federalist position reiterates the productivist dichotomies of representation under the new roof. By 1788, then, an array of class-constituting architectures—from the medical to the economic—joined themselves to the mechanical arts to declare the old roof of the Articles of Confederation defunct and to raise the new roof of the extended republic in its place.

The Lunacy of Antifederalism

In yet another literary artifact of the procession, titled "The New Roof," Hopkinson approached the raising of the new roof through satire, lampooning the politics of antifederalism as lunacy, bad variety, unhealthy excess, a mélange of unincorporable stimuli. In "The New Roof," Hopkinson pursued the conceit of the nation as edifice to the point of referring to the Articles of Confederation (1781–89) as "the old roof." His satire opens by comparing the new Constitution to the defunct Articles, "the old roof," which was "so flat, as to admit the most idle servants in the family, their play-mates, and acquaintance, to trample on and abuse it."[71] Because of the failures of this old "flat" roof, the new roof must be "raised"—but not only in the sense of simply being put into place (designed, ratified, and instituted). It must also be elevated—or raised at its center, pyramid-style—in order to keep its "servants" down, in their place, and, presumably, at work. A worthy group of architects gathers, therefore, to offer "a drawing or plan of a new roof, such as they [think] most excellent, for security, duration and ornament," and their proposal for a new roof becomes "the principal subject of conversation in the family."[72]

But what begins as a family conversation is soon transformed into a debate between the architects alone—that is, the Constitutional Convention of 1787—led by one "James." This James, we are told by Hopkinson's footnote, is James Wilson himself, the Philadelphia merchant and federalist: "On a certain day the servants of the family had assembled in the great hall to discuss [the roof]. Among these was James the architect, who had been one of the surveyors of the old roof, and had a principle hand in forming the plan of a new one."[73] At this juncture (as the debate migrates from "the family" to "the architects") the site of discussion itself shifts from the household setting of the mansion to "a great hall." Hopkinson's footnote identifies this great hall as the Pennsylvania State House. With the move to "the great hall" the household scene of the mansion suffers a dislocation that is inseparable from a radical slippage in the referent of the word "servants." In the great hall, it is the federalist architects themselves who are now called "servants of the family," whereas the first referent of "servants" (i.e., the "idle servants and their play-mates" trampling over the old, flat roof of the Articles of Confederation) had been to that category of indentured or enslaved "servants" living and working in preindustrial, extended families and households. Here it becomes clear, in retrospect, that the earlier "idle servants" must also have referred to political figures (or public servants), specifically to those antifederalists in city and state assemblies who opposed a stronger central government in the interests of maintaining local, state, and family power.

In manufactory-era Philadelphia, of course, the category of "servants" had a wide range of referents. It embraced male or female African-American "servants," enslaved or free; male or female European-Americans living as indentured servants in a household and/or shop; and men indentured by master craftsmen as journeymen and apprentices to a trade. In 1788, indentureship and the apprentice system were both still very much intact. But federalist Philadelphia was also, of course, in the midst of a gradual and uneven reorganization of craft production in which artisan shops were, very gradually, giving way to manufactories, and journeymen were increasingly becoming wage laborers.[74] Crucially then, in Hopkinson's "The New Roof," when congressional or state legislators and members of the Constitutional Convention are suddenly called "servants," a social relation is displaced into a structure of representation. This displacement occurs at precisely that juncture where the political architecture of federalism was structurally engaged with an ongoing, cultural creation of waged labor and working subjects.

Further, with the shift in the referent of "servants" and the move to the great hall comes yet another dislocation. When the architects begin their debate as public servants in the great hall, a number of the mansion's tenants suddenly find themselves "out of doors," where they are transformed into spectators and excluded, not only from the great hall, but from the mansion altogether. "A great number of the tenants," Hopkinson tells us, "had also gathered out of doors, and crowded the windows and avenues to the hall, which were left open, that they might hear the arguments for and against the new roof."[75] Neither servants nor architects, these "tenants" have been translated into listeners and viewers, positioned at windows and doorways. However, while this audience begins to assemble around the hall of the debate, opposition to the New Roof is orchestrated by "an old woman" named Margery—who is identified in a note as a well-known antifederalist, the "reputed author" of a series of essays signed "Centinel" (probably Samuel Bryan).[76] This antifederalist Margery is said to have "got a comfortable apartment in the mansion house" and to be a great "mischief maker," who "kept the house in confusion," sowing "discord and discontent among the servants."[77] (Here, again, the referent of "servant" is multiple, referring variously to political representatives, federalist or antifederalist authors, artisanal laborers, and household servants.) Finally, while support for the Constitution comes from a group of virtuous and learned "architects," opposition is articulated on the other side by a counterassembly of characterless characters who manage to vacate the possibility of representation altogether: madmen, old women, idle "servants," sectarian religious fanatics. Neither the architect of the structure nor its viewers, these nonpersons irrationally oppose the reroofing of a structure badly in need of repair.

These excluded "minions" of Margery's have endless hypochondriacal fears about the new roof: that "the chimney should take fire" and that "the walls might crumble away," leaving the roof "suspended in air, threatening destruction to all that should come under it."[78] But these crazy-sounding objections fail to discourage the family at the windows from listening to their architects, and it is here that Margery, now desperate, hires a lunatic to inspire fear in the family, filling "a half-crazy fellow" with "terrible apprehensions from the new roof" and making him believe "that the architects had provided a dark hole in the garret, where he was to be chained for life."[79] In the end, antifederalism is voiced by the prophetic warning of a lunatic, who opposes the new structure for a mixture of fanatically religious, economically interested, and socially paranoid reasons:

> oh the architects! the architects!—they have seized the government, secured power, brow-beat with insolence and assume[d] majesty—oh the architects! they will treat you as conquered slaves—they will make you pass under the yoke, and leave their gluttony and riot, to attend the pleasing sport—oh that the glory of the Lord may be made perfect—that he would shew strength with his arm, and scatter the proud in the imaginations of their hearts— blow the trumpet—sound an alarm—I will cry day and night—behold, is not this my number five? —attend to my words, ye women labouring of child— ye sick persons and young children—behold—behold the lurking places, the despots, the infernal designs—lust of dominion and conspiracies . . . [80]

With this passage, Hopkinson represents antifederalists as members of a lunatic "fringe." But in fact it was precisely this apocalyptic voice of sectarian, Protestant millennialism, prophecy, and revelation that had been raised since the English Civil War against kings, tyrants, and large centralized systems of power in Britain and her colonies. And it was this voice that would be allied with artisan radicalism in Britain and the United States through the 1790s.[81] In July of 1788, in the middle of the raising of a new federal state, this strain of prophecy and apocalypse, now exiled and repressed, returns in the words of Hopkinson's lunatic, a shadowy outcast of federalism's official self-construction.

Legal historians argue that by the 1840s, a laissez-faire ideal of the wage contract and of the rights of employers versus employees in the wage relation gradually won out over preindustrial concepts of fair or just price and customary rules regarding relationships between masters and servants.[82] Such changes involved imagining a world of contractual subjects who, as free and equal agents, could sell their labor in an open marketplace. The open market was also, however, a representational concept and a spatializing architecture that imagined its collectivity of contractual subjects not merely as commodity producers but also as a crowd of individuated spectators. What Margery's lunatic points out in this regard was that the open field of this laissez-faire landscape was, in fact, structured and divided by the elevated forum of "the great hall." Among the divisions constituted by the great hall, then, were not only the distinction between servants and architects but also the distinction between those who produced and those who watched the performance of production.

Already in 1788, well before the arrival of factories, shopping arcades, and widespread waged labor, contracting persons were being projected by the bipartisan structure of a grand federal Enlightenment that divided them, not only into labor and management, but also into producers and viewers—or spectators. In Carey's *Museum*, however, the violence of this framework and its divisions could only be expressed, lunatic-style, as fear of confinement in a garret or in darkness. Margery's spokesman is a lunatic then, not only because he will not ratify, but because he cannot, or will not, be made into a self-viewing, self-making subject and object from the federal point of view. He cannot ratify the new roof because he cannot learn to see—or read—federally; he will not or cannot interiorize federalism's elevated perspective (and so he also does not recognize the new subject-making disciplines of political economy). Despite his Manichean rhetoric of apocalypse, the lunatic does not know how to divide "the light" from the darkness, Enlightenment-style, so as to become a self-creating, self-maintaining subject under the "new roof." He does not even, therefore, find a place for himself in the crowd standing at its apertures, doors, or windows.

From this perspective, the lunatic's gothic fear of being "chained to a dark hole in the garret" is a reaction to a recreational reorganization of work accomplished by the multiple representational structures that joined authorship not only to commodity production but also to spectatorship. At the end of "The New Roof," the architects' plan wins out over the lunatic. But the last word is, nevertheless, given to the lunatic and his "rhapsodies," as a way, Hopkinson writes, "of exhibiting the stile and manner in which a deranged and irritated mind will express itself."[83] But Margery's lunatic does more than represent antifederalism, because the address of his rhapsody is to those watchers, listeners, and other shadowy (nonwhite/ not dimorphously sexed?) figures outside the framework of the federal debate: "women laboring of child," "sick persons and young children," and idle, incompetent, or excessively religious men. These excluded nonpersons or noncitizens include anyone too insane, idle, ill, or undifferentiated to ratify, even by viewing, the logical elegance of the architects' design. Indicated rather than represented by the lunatic's raving, they stand outside the binary divide of federalism versus antifederalism—even while, in their absence, they reveal the Roof to be a spectacular representational structure extending far beyond the institutions of the national government per se.

As a metaphor for Constitution writing, the "New Roof" reproduces the familiar federalist trope of the Constitution as a well-designed frame. But this frame was also more than just another trope for the text of the Constitution. Contrary to the lunatic's belief ("Oh the architects, the architects!"), the construction of a virtual citizenry of spectators, and of spectatorial readers, was not the conscious plan of conspiring architects and their friends. Rather, it also emerged via the cultural constructions of working, writing, and viewing elaborated outside the "New Roof" of the written Constitution itself—and quite beyond the control of federalists and antifederalists alike. Not reducible, in fact, to the dynamically reproductive binaries of its own self-representation, federalism was raised by a multiplicity of representational and reproductive technologies that were making a world of things by creating (and organizing) both labor and looking together.

Ultimately, Margery's lunatic tells us that constitutional government was only one aspect of a frequently inadequate, structurally discontinuous culture of production. Performed in the streets of Philadelphia, the forging and framing of the federal state was a dynamic display of American manufacturing, a performance of production articulated by an array of diverse representational structures: oration, collection, observation, description, publication, and exhibition. Considered from this point of view, as a multiply mediated event occurring between and among these modes of (production's) representation, the procession reframes the writing and ratification of the Constitution as merely one political "occasion" raised within an extended, Grand Federal, exhibitionary complex.[84]

FRAMING THE SHIP *PHILADELPHIA*: BIRCH'S *VIEWS* OF *PHILADELPHIA* IN *1800*

Engraved in 1798–99, more than ten years after the procession, William Russell Birch's *Views of Philadelphia* rehearse once again the centrality of viewership to the successful raising of the federal frame. In the process, as engravings, they bring further into view the variety of (technographic) arts that accomplished that raising. Originally titled *Philadelphia in 1800*, Birch's twenty-nine views are a series of logically interconnected street scenes, accompanied by a map and organized as a series of fourteen contrasting pairs. The fourteen paired plates are presented as a series of contrasts between, for example, "Old" and "New" Philadelphia; finished and unfinished construction; northern and southern locales in the city; open

and confined spaces; transparent and opaque vistas. The Janus-like reversibility of these pairs is epitomized by such plates as "The New Lutheran
Church, in Fourth-street," versus "The Old Lutheran Church in Fifth-
street" (Birch, plates 5e and 6); "High street from the Country Marketplace" versus "High street from Ninth street" (Birch, plates 11 and 12);
"The [finished and empty] house intended for the President of the United
States in Ninth-street" versus "An unfinished [and empty] house, in Chestnut street" (Birch, plates 13 and 14).[85] Together with an opening grid of
the city streets, the dichotomous organization of the engravings offsets
and contains the threat of randomness implied by the collection's imitation of an actual tour of the city.[86] Prefacing the collection, the grid represents a bird's-eye view of Philadelphia, which reader-viewers are to use as
a tourist would, to orient themselves in relation to particular views (fig. 3).
The map unites the collection and reiterates the ideal of union through
elevation articulated by the Grand Federal Procession even as it constitutes
the elevated view of the reader-viewer of the collection as a whole. Birch's
Views thus elaborate a self-contained, circular, and nonprogressive kind of
progress.

It is in plates 11 and 29 (figs. 1 and 4), in particular, that the roof-raising
performance of collectivity is seen to be definitively rooted in the eyes of
tourists, viewers, and spectators: these plates represent a view of Humphreys's shipyard in the southern suburb of Southwark (Birch, plate 29)
and a view of the crowd of spectators at Philadelphia's Funeral Procession
of 1799, commemorating the death of Washington (Birch, plate 11). Together, these plates reiterate and summarize the framework of spectatorship that floated the federal ship of state in the Philadelphia procession
of 1788. For Birch, as for Hopkinson's Committee of Arrangement in
1788, both shipbuilding and mansion making represent the pyramidal
unity of base with superstructure and of artisan craft with commerce; like
the Federal Procession, Birch's *Views* privilege the building trades, focusing upon ships and mansions. In the Grand Federal Procession, the Federal Ship *Union* sailed near the head of the procession, behind *The New
Roof.* Thirty-three feet long, it was surrounded by a huge skirt of blue canvas (representing the sea) and accompanied by the city's merchants and
traders, the Marine Society, and the shipbuilding crafts. The men aboard
the *Union* performed all the ceremonies of a voyage, from "setting sail"
and "receiving the pilot" to "trimming her sails to the wind according to
the several courses of the line of march." In his "Account" Hopkinson
describes the ship itself as

> a master-piece of elegant workmanship, perfectly proportioned and com-
> plete throughout; decorated with emblematical carving. And what is truly
> astonishing, she was begun and completed in less than four days. . . . The
> workmanship and appearance of this beautiful object commanded universal

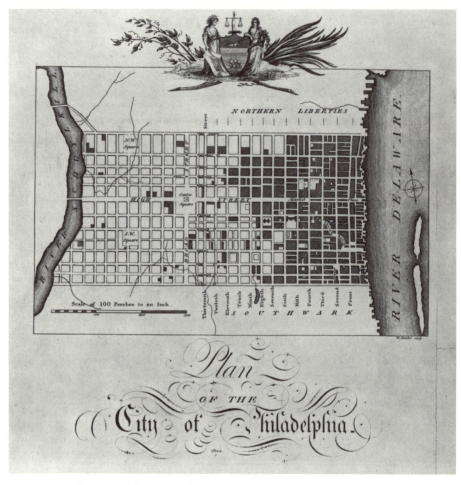

Figure 3. William Russell Birch, "Plan of the City of Philadelphia,"
in *The City of Philadelphia in the State of Pennsylvania North
America as it appeared in the Year 1800* (Springfield Cot, Pennsylvania:
William Birch, 1800), plate 3. (Courtesy of the Library
Company of Philadelphia.)

admiration and applause, and did high honour to the artists of Philadelphia,
who were concerned in her construction.[87]

But, of course, this celebration of collective construction belies a hierarchy: the merchants lead the way, carrying a flag with a globe and a scroll
inscribed "*par tout le monde*," while their clerks and apprentices march behind, led by "mr. Saintonge, bearing a large ledger."[88] The eighty-nine
member Marine Society follow, carrying spyglasses, trumpets, charts, and
quadrants; behind them, and most numerous of all, are the shipbuilding

Figure 4. William Russell Birch, "High Street, from the Country Marketplace Philadelphia: With the procession in commemoration of the Death of General George Washington, December 26th 1799," in *The City of Philadelphia in the State of Pennsylvania North America as it appeared in the Year 1800* (Springfield Cot, Pennsylvania: William Birch, 1800), plate 11. (Courtesy of the Library Company of Philadelphia.)

craftsmen: mastmakers, caulkers, ship's carpenters (or "white oaks"),[89] carvers, boatbuilders, sailmakers, ship joiners, ropemakers, and ship chandlers. As Hopkinson reports in his meticulous "Account," 330 mastmakers, caulkers, and ship's carpenters marched beneath "a flag bearing a ship on the stocks." In their hats they wore "a green sprig of white oak" and a badge (also representing "a ship on the stocks"). The ship joiners wore cedar and carried their "company's arms on a flag, viz. a binnacle and hencoop, crooked planes and other tools of that profession"; their motto, "by these we support our families."[90]

In the port city of Philadelphia, the phenomenon of a ship sailing in the streets punningly materialized the union of merchant and mechanic interests in a reviving urban economy that would, presumably, be reinvigorated by federal trade laws under the Constitution. Merchants and mechanics both depended, in other words, upon a commercial ship of state

that would "float." On these grounds, Hopkinson's Committee of Arrangement similarly linked the streets to the sea in the opening salvo of the
Federal Procession. At dawn on the morning of the parade,

> The rising sun was saluted with a full peal from Christ church steeple, and
> a discharge of cannon from the ship Rising Sun . . . anchored off Market-
> street, and superbly decorated with the flags of various nations. Ten vessels,
> in honour of the ten states of the union, were dressed and arranged thro' the
> whole length of the harbour . . . . New Hampshire opposite to the Northern
> Liberties; Massachusetts to Vine-street; Connecticut to Race-street; New-Jer-
> sey to Arch-street; Pennsylvania to Market-street; Delaware to Chestnut-
> street; Maryland to Walnut-street; Virginia to Spruce-street; South-Carolina
> to Pine-street; and Georgia to South-street.[91]

The gridlike streets of Philadelphia are also to be found in the opening
engraving of Birch's *Views*. Individuating, egalitarian, and homogenizing,
the grid translates space into interchangeable and identical parts. In another of Birch's plates, however, the egalitarian division represented by
the grid also explicitly presumes elevation, hierarchy, and class distinction.
Titled "Preparation for WAR to defend Commerce," plate 29 depicts the
building of "the Frigate Philadelphia in Humphreys' shipyard in Southwark, a southern suburb of Philadelphia"[92] (fig. 1). In this engraving, the
men at work in the shipyard are watched by at least three observers: the
man and woman who appear to be touring the site (at lower left) and
the gentlemanly military figure (lower center). This last figure is further
distinguished by his dress and pose as either the manager of the worksite
or, perhaps, as the future captain of the ship *Philadelphia*.

The scene is, above all, a worksite, with workmen clustered below and
upon the roughly pyramidal framework that surrounds the ship. Here the
skeletal apparatus of the scaffolding resembles a grid laid across the picture space, dividing and reframing the scene. At the same time, however,
the scaffolding is composed to figure a triangle, reiterating, in effect, the
elevated slope of federalism's "new roof." In Birch's shipyard scene, as in
the Federal Procession, workmen perform various acts of construction:
the beam, being raised into place with ropes and pulley at the top of the
scaffold's ramp, reiterates the trope that structures the *Views* throughout—
the raising, or "rise and progress," of the port city—while the juxtaposition
of workers with viewers, labor with looking, reiterates the message that
production must be performed in the presence of an elevated view that
can (via representation) articulate and incorporate all. The pyramidal
shape of the ship carpenters' scaffolding is one more version, then, of the
federal frame, raised to keep it out of the hands of "idle servants." Here,
though, the raised or elevated point of view is inhabited not by architects
and speech makers but by tourists, who stand on the ground below and
among the workmen.

The touring couple and the military gentlemen (together with the background sentry in his guardhouse, at lower right) all figure viewership within this scene of work. Their viewing presumes the grid of streets that opens the *Views*; the onlookers take in the scene in ways that the workmen do not, representing within the picture itself the point of view of the spectatorial reader of the whole collection.[93] In Birch's shipyard scene, where viewership means elevation, class difference is constituted primarily through acknowledgment of the frame of viewing itself (of the grid itself as scaffolding and collective point of view). Birch himself described the view of the shipyard like this: "The scenery . . . represents, with the Swedish church, the exertion of naval architecture to protect . . . [the city's] commerce."[94] The "Swedish church" mentioned here refers to the church in the center background of the shipbuilding scene in plate 29, represented by the steeple and cross rising in the distance, above the worksite. This church, called "Gloria Dei, or Old Swedes," was a Philadelphia landmark; built between 1698 and 1700, it was one of the oldest buildings in the city.[95] The cross and steeple of Gloria Dei in the center background of the plate are echoed in the left middle ground by four men walking up the scaffolding with a beam on their shoulders—a beam that forms another "cross" with the vertical post they are passing. Here, the past in the form of the "Old" church and its cross is reconstituted in the foreground grid of the scaffolding, now seen as a frame not only for building but for viewing and for reading. The church is also reconstituted in the foreground, however, by the opaque hull of the leviathan-like ship itself, built in preparation for "WAR to defend Commerce."[96] Here, by way of the steeple, the foregrounded work of shipbuilding connects the colony's historical founding in the late seventeenth century to its commercial present in the late eighteenth century via a gridwork that is not only man-made but also of providential design: American shipbuilding is part of the Creator's original plan, visible and ongoing in the present.

If the Swedish church in the background of Birch's plate 29 figures a providential design made visible in the mechanical art/work of the present, his plate 11 figures the Maker's absent presence in the death of the nation's founding "Father," General Washington. Plate 11 memorializes the Philadelphia procession held on the occasion of Washington's death. In this plate, the visual framework of the grid is echoed by a memorial arch of market stalls, which open out onto the parade scene. Several figures are framed in the illuminated gloom of the market, including a man at far right who is weeping. Five other figures, by contrast, are comparatively without affect, being absorbed in the procession to the point of unreadability: behind the weeping man, a woman and child watch the procession, their backs to us; a couple perches on the stall above them; while a lounging man reclines in a stall at the far left middle ground. The weeping man is dressed in military costume; he seems to have stepped out of the procession and is, perhaps, a member of the Revolutionary "Society of the Cincinnati" or a former officer in the Revolution; he wears clothing reminiscent of that which Washington himself might have worn as general.

The black-draped coffin in this procession was, in fact, empty (as has been the case in state funeral processions in the twentieth century), and thus it is here an empty coffin that figures the missing founder or father, whose "creation" is a viewing public that goes on without him, in the form of a state-making spectatorial frame/work, a frame/work associated, in Birch's plate, with the market. The weeping man's affect fills the empty frame of viewership, while his body figures what is—and is not— inside the dark coffin at the picture's center: the body of the founding father. By contrast with the figures in the foreground, a relatively undifferentiated crowd fills the windows and balconies in the background. Within the engraving, window frames define and individuate an anonymous crowd. And, as was the case during the Grand Federal Procession of 1788, women and children are found here among the spectators. In short, Birch's representation of a federal spectacle in plate 11 argues that the missing body of "the maker" lives on in the skeletal constructions of visible and legible viewership—in the employment of virtual citizens in the practice of spectatorship.

In its July 1788 issue, Carey's *Museum* offered another extensive report on the Baltimore parade, after which Baltimore's "Federal Ship" was presented as a gift to Washington himself. Built by the city's shipbuilding trades, the miniature sailing ship was literally floated down the Potomac to Mount Vernon. The *Museum* reprinted the letter from General Washington (dated 8 July 1788), in which he thanks the Baltimore Committee for the gift. "I pray you, gentlemen," writes Washington from Mount Vernon,

> to accept the warmest expressions of my sensibility for this specimen of American ingenuity; in which the exactitude of the proportions, the neatness of the workmanship . . . (which make your present fit to be preserved in a cabinet of curiosities) at the same time they exhibit the skill and taste of the artist, demonstrat[e] that Americans are not inferior to any people whatever in the use of mechanical instruments.[97]

Here, the arts of mechanical assemblage and of museum display combine in Washington's identification of technical ingenuity with its exhibition in "a cabinet of curiosities" displayed before an imaginary world audience ("not inferior to any people whatever").[98] The cabinet of curiosities in which Washington imagines his ship displayed is the exhibitionary parallel to the *American Museum* itself. The reference points to the shared exhibitionary/spectatorial field that linked the procession as a display of American manufacturing to Carey's *American Museum* as an assemblage of

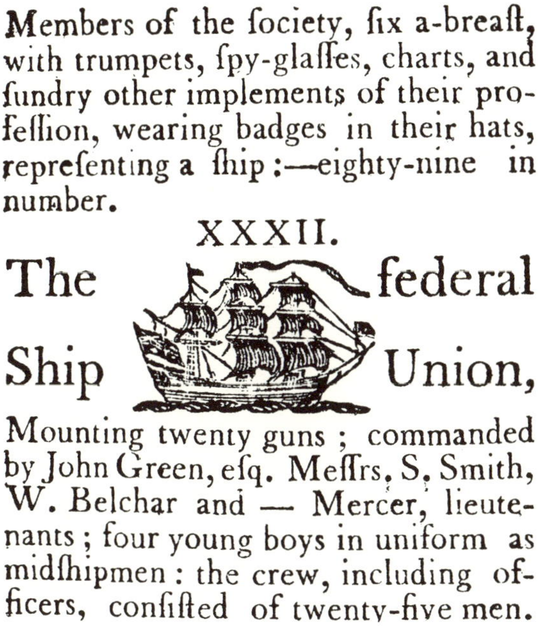

Members of the fociety, fix a-breaft,
with trumpets, fpy-glaffes, charts, and
fundry other implements of their pro-
feffion, wearing badges in their hats,
reprefenting a fhip :—eighty-nine   in
number.

XXXII.

The federal

Ship Union,

Mounting twenty guns ; commanded
by John Green, efq. Meffrs, S, Smith,
W. Belchar and — Mercer, lieute-
nants ; four young boys in uniform as
midfhipmen : the crew, including officers, confifted of twenty-five men.

Figure 5. The Federal Ship *Union.* "An Account of the Grand
Federal Procession." *American Museum and Repository of Ancient
and Modern Fugitive Pieces, &c.,* July 1788, 61.

writing in print. As a cabinet of assembled articles, the *Museum* reiterates
what the floats and badges, mottoes and devices, buttons, barrels, ships
and saddles of the Grand Federal Procession also (reportedly, as in fig.5)
displayed: all ranks and representational forms could be conjoined in
(and as) the production and display of American manufacturing.

In his discussion of American melodrama in the nineteenth century,
Bruce McConachie argues that widespread anxiety about the theater sent
many lower-middle-class families to the performative space of popular museums such as Barnum's New York Museum or Kimball's Boston Museum.[99] McConachie holds that it was an admixture of Finneyite Christian
evangelicalism in the republicanism of these museum-going audiences
that made the moral melodramas performed at Barnum's and Kimball's
museums so appealing. Focusing on the nineteenth century, McConachie
distinguishes sharply between the midcentury visual space of the museum
and earlier, federalist-era museums, in the main dedicated to natural history, such as Charles Willson Peale's Museum of Art and Nature.[100] Certainly an emphasis on Linnaean science distinguishes Peale's museum
from Barnum's or Kimball's. But in fact the differences between Peale's
and Barnum's or Kimball's museums are overwhelmingly outweighed by

the structural similarity between the field of visibility and legibility opened by Peale's museum and that offered some thirty years later by Barnum and Kimball. Federalist-era natural history museums in the United States may have been few in number, but they were intensely performative exhibitionary spaces. And, like Rousseau's defense of republican assembly, they advertised themselves as republican entertainments by way of contrast to the immoral or amoral theaters of Europe.[101] Furthermore, in late-eighteenth-century Philadelphia, the word "museum" referred equally to collections of objects and to magazines and miscellanies dedicated to the preservation of print ephemera. Ultimately, not only the melodrama in Barnum's museum but federalist-era republican festivity must be identified with the performative and exhibitionary framework of the American museum writ large, where the museum serves as a grand federal mechanism for the creation and division of labor and the constitution of an American working class.

The *American Museum* reports that on the evening of 4 July 1788, at the end of the procession and the feast on Union Green, the Grand Federal Edifice was carried "back in great triumph, and with loud huzzas, to the state-house, in Chestnut-street."[102] Juxtaposed with its symbolic original (the Pennsylvania State House, or Independence Hall), the miniature edifice deposited beside the State House was a pun on federalism as both museum and mass culture and on the procedures of representation in the extended republic as the mechanical reproduction of symbolic originals. It also reiterated the connection between political power and a public culture, where culture means a display of the collective arts of self-production.

The miniature Edifice beside the State House articulates several meanings. On one hand, it juxtaposes an elite structure, a mansion, with the State House, a site of national self-making and political representation. In addition, Carpenters' Hall—the traditional meeting-place of Philadelphia's elite, guildlike Carpenters' Company—was situated next to the State House, and the juxtaposition of the buildings articulates the longtime social and economic links between the two structures.[103] On the other hand, however, the miniature mansion was not the solid and actual State House. In fact, it made visible the floating of the state: the continual (re)creation and dissemination of federal law and republican orderliness accomplished by the multiple structures of representation that authorized law and order together on the grounds of production.

CHAPTER TWO

The Mechanic as the Author of His Life:
John Fitch's "Life"
and "Steamboat History"

> The house that I was born in was upon the line between Hartford
> and Windsor but as the biggest part of the place was in Windsor
> it was said that I was born in Windsor but from the singularity of
> my make shape disposition and forturne [sic] in this world I am
> inclined to believe that it was the design of heaven that I should
> be born on the very line and not in any township whatever.
>
> John Fitch, "Life"

In 1792, just two years after Benjamin Franklin's *Autobiography* was published, a Philadelphia metalworker named John Fitch finished writing his
own manuscript "Life" and "Steamboat History." Part autobiography, part
technological disquisition, Fitch's manuscript intersperses familiar modes
of discourse (travel literature, sermons, captivity narratives, pamphlet debates) with self-justifying tirades concerning his five-year race with rival
inventor James Rumsey to build and patent the first working steamboat in
North America. Fitch's manuscript falls into two parts: the autobiographical narrative (his "Life") and a shorter "Steamboat History." Part appendix, part unfinished pamphlet, the "Steamboat History" traces the vicissitudes of Fitch's invention and his struggle for patent priority. Like
Franklin's *Autobiography*, most of Fitch's "Life" covers decades prior to the
Revolution. But for both Fitch (1744–98) and Franklin (1706–90), it is
the Revolution that calls forth the project of bridging, through autobiography, a whole series of Revolutionary divides: colonial versus national identity, childhood versus adulthood, apprenticeship versus independence.

In many ways, Franklin's *Autobiography* constitutes a far-from-seamless
passage over these Revolutionary divides. One thinks, for example, of the
gaps between its four "Parts" and, in particular, of the rupture between
Franklin and his Loyalist son William which divides Part One from Part
Two.[1] But, while Franklin's *Autobiography* discovers its own gaps and limits,
it nevertheless thrives upon the possibility of representative self-making,

of personality displayed as an artifact of American ingenuity.[2] The *Autobiography* participates unevenly, but unambivalently, in the federal fantasy that subjectivity could be performatively produced, in print and in life, to the point of an author's becoming entirely one with himself as the object of his own creation. Just like the numerous companies and corporations he founded—the Philadelphia Fire Company, the Library Company, the "Junto," and The American Philosophical Society—Franklin's life-in-letters is a monument to the federal fusion of words and things, private profit with public goods.

Fitch's manuscript, by contrast, constitutes no such ironic-but-monumental passage. Just as his attempts to found corporations and "Societies" were all short-lived, so his unpublished "Life" and "Steamboat History" fail to demonstrate the living truth of federalism or to frame a workable bridge between nation building and self-creation. Whereas Franklin's *Autobiography* is a do-it-yourself demonstration of how to transform social contradiction into profitable representational and economic structures (with the printer-made-good on top), Fitch's "Life" and "Steamboat History" present a pattern of repetitive failure and impotent railing at those "worthies" of the early republic who failed to support him in his struggle to patent his steamboat. Fitch's "Life" shares some of the generic features of Franklin's *Autobiography*, such as the attempt to legitimate the writing of autobiography itself as the dissemination of useful knowledge.[3] But, in an inversion of Franklin's how-to story of successful self-production, the tirades and incoherences of Fitch's manuscripts articulate precisely the politics of rage and the open economic ambition that more worthy republicans were warning against—but which republican representational practices also worked to elicit.[4] In their failure to mesh with the gears of federalism, Fitch's "Life" and "Steamboat History" fail, then, to translate Revolution into Union, private interest into public good, or words and persons into things. Like the Connecticut farmhouse in which he was born, his writings sit, counterproductively, "on the very line" of such divides. Unpublished until 1976, Fitch's "autobiography" is the tale of a would-be Benjamin Franklin who neither escaped the tyrannical apprenticeship of his youth nor found his way to fame and independence.

Fitch's manuscripts bristle with libelous accusations—of deceit, self-interest, and outright lying manipulation (or lack of "candour")—against such celebrated republicans as Franklin, Washington, and Washington's secretary of state, Thomas Jefferson. Fitch later claimed that it was because of his manuscripts' expressions of resentment against the "first officers of the Government" that he "sealed" them in the Library Company of Philadelphia, with instructions that they remain unopened for thirty years: "[T]he warmth of the present age," he writes,"is so much in favour of the first officers of the Government whom I have so strenuously called in question their candour that I much fear that [the manuscripts] would be destroyed without ever giveing the world an opportunity of knowing in what manner I have been treated by them."[5]

The most immediate cause of Fitch's rage was that in 1791 the first national patent commission (headed by Jefferson) denied him patent priority for the steamboat, despite the fact that Fitch had assembled not one but two working steamboats between 1787 and 1790, under extremely difficult financial and technological conditions. Instead, Jefferson issued a joint patent to both Fitch and his rival James Rumsey.

Historian Thomas Boyd argues that in the late 1780s Fitch lacked crucial support from Washington and his administration because he openly advocated deploying his steamboat on the Mississippi, at a time when the United States had just signed a treaty with Spain relinquishing control over the river's trade through New Orleans. Fitch's first petition to the Continental Congress for support in 1785 was allowed to die in committee because of its opening paragraph, which frankly declared the steamboat "[adapted] especially to the waters of the Mississippi."[6] By the mid-1780s Washington and many members of Congress feared that the growing flood of settlers into Ohio and Kentucky would not only antagonize Spain but undermine the political and economic integrity of the original thirteen colonies. Washington therefore supported Fitch's rival James Rumsey, an engineer of canals in Virginia who had been working on a steamboat since 1784. Washington's support of Rumsey, a fellow Virginian, aimed to redirect the trade of the interior to the rivers and canals of the eastern seaboard; he expected that, eventually, western produce would find an outlet via eastern rivers like the Potomac, thus preserving the economic power of the Atlantic seaboard states.[7] For these reasons, among others, Washington not only sided with Rumsey on the question of steamboat priority but also employed Rumsey in Virginia to make improvements on the Potomac River, as a way of fulfilling his dream of making the Potomac, rather than the Mississippi, the primary outlet of western trade.[8] Where Rumsey was a Virginian with eastern connections and eastern ambitions, Fitch, by contrast, had made a trading trip of his own down the Ohio to the Mississippi (from Pittsburgh, with a load of flour) and had spent years in the early 1780s as a landjobber and surveyor in Kentucky and Ohio. Born and raised on an impoverished farm in Connecticut, Fitch never considered binding the West to the East by drawing trade to the eastern seaboard via canals. He was not, like Rumsey, an engineer of canals; apocalyptic war canoes were more to his taste. He declared his steamboat "a first Rate man of war," which would navigate "the Western Waters . . . by Fire," make the Mississippi "as Navigable as Tide Water," and "raise the value of our Western Territory three or four times what it then was."[9]

Ultimately, however, Fitch's explicit statements about dominating the continental interior are not the sole explanation for his difficulties in gaining patronage and patent priority: Fitch was also intolerable to leading federalists because he took so literally federalism's advice to the mechanical artist to raise himself while raising a nation. And, what was perhaps even more damaging, in the process he made explicit one of the open secrets of the extended republic: its continuing dependence upon personal face-to-face relations of patronage and subscription—relations that, despite the official emphasis on disinterest and detachment, remained virtually unmediated by the republican principle of representation, even at the highest levels of the federal government. Fitch was intolerable to "the first officers of the Government" because he could not hide his dependence upon their personal patronage (letters of recommendation, social connections, and subscription), even while he took literally, or to the point of lunacy, the federal fantasy of representative self-production.[10] "[T]here is now," Fitch writes to one Reverend [Nathaniel] Irwin, a preacher in Neshaminy, Pennsylvania,

> the greatest opening for a man of Tallents . . . to make himself the Greatest which ever lived. Moses Jesus Christ Alexander or Mahomet would stand but Cyphers to him. . . . Was you Sir to step forward and form a Society upon generious Principles and give public lectures on questions every sunday . . . you would in the first place soon make a fortune. In the 2nd Place you would do real and great good to mankind. 3d, you would soon have connections with other Societies belonging to you which would take Rise from yours throughout the continent and first become a Membre of Congress for a District and finally a President of the United States and fix a new Era that all the world would remember when the names of Jesus Christ or Washington is Lost.[11]

In 1791, just three years after the Grand Federal Procession, Fitch made all too graphic the corporate juncture of man making with world making. In this passage, Fitch encourages Irwin to become the artisan-lawgiver of a technological millennium that would unite time and space, "Era" and Area, through the universal laws of God-in-mechanism. These laws were as yet imperfectly known, Fitch acknowledged, but the man who comprehended them all would "be made infallibel, and consecrated Pope for one year."[12] Taking rise through a social system that linked individuals with each other and with the world, this technological genius would not rise solely on his own but through the dynamic interaction of his mechanical know-how with the representational machinery of interlocking social organizations: the corporations, companies, and learned societies that constituted and mediated the interplay of public disinterest with private investments. By using the techniques of incorporation that structured learned and self-improvement societies as well as religious organizations—"to step forward and form a Society . . . and give public lectures on questions every sunday"—any mechanic or obscure preacher might emerge on a global stage, first "a Membre of Congress for a District and . . . [then] President of the United States." Here Fitch's dream of a fusion of private interests ("to make a fortune") with public virtue (to "do real and great good to mankind") is a literal-minded replica of the federal design celebrated in Philadelphia's Grand Federal Procession of 1788. But in his words, federalism's "New Roof" is a ladder or, more precisely, a global system for emerging from obscurity via myriad social connections, for mounting to the top of a pyramid whose vertical height is matched only by its imperial sprawl ("taking Rise throughout the continent").

Nevertheless, although Fitch saw the federal pyramid raised above him, he failed to inhabit its architecture, and his "Life" and "Steamboat History" never became well-preserved articles in the museum of federalism. Fitch's manuscripts would remain unpublished in the Library Company for more than 180 years, until the American Philosophical Society printed them in a Bicentennial edition of its *Memoirs* under the title *The Autobiography of John Fitch*. Even in the form of a book—transcribed by Frank D. Prager, together with a selection of letters and textual fragments called "postscripts"—Fitch's autobiography is a pastiche of genres, impossible to organize into any neat, narrative sequence or self-identical whole, even by the most skillful editor. The remarkable range of genres, styles, and discourses in Fitch's writings testify to the innumerable representational structures that functioned in early industrial America to classify and organize persons as objects in an expanding world of things. But, as pastiche, the modes of discourse Fitch employs (only to drop) never become what Bakhtin called "dialogic," despite their conglomeration of genres, styles, and grammars.[13] Disintegrating rather than integrated, Fitch's life in letters never "novelizes" the discourses through which it churns; his unruliness never translates into a lesson well learned.[14]

Several months after the patent decision of 1791, Fitch, resenting Jefferson's decision as an insult and a disaster for his Steamboat Company, made his will and sealed his manuscript in the Library Company. Not long afterward, fired with new hopes, he sailed for Europe, where, in 1793, he made unsuccessful attempts to build steamboats for revolutionary France. Eventually, in 1798, after wandering from France to England to Massachusetts, Fitch killed himself with an overdose of opium in Bardstown, Kentucky, near the Ohio River, where he had once hoped to conquer "the Western waters" of the interior. Fitch's deposit of his "Life" in the Library Company was never a simple suppression of unutterable truths. The "sealing" of his "speach" was itself part of his rage for personhood—his desire to produce himself and to be produced as a public property, an embodiment of republican legitimacy, and a monument to freedom, like the exemplary figures of state upon whom his life and steamboat depended. Despite his fear of exposing his transgressive rage, Fitch clearly believed that an eager audience was waiting somewhere for his "Life" to emerge, incarnate, in a well-edited print edition: "[A]s I am no grammarian," he writes, "I wish the whole of my works revised . . . whenever a person would come forward and pledge his honor that he will . . . do them justice and spare no man however high in office."[15]

Fitch unquestioningly absorbed the claims of a productivist culture that presented graphic design, visual access, and a candid correspondence of word with image, or inner with outer man, as the bases of both social cohesion and individual celebrity. In the end, however, he failed to hide his literal-minded fusion of personal power with national power and territorial expansion: he could not ironize his combined economic and emotional investments, nor distinguish private from public interest. Fitch's "problem" was that he had no proper—or property-acknowledging—sense of a subjective interiority. He could neither bring himself into view nor display himself as a properly detached subject who had learned to regard himself as an object. Fitch hungered to make his appearance in the history of the world, but he was unable to integrate words with things or persons with objects within the new republic whose fields of enterprise were emerging all around him. He failed to make his life a coherently self-divided work, or a fulfillment of the patent and copyright clause in the new Constitution, which linked authorship and mechanical invention together on the grounds that both produced intellectual "properties." In marked contrast to the cultivated irony and performative self-consciousness of Franklin's *Autobiography*, the contradictions and failures of Fitch's writings simply never translate into that edifice of modern subjectivity: the citizen as the object of his own making.

CHILDHOOD AND REVOLUTION

In Philadelphia, as in France and England, Enlightenment projects of social, legal, and penal reform aimed at creating free citizens by liberating the collective body of the people from savage or superstitious tyranny. As an early national mechanism of social engineering, liberal humanitarianism opened new channels of cultural reproduction, expression, and control. In Franklin's *Autobiography*, for example, public projects—from newspapers and autobiographies to street lighting and improved stoves—are presented as mechanisms for doing good and for marrying public with private interest. In Fitch's "Life" and "Steamboat History," by contrast, the body's liberation from one repression only subjects it to another. Throughout his long life of effort, Fitch experienced the humane lifting of labor from his body only as an increase in its repression and control, rather than as an internalized, self-historicizing advance. Whereas Franklin's *Autobiography* traces his steady rise from the obscure rank of printer's apprentice to his appearance as a celebrated character on an international stage, Fitch worked his way through life variously, as a clockmaker, brass-founder, silversmith, gunsmith, buttonmaker, engraver, surveyor, and Kentucky landjobber, before turning to steamboats in the early 1780s. And, where the myth of independence in Franklin's *Autobiography* begins with the author's flight from an oppressive apprenticeship under his brother in Boston to freedom and independence in Philadelphia, Fitch's "Life" remains irredeemably bound to corporate forms of patriarchal "tyranny."

Fitch was raised on a Connecticut farm during the 1740s and 1750s, by a father who "was educated a rigid Christian and was a bigot and one of the most strenuous of the sect of Prisbertereans." His mother died when he was four, and Fitch was allowed to go to school only until he was eight or nine, and even so only because it cost his father nothing. Thereafter, except for one month each winter, he was kept home for the value of his labor. The youngest of five children, Fitch was forced to work almost continually for both his father—a "mean nigardly wretch"—and his older brother Joseph: "This tyrant brother would make me hoe row and roe about with him till I was ready to faint and fall down in the field and dare not stop for one minute to rest myself as knowing his cruil hand. And . . . [my father] indulged him in it as I suppose because he thought he could get a few hills of corn more hoed." He later adds, "I enjoyed myselfe as well as most of the Virginia slaves."[16]

At the age of seventeen, Fitch finally managed to escape his father's farm, only to enter a long and miserable apprenticeship to two clockmak-ers, Benjamin Cheany and (later) Benjamin's brother Timothy. But this apprenticeship resulted in neither mastery nor independence. Timothy Cheany in particular employed his apprentice just as Fitch's father had, to "work his place": "Nay Sir I did there demean myself to the washing of dishes and never complained of it to mortal man till this day."[17] The best that Fitch can say of his two-and-a-half-year apprenticeship is that "I generally had my belly full of something or other altho much more indifferent and coarse than I was accostomed to at my father's house."[18] Worst of all was the clockmakers' failure to teach their apprentice the secrets of the trade. Timothy Cheany, for example, never showed Fitch "any of his tooles for watch-work as he had a drawer where he was particu-larly cairful always to lock them up as if he was affraid I should know their use and by that means gain some information of the business. And he never would nor never did tell me the different parts of a watch."[19] On this occasion, as on many like it, Fitch's narrative of deprivation and inequity in early America is marked by "oddities," or grotesque details, that sit curi-ously (as the products of, and at odds with) the matter-of-fact empiricism of his autobiographical narration: "My master was a pretty good sort of a man but possessed with a great many oddities and considerably deformed with the rickets in his youth especially his head which was near double the size of common proportion. And [he] was a man of som considerable genius."[20]

Years later Fitch was able to teach himself clockmaking by trial and error—as he claimed to teach himself virtually everything throughout his life. The unresolved struggle to appropriate skill, comfort, and security left its marks, however, and Fitch repeatedly uses the word "meanness" to describe the mixture of emotional and economic deprivation that marked both his failed apprenticeship and his upbringing on his father's farm. In his telling, the "meanness" of his childhood—grinding poverty, endless labor, and social humiliation—is never left behind but simply repeated in the rejections and failures of his adult life. In Fitch's "Life," such accusations of "meanness" are never mere expressions of rebellion against traditional forms of deferential behavior; rather, they indicate the breakdown of those forms. The resentment and rage that mark Fitch's life are directed less against hierarchies of rank and patriarchy per se than against their frequent failure, under the conditions of Anglo-American market expansion, to fulfill their promise of protection, security, and legitimacy.[21]

Deferential behavior toward one's betters was supposed to bring in return a paternalistic promise of protection and loyalty. As a manifestation of social interdependence, deference included signs of condescension from social superiors and of obedience from those upon whom would-be governors or representatives depended for support.[22] While deference persisted after the Revolution, the class relations it mediated were increasingly intertwined with market mechanisms of representative self-making. As a way of getting ahead in the post-Revolutionary marketplace, deference was a deeply ambiguous cultural practice: a simulacrum of interdependence embedded in a market that was working to dissolve the very structures of cohesion upon which that market also depended.

The failure of the deferential social connections that characterized Fitch's life before, during, and after the Revolution—and the "meanness" that resulted—are epitomized in his "Life" by a confrontation that occurred long before the Revolution, in 1752, when he was eight years old. The Fitches' Connecticut farm lay next to the estate of Roger Wolcott, the governor of the province from 1750 to 1754. As a child, Fitch occasionally assisted the governor in surveying his fields, both for the honor of carrying the chain and in "expectation of some pennies." Fitch was eager to help, and Wolcott's requests were "easily granted," he writes, "as [it] is common for poor men to exert themselves to oblige the great."[23] In the view of Fitch's older brother, however, Wolcott was not always forthcoming on his side of the social bargain with the men whose property adjoined his. It was "the custom" for rural people laboring out of doors "to keep a bottle of

rum and offer every traveler which passed a dram." From this they expected a generous gift of money and "frequantly received as much as
would buy a whole quart." One day Fitch's oldest brother and a number
of other men were working to mend the highway when Governor Wolcott
passed by in a scarlet coat. According to "custom," the governor was given
a drink, but he gave "one copper only" in return. Fitch's brother retaliated
with rage:

> [M]y oldest brother who was possessed with quite as much meanness as ei-
> ther my father or Governour Woolcutt brought the copper to my fathers
> and punched a hole thro' it and got a piece of scarlet cloth and went and
> sat a post in the ground so near the road that every traveler must see it. I
> stood by and see him punch the hole in the copper and went with him and
> see them plant the post and nail the copper and scarlet rag and heared many
> invectives thrown out against him for his meanness.[24]

The post by the road, with the copper and the scrap of red coat at its
center, marked a failure of "custom" all around. In a confused analysis of
the situation, Fitch diagnoses "meanness" on both sides: "This undoubt-
edly is the meanest and most unjustifiable way of getting money that can
be persued . . . but I thing [sic] the Governor took a very improper way to
suppress it and very imprudent in the first officer of government."[25] The
confusion here arises from the fact that Fitch finds it impossible to ally
himself with either his "tyrant brother" or the governor. In fact, a few days
earlier, Wolcott had honored Fitch with his patronage and then let him
down too. The governor had asked the boy to help him with some surveying and, "being proud of the office," Fitch "executed it faithfully." Later,
when the work was done and Wolcott came to get the surveying chain,
Fitch "fetched it to him with the greatest expedition and expectation of
some pennies." But the governor only took the chain and, putting it in his
saddlebag, "rode off without saying a word more to me." Fitch's "mortifi-
cation" was overwhelming: this was "a meanness," he writes, "which [even]
my father would never be guilty of"; yet he remains "persuaded" that "the
Governor was an honest man."[26]
As a deferential custom, a gift of money to workers on the road would
have been an affirmation of interdependence in which the social power
of the laborers was recognized while some of the community's total wealth
was redistributed, if only symbolically. By refusing to offer this gift to the
men working on the highway, Governor Wolcott set himself apart as a
private person and independent economic actor while at the same time
maintaining the privileges of his rank. For these reasons, Fitch and his
brother called the governor's assertion of independence from custom an
act of "meanness." Recollected by Fitch in 1792, the penny and the scrap
of a red coat are an early signpost of the American Revolution that, for

Fitch, was never really begun or concluded. The post in the road, with its copper and red cloth, articulate an unproductive social division wherein the withholding of "spirits" does not translate into a republican spirit of unity between ranks or a compromise between interests, as it would in the Grand Federal Procession of 1788. Rather, the post in the road testifies to a painful dislocation between the forms and local dependencies of a colonial hierarchy and the multiply mediated investments of imperial commerce and private property. Asserting transgression and independence on both sides of a class border in formation, the coin and the red cloth stand at a juncture where traditional forms of interdependence were being assimilated to new, market forms of institutional and corporate connectedness. It was at this history-making (dis)juncture that Benjamin Franklin began to make his mark in the 1730s and 1740s, learning to swim, or float himself, as a representative personality.[27] Unlike Fitch, Franklin was adept at exploiting the changing forms of social interdependence precisely where they were being painfully, unevenly transformed by the representational concerns of early industrial commercial expansion.

As a harbinger of nation making, then, the money and the red coat on the post articulate an unintegrated juxtaposition of social ranks, where rank was becoming class and class was emerging in and as national history. Fitch figured his engagements with this history-making culture, and his failures to embody its developmental narratives, as the disintegration of corporeal unity. While other observers perceived him as tall and "powerful," Fitch claimed that endless work and poor food stunted his growth, and he repeatedly deprecated himself as "little Johney Fitch."[28] He attributes what he calls his "disproportioned shapes" to a childhood passed in oppressive labor, followed by a sudden release or burst of natural growth at "seventeen or eighteen years of age," the age at which he left home:

> Sir the first part of my life has been thus far the severest task I have met with as to bodily labour. Which I believe stunted me and kept me from growing till I was seventeen or eighteen years of age and then as nature required growth [I] started up all at once without giving nature time to consult herself into my disproportioned shapes as you see me at present. For which I do not thank my unfealing father . . . and abhor to this day my tirant brother.[29]

The metaphor of disproportioned, grotesque, or uneven growth runs through Fitch's writing. But this grotesquerie is not simply a parodic inversion of federalism's social machinery.[30] Nor can it be explained as the pathological symptom of uneven, damaged, or thwarted "psychological" development.[31] The disproportioned shapes of Fitch's "Life" can be fully comprehended only as an articulation of historical time-in-the-making; they mark the uneven creation, rationalization, and reorganization of labor (as works) by proliferating technologies of production and representation. Disproportion marks the places in Fitch's "Life" where the representational frameworks that produced and divided persons and classes were resisted, and where, warped by resistance, such frameworks were emerging into visibility and legibility. Instead of the author as representative producer, then, Fitch's "Life" figures the uneven emergence of a culture of production. Although he was raised as a child laborer on a farm in Connecticut, Fitch was never a "husbandman." Likewise, although he had worked as a landjobber and surveyor in the Ohio territory and had engraved and printed one of the first accurate maps of the Ohio interior, he was never a "frontiersman." As a would-be founder and framer, Fitch was a metalworking mechanic employed at junctures where diverse spaces and times were emerging as collective history via the representational construct of the extended republic. Even as he was launching his steam-driven paddleboat (the *Perseverance*) on the Delaware, Fitch labored elsewhere, throughout his life, in a territory articulated with—but never fully entering—the new nation's extended sphere of visibility, its frameworks of representative self-production, and its museums of American manufacturing.

FITCH AMONG THE DELAWARE

At the beginning of the Revolution, Fitch was a silversmith in Trenton, New Jersey, where he was also employed as a gunsmith, supplying and repairing guns for soldiers in the militia and the Continental army. In the late 1770s, Fitch also served for a brief period in the New Jersey militia, but he viewed the assignment primarily as an opportunity for promotion and quit his company in a rage when he was refused an appointment to lieutenant. Fearing he would be prosecuted for desertion, he fled to Bucks County, Pennsylvania, where he discovered that his tools and his household furniture had been destroyed by the British: "My Desk was split up for fuel and Windsor Chairs the arms and upper parts were cut off I suppose for the same purpos and nothing but the stools left."[32] He had buried his stock of silver and gold in the woods outside Trenton, but this too was stolen, and, in the inflation that ensued near the end of the war, his savings of "som 4000 Dollars" became worth "no more than one hundred." It was at this juncture that Fitch looked west for a new route to property and position: "finding all my money gone," he writes, "the distresses of my mind was amazingly great and [I] could see no other way to realize my money but to go to Virginia and lay it out in Land Warrants and to Kentuckey and lay those Warrants on the most valuable Lands I could."[33]

Between 1780 and 1785, Fitch made four separate trips into Ohio and Kentucky as a surveyor.[34] It was during the second of these trips that he was taken captive by a group of Delaware Indians while ferrying a boatload of flour from Fort Pitt to New Orleans in search of quick profit. After a gunfight at the mouth of the Muskingum River, near present-day Marietta, Ohio, he was captured, together with eight other Anglo-Americans, by a group of eight Delaware.[35] From March to May of 1792, he traveled north with his captors, until he was traded to the British at "Prison Island opposit Cotedelack," where he was held until November. Fitch's narrative of his six-month captivity is the longest single episode in his "Life"; with the exception of his struggle with the steamboat, it is the one event to which he gives sustained attention. In fact, Fitch's captivity narrative is positioned as a bridge between the account of his early life and the "Steamboat History." Like most of the events in Fitch's narrative, however, it is a very curious kind of bridge, which affords no narrative progress and only very tenuous connections to other events in his "Life" or "Steamboat History."

The sheer length of Fitch's captivity narrative can, in part, be explained by the popularity of the genre, as well as by the celebrity accorded to naturalists, explorers, and travelers by a late-eighteenth-century print market that thrived on curious relations of new specimens, observations of the "manners and customs" of non-Europeans, and monumental works of useful knowledge illuminating new sites of Euro-American market expansion.[36] But Fitch's captivity among the Delaware (and later among the British) results in very little "useful information." Neither does it conclude in Calvinist resignation or surrender to God's will, as in the classic New England genre. Fitch never presents his captors, Puritan-style, as the agents of heaven or of hell and, though he tries sometimes, he never really comes to regard them as a naturalist or ethnographer might, as objects framed for study, comparison, and classification.

Indian captivity may be said in part to figure for Fitch as a trope for his life as a whole, with its repetitive failures and lack of conclusion—as in the following passage, in which he compares his career to the experience of torture by savages: "it seems that heaven had designed me for some more cruel fate whose only pleasure should be to sport and tyrinize with me as if he had been educated amongst savages for thousands of years for the very purpose."[37] At the same time, however, even while captivity was just one more experience of helpless dependence, it was also, initially at least, a brief opportunity for rest, a chance to let someone else do the work. At the moment of his capture, for example, Fitch's primary experience is one of relief, a lifting of the burden of continual effort. His first act after being taken by the Delaware is to go immediately to sleep: "being amazeingly fateagued with my days work before and doing near double duty on sentry and fully resigned to my fate [I] felt myself perfectly easy and . . . requested the Indian who could speak English to permit me to lay myself down and sleep. Which he granted." Fitch slept only briefly, being awakened and forced to march after only fifteen minutes. But, Fitch observes, even while they had control over his body, "proportion" was in some degree restored in their company. In a display of fairness that Fitch's own father had never shown, the Indians distributed packs to their captives according to the size and experience of each man: "the Indians . . . made up Bundles for each of us to carry and in the most juditious manner according to our appearance the man who looked healthy and strong they gave a heavy Load and lighter ones to the weaker. They did not give me above seven or Eight Pounds wt. but some near 30 lb. But none to be compaired to what they themselves carried. I am confident that some of their packs would weigh 6o lb."[38] The prisoners were also tied loosely ("I think as a Badge of Captivity rather than for use"), and Fitch was particularly "pleased to see the good order which was kept up amongst them and whenever we came to camp and a fire kindled I knew the spot where every one was to lie."[39]

In captivity, for the first time, Fitch experienced rest that was not leisure and order that was not a representational order of things. However, these periods of rest and proportion were interspersed with moments of terror that recalled the frustrations of his youth and anticipated his struggle with the steamboat. When he fell asleep at the moment of capture, for example, he was awakened by an Indian standing over him with a tomahawk, ready "to sink it into my head": "I looked him full in the face," Fitch writes, "and felt the greatest composure to receive it that I ever felt to meet Death unless it is since I began the Steam Boat."[40] Used here as a metaphor for the steamboat struggle that would follow his release, the force used against him in captivity is represented as simply a continuation of the demands to work and to move that characterized his life before and after captivity.

While the Delaware never emerge in Fitch's narrative as a particular enemy, they do evoke the same oscillating responses that typified his relations with patrons and other men of rank throughout his early life. In keeping with the analogy between Indian captivity and his struggle for recognition as an inventor, Fitch names one of his Delaware captors "Captain Washington" in an obvious allusion to the military hierarchy of the Continental army and state militia. But "Washington" is, of course, also an allusion to the man who would eventually support James Rumsey in the race to patent a steamboat. On the one hand, Fitch's captivity presents him with rest and a redistribution of labor that is outside of his experience. During the journey northwest from the Muskingum to western Lake Erie, for example, "the Game was exceeding scarse," and there was not food enough to support the nineteen men on their march. Under these conditions, Fitch notes, "[t]he Indians was very particular when provisions grew scarce to give everyone an equal share and gave the Prisoners equal to themselves that we had no just cause of complaint."[41] On the other hand,

such experiences never cause Fitch simply to identify with the Delaware.
Captivity instead reiterates his own long battle with scarcity and humiliation, and as he rather matter-of-factly reports, the Delaware force Fitch to
undergo various forms of ritual humiliation, which include the running
of a gauntlet. But even the gauntlet evokes no particular response or reflection. In every stressful episode, Fitch's primary point of reference is,
finally, neither ethnographic anecdote nor theological moral but his own
volatile "fealings." At one council dance, Fitch refers to himself as an Indian, but the comparison is emphatically not one of identification. Rather,
the comparison is only another way of expressing his feelings of isolation
and exclusion: "Every one of the Prisoners except myself danced . . . but I
felt as sulky as an Indian. I scarcely ever felt such fealings before or since."[42]

Early on in their captivity, the white captives were divided up, and Fitch
was given to "Captain Buffaloe." Fitch's relationship to this captor in particular reproduces the emotional gauntlet of Euro-American situations of
patronage and petition. In a moment of panic, for example, fearing that
all the captives were about to be killed, Fitch throws himself on the mercy
of "Capt. Buffaloe" by drawing a three-legged stool "long side of" him: "[I]
seated myself on it and layed my arm over his Bare thighs and sat dureing
his stay in the House looking upon him." For the moment Buffaloe pro-
tects Fitch, allowing—and in fact ordering—him to remain safe in the
house. But, at the end of this episode, Fitch reports that his fellow captives
"seemed to be extreamly angry with me and said—You are a great Friend
of the Indians I suppose."[43] Fitch's composure is shaken not so much by
Indians and tomahawks as by his fellow Anglo-Americans, who quickly become his "Enemies." By the end of the long trek to Canada, two of these
white men, "Parkerson and hopkins," represent Fitch to the other prisoners "as the damdest Tory that remained unhung and it was generally believed and told many dismal tails of me."[44] Thus, just as Fitch fails to charac-
terize the Delaware ethnographically, he also fails, in the end, to recognize
or represent them as the cause, or agents, of his captivity: throughout the
long march with the Delaware to Canada, Fitch's most acute experiences
of humiliation, oppression, and displacement were caused not by the Indians but by his fellow Anglo-Americans. In fact, if any single, overriding
issue is raised for Fitch by captivity, it is the question of whether the experience proves his cowardice or his bravery. True to form, he oscillates on
this issue, sometimes despising cowards while at other times celebrating
his own acts of cowardice as caution or good sense. Ultimately, though,
even the question of cowardice versus bravery becomes just one more unresolved dichotomy through which Fitch attempts to establish social definition and gauge his social position vis-à-vis other white men.

Fitch traces the hostility of "Parkerson and hopkins" to an episode in
which he refused to work. Not long after their capture, the white captives

were divided among "Capt. Washington," "Capt. Buffaloe," and "Capt. Crow." Captain Buffaloe took five of the eight men, including Fitch, to his "Town," where he tried to put them to work to "build a house for him." Fitch refused to do his part of the labor of house-raising:

> I informed the other Prisoners that I was not able to do any thing toward
> [building the house] but that would not satisfy them but the unfealing Pris-
> oners Perkerson and hopkins laid hold of me and by main force draged me
> to the place of work. My resentment was much roused at the unfealing men-
> ace. . . . I further told them that I was not fit to work neither would I and if
> I must die it should be by the tommyhawk and not by inches. They might
> do as they pleased obey their masters orders or risque the tommyhawk as to
> my own part I had made up my mind on the matter. And turned about and
> walked into the Cabbin. But these sevear reflections was never forgot by
> hopkins Perkerson and Johnson but was ever afterwards my most inveterate
> Enemies.[45]

Enraged by Fitch's behavior, the other prisoners try to isolate and pun-
ish him. "Captain Buffaloe" again intervenes and, instead of forcing Fitch
to work, gives him calamus root: "Instead of Buffaloe useing severities with
me for refusing to work he went and got som calimus root and ordered
me to take it which I did more to please him than a belieff of its being of
real service to me." Relieved of house construction, Fitch gathers wild on-
ions and artichokes and goes fishing, sharing his catch "equally amongst
the Prisoners," and claiming, in the end, that this "was of greater service
to them than my Labour could have been."[46]

Accused of being a Tory and "a great Friend of the Indians," Fitch never
articulates a consistent identification with any collectivity and has no clear
national loyalty. Whenever he is angry, furthermore, he contemplates
switching his allegiance. When he deserted the New Jersey militia, he
"marched back to Trenton alone and wished to have my judgment con-
vince me that Great Britain was right."[47] Later, in 1785, denied support
for his steamboat by Congress, he contemplated serving "the Day [Dey]
of Algiers" and applied to the Spanish foreign minister for assistance from
"his Most Catholic Majesty," the king of Spain.[48] The incoherence of Fitch's
shifting loyalties is most vivid at the end of his captivity, when he finds
himself in a British prison. On "Prison Island opposit Cotedelack," Fitch
neither rests nor resists; rather, he becomes, for a time, contentedly
"Crusoe-like." A Canadian prison seems to be the perfect place for him.
He plants a garden, makes himself a lathe, sets up a buttonmaking establishment, and, before long, is constructing wooden clocks in the barracks.
He finds great demand among the British officers and guards, and even
takes an apprentice: "one John Segar from the Massichusets an ingenious
handy Lad that lived in my Barrack . . . but he being so worthy a lad and

so attentive to businiss I gave him generious wages for his work."[49] With the proceeds from his shop he manages to enact in prison the ethic of solitary productivity represented by "Roberson Cruso": "I cloathed myself in a superfine suit with a Great Pleanty of coarse working cloaths for the Winter. I also had a good Russia sheating Hammock hung in the Middle of my Barrack to keep me from lice and had . . . five Blankets . . . and my Barrack fitted up in the warmest manner in short Sir in about four months I got to be as rich as Roberson Cruso."[50] If, to adapt Max Weber's argument, the work ethic of capitalist cultures reproduces the structures and strategies of the Puritan experience of life as a form of captivity, then in Fitch's case the transformation from terrified captive to solitary worker is a profoundly ironic one. Fitch's enactment of the Crusoe story on Prison Island only parodies and ironizes the person-making representational structures of an Anglo-American empire that produced Robinson Crusoes not merely on desert islands but in the colonial bureaucracies and urban seaports of early industrial North America.

Fitch was so content on Prison Island, in fact, that when the time came for him to be released he didn't want to go: "The officers came into my Barrack and congratulated me on my Releas I informed them that I could not get ready to go on so short a notice which they made themselves very merry about."[51] Forced to leave Canada, Fitch made his way back to Philadelphia by ship in great misery, plagued by lice, constantly seasick, and in terror of shipwreck. After ten weeks on the water, he finally arrived in New York and traveled overland to Philadelphia, where he arrived destitute. The conclusion of his captivity narrative is perhaps the most revealing aspect of its relationship to the Puritan genre. Puritan captivity narratives conventionally conclude with a chastened return to and reunion with the spiritual and material community of saints. When Fitch finally returned to Pennsylvania, he too visited a church; his purpose in going, however, was not to give thanks for deliverance but to obtain money, which he needed to survive—and to reinvest. Fitch claims he was once a Methodist and, arriving in Bucks County, together with another captive (John Burnet, a Baptist), he attended the Southampton Baptist meeting. There, Fitch writes, "we had public thanks returned for our safe delivery from Captivity to God almighty and to Jesus Christ Both. At any rate it was as good as an advertisement in the newspaper and the whole story [was] told them as far as the parson knew. And he did a real good for he collected that day for Burnett about 12 Dollars to take him to Kentuckey which was much better than the methodists did by me."[52]

Though "the methodists" never helped him, Fitch too soon gathered the money needed to take him west again, where he set to work once more as a surveyor in Kentucky. By 1785, he had laid out warrants on tens of thousands of acres of land in both Ohio and the Kentucky territory—over two hundred thousand acres, he claimed. Within just three years after his release, then, Fitch was fully reengaged by the cyclical ups and downs of making himself in early industrial North America. Captivity makes very little difference in the shape of Fitch's "Life," despite the fact of its narrative position as the wartime passage between his youth and his steamboat career. Just as the Revolution fails to be revolutionary in Fitch's "Life," so his experience as a captive yields neither insight nor change, and his captivity narrative is devoid of moral or reflection.

Fitch's journeys west did, however, provide him with hints, information, and powerful metaphors regarding new fields of enterprise. Back in Philadelphia in 1785, the rise and fall of his financial condition began to be accompanied by a recurrent ebb and flow of ideas. Since the beginning of the Revolution, he had been suggestible, easily seized with ideas for investment. After the Revolution, these ideas took on a new cast as he began to think of his schemes as inspiration or even as the valuable products of mechanical genius. In fact, if there is any link between Fitch's captivity narrative and his steamboat history, it lies in the category of "genius," where the opening of new territories in the western interior is linked inseparably to the (violent and painful) forging of new territories of subjective interiority, or new "mental properties."

THE GENIUS AS COMPANY MAN

While metalworking technology was critical, the success of Fitch's steamboat depended equally upon the subscription and recommendations of influential men, particularly the men of the American Philosophical Society, who were among the best connected. In Fitch's case, however, that support was not forthcoming. Most of the members of the American Philosophical Society backed James Rumsey, a Virginian with influential cousins, who was able to finance his steamboat partly with family funds.[53] And Rumsey had something even more important: the recommendation of Washington, with which he made a sweep of the Philosophical Society. Fifteen of the twenty-one members of Rumsey's steamboat society (dubbed "the Rumseian Society") were members of the Philosophical Society and immediately elected Rumsey to membership. By contrast, Fitch was never invited to join, though five of the Philosophical Society's members subscribed to Fitch's various steamboat companies. Not only did the Rumseian Society subscribe one thousand dollars to send Rumsey to England, where he could meet with Matthew Boulton and examine the Watt engine, but the social power of the American Philosophical Society was also arrayed, and none too subtly, *against* Fitch. Both Jefferson and Franklin entertained Rumsey in Paris and furnished him with letters of introduction. In a letter of introduction to Benjamin Vaughan in London, Franklin warned that Fitch was a pretender to "a prior right of invention," and in a letter of 1788 to John Lettsom in England, the Philadelphia physician Benjamin Rush described Fitch as "licentious." As a result, while Fitch and his partner Voight were able to find enough subscribers to continue work on their steamboat until 1791, they could never sustain consistent investment and commitment.[54]

Fitch was forty-one years old when he first wrote to Franklin and Washington in 1785, "praying [their] patronage" for his steamboat idea. When Fitch came to call on him in 1785, Franklin listened, was unresponsive, and reportedly tried to give him four dollars.[55] Later that year, Fitch called on Washington at Mount Vernon, where he described his steamboat and even spent the night, but got no further than he had with Franklin. Fitch recounts Washington's coldness—and his partiality for Rumsey's design—in a mixture of outraged and deferential language that oscillates between accusations of conspiracy and pious reminders to himself that, despite the temptation, "it is impious to worship any one as Deity":[56]

> When Moses Alexander Ceasar and Franklin have made themselves great by Fomenting Wars Murder Rapine and depopulating Countries, the more noble Washington has made himself greater than all without wadeing thro those seas of Blood. . . . How hard it is in my dying speach to suggest that so amiable a character would Injure an indigent citizen to save his own reputation, and send an express to Rumsey . . . to urge him to compleat the Boat, or others would run away with it.[57]

As Fitch explained in a similar letter to Jefferson (also "sealed" and never sent): "The injurys which I have received from my nation or rather from the first officers of government has induced me for a lesson of caution to future generations to record the treatment which I have received."[58] Here, Fitch uses the language of public utility ("as a lesson to future generations"), but hesitates over the distinction between the nation and its first persons ("from my nation or rather from the first officers of government"). The hesitation marks the difficulty of locating the source of "injury" in a situation where "my nation" was an assemblage of representational forms that distinguished sharply between representative persons and unrepresentative nonpersons such as Fitch—whose productive "powers" were nonetheless called forth by that very line of demarcation.

In his essay "The Worthy versus the Licentious," Gordon Wood argues that during the 1780s the leaders of the American Revolution became increasingly concerned about the large numbers of "new men" who had been introduced into political participation by the upheaval of the war: "The emigration of thousands of Tories, the intensification of interest in politics, the enlargement of the legislatures and the increase in elections, the organization of new militia and political groups, the breakup of old mercantile combinations and trade circuits, the inflation and profiteering caused by the war—all offered new opportunities for hitherto unknown but ambitious persons to find new places for themselves."[59] In Wood's view, the federal Constitution of 1787 was a device for resolving the tensions produced by this social transformation and for containing the threat that "licentiousness" posed to "worth." In an "amazing display of confidence" in the "efficacy of institutional devices for solving social and political problems," the authors of the Constitution aimed "to turn the political and social developments that were weakening the place of 'the better sort of people' in government back upon themselves and to make these developments the very source of the perpetuation of the natural aristocracy's domination of politics."[60] Wood notes the irony of an "elitist theory of democracy" that actually reaffirmed the dominance of a "natural" aristocracy— a club to which any man of talent could theoretically belong. Federalism, in other words, only reconfirmed an "organic conception of society" at the very moment the federalists were themselves developing "distinct professional, social, or economic interests."[61] For Wood, the key to this irony lies in the fact that an "organic conception" of inherited, patriarchal privileges and fixed, inborn, or "corporate" social status was, in fact, "finally and avowedly dissolving."[62] Fitch's "Life," however, demonstrates that this "organic conception" of social hierarchy was not so much dissolving as migrating into (and by way of) the visual and verbal arts and, in particular, new works of American science and technology. The institutional devices that "the better sort" were turning to their own ends extended far beyond the institutions of representative government per se to multiply mediated and proliferating representational structures for ordering persons and groups generally.

Nowhere is this clearer than in Fitch's account of the coming of the steamboat idea itself, in which the steamboat emerges at precisely this joint of (the changing forms of) social inequality. Fitch was walking along a road outside Philadelphia, on his way home from hearing his preacher friend, Reverend Irwin (whose sermons he valued not for their content but for their inventive genius).[63] Fitch was on foot because he had let his horse "out to work for its liveing." Suddenly, he felt "Rheumatism . . . seize me pretty severely in one of my knees." At the very same moment, "a Gentleman passed me in a Chair with a Noble Horse. A thought struck me that it would be a noble thing if I could have such a carriage without the expense of keeping a hors. A query then rose in my mind Thus viz what cannot you do if you will get yourself about it."[64] Here, the idea of a self-powered vehicle emerges at the social divide between gentleman and mechanic. As in the case of John Bertram's insight into the organic structure of a daisy, inspiration comes in the form of a voice of uncertain origin. Addressing Fitch in the second person—"what cannot you do if you will get yourself about it"—the "query" could be either divine inspiration or some learned question imbibed, Lockean fashion, from self-improvement literature or lectures on perseverance. From one point of view, the indeterminate origin of Fitch's "idea" might be called a secularization of revelation. It also suggests the marketplace mixture of encouragement and control, interest and disinterestedness, that was producing collective subjects on the pattern of mechanical and literary works. Fitch's rheumatic kneeling mingles religious with social deference while articulating the penetration of both by a new (organic) conception: a representational mechanics of social production.

Fitch was similarly "struck" with the idea of the steamboat in 1785, immediately after he had returned from the last of his surveying trips to Ohio. He had recently arrived in Philadelphia, hoping to find that he had been appointed by Congress to the position of "surveyor of the Western Territories," an appointment he had sought and fully expected to receive. But, in a repetition of Governor Wolcott's failure to "reward" him for carrying the chain earlier in life, Fitch was turned down by Congress and, with the Northwest Ordinance of May 1785, all his landjobbing investments were negated. The ordinance prescribed that the surveyed western land would be sold "at public Vendue"—and so, standing again at the juncture between public and private works, he writes, "from an immense forturne [I] was reduced to nothing at one Blow."[65] In the face of this new disappointment and return to poverty, Fitch conceived the steamboat; penniless and humiliated, he began to design "a first Rate man of War." The idea was clearly tied to his travels west and to his thwarted dreams as a landjobber: he aimed first of all to "revenge [himself] on the Committee of Congress." "[M]y grand views," he writes, "were to Render service to my Country, and Chastize the Ignorant Boys of Congress." And Fitch believed that, with the help of a federal patent, his boat would make him famous and powerful while "convert[ing] our vast territory on those waters into an inconceivable fund in the treasury of the United States."[66]

Remarkably, within just two years, Fitch and his partner, Henry Voight, had their man-of-war afloat on the Delaware and, in the summer of 1787, were offering free rides to the members of the Constitutional Convention assembled in Philadelphia. This first steamboat was a "crank-and-paddle" design that, Brook Hindle speculates, may have been derived from the Indian war canoes Fitch had observed on the rivers of the interior during his travels and captivity. Propelled by two steam-powered rows of oars suspended on either side of the hull, the *Perseverance* was shaped like a large canoe, while its "banks" of oars recalled Indian warriors paddling in unison.[67] Although neither Washington nor Franklin appeared on board, many other delegates did: Edmund Randolph and Samuel Johnson, for instance, gave written testimonials of their "satisfaction," while David Rittenhouse and John Ewing were especially enthusiastic and certified that they had "frequently seen Mr. Fitch's steamboat, which with great labor and perseverance he has at length completed."[68] Rembrandt Peale, Charles Willson Peale's son, was busy painting portraits of the republican worthies gathered for the convention when he chanced upon a trial run of Fitch's paddle steamboat and became its reporter:

> hearing there was something curious to be seen . . . I eagerly ran to the spot, where I found a few persons collected, all eagerly gazing at a shallop at anchor below the bridge, with about twenty persons on board. On the deck was a small furnace, and machinery connected with [a] coupling crank projecting over the stern to give motion to three or four paddles, resembling snow shovels, which hung into the water. When all was ready and the power of steam was made to act . . . the paddles began to work, pressing against the water backward as they rose, and the boat to my great delight moved against the tide, without wind or hand.[69]

While the sight of Fitch's curious boat, as here framed by Rembrandt Peale, may have been a delightful novelty, the crank-and-paddle design suffered repeated breakdowns, and the boat never achieved commercial success. (It would be twenty more years before Robert Fulton, who is usually remembered as the inventor of the steamboat, used a Watt engine imported from England to assemble the first commercially successful steamboat, the *Clermont*, in 1807.) Fitch and Voight assembled a second steamboat in 1790 that proved much more successful from a mechanical point of view but likewise failed to turn a profit. Traveling upwards of eight miles per hour and more than eighty miles per day, the new boat transported passengers all summer long between Philadelphia and Trenton (or Chester).[70] True to his oscillating fortunes, however, by 1791 Fitch was again penniless, reduced to "a pair of breeches" and one coat, of which he writes, he could not "tell the exact age and constant wear of it, but it is broke in every part, especially the lining, elbows, about the wrists and under the armes."[71]

Simultaneously social, economic, emotional, and cognitive, such ups and downs structure Fitch's account of his steamboat career throughout. If labor was the origin of all property, its counterpart in the realm of "mental enterprise" was the genius who transformed ideas into objects. Likewise, where the production of production meant the making of geniuses, genius was viewed, like labor, with profound ambivalence by republicans who relied nevertheless upon its artifacts and anecdotes. Insofar as Fitch aspired to the status of genius and ended up instead a "crack-pot"— that is, an unsuccessful, inadequately funded, or would-be genius—his failures cannot be traced merely to his own economic, intellectual, or psychological limitations but to the fact that he was himself a *product*: a production of production and a creature of (the culture of) creation.

Just ten years after Fitch's death, the May 1809 issue of the Philadelphia *Port Folio* would display an engraving of "McBride's Machine for Ginning, Carding, and Spinning Cotton."[72] Titled "The Columbia Spinster," this device was invented by a Mr. John McBride of Tennessee. According to the *Port Folio*, McBride was "an American Arkwright" who, like the inventor of the spinning frame in Britain, Sir Richard Arkwright (1732–92), rose from a lowly station by virtue of his genius. The magazine, however, expresses significant ambivalence about mechanics become suddenly great, describing Arkwright as an illiterate barber whose meteoric rise is both awesome and despicable: "Many of these improvements are the inventions of illiterate characters, to whom the science of mechanics, and the theory of the mechanical powers are almost wholly unknown; they are generally the result of an ardent mind, bent to the accomplishment of a particular object, goaded by necessity, or allured by the prospect of immediate wealth"[73] Not only did Great Britain owe "much of her wealth and power . . . to the halfpenny barber, Arkwright," the United States, too, was in debt to "this same barber": it is to Arkwright that the United States must trace its own cotton culture, "the culture of one of its most considerable sources of wealth and many a southern planter . . . his gilded carriage and splendid equipage."[74] Here, praise and condemnation cancel each other out in a bland acknowledgment of American manufacturing's resemblance to British industrial development and the complicity of both with plantation slavery in the South and the Caribbean.[75]

Fitch's own turn to steamboat construction was likewise a product of cultural constructions of the uncultivated or half-cultivated inventor. Representations such as the *Port Folio*'s authorized new technology by bringing mechanical innovation together with the figure of the untutored, or natural, genius. According to this early industrial creation myth, a member of an underclass became socially useful or resourceful (i.e., a human resource) by means of creative genius. As an inexplicable gift, like money from heaven, genius figured the Creation, or the unknowable, inchoate invention of the world itself. As the power of creation, genius was contemplated, therefore, with considerable anxiety by organs of collection and observation that nevertheless relied upon the category as a way of authorizing their own legitimacy as re-creational constructions, or little worlds. Such organs included not only miscellaneous magazines like the *Port Folio* but also works of natural history, such as Jefferson's *Notes on the State of Virginia*. In fact, the ambiguous figure of the genius as creator marks one of the deep points of identity between such disparate works as the *Port Folio*, Fitch's "Life," and the early industrial texts of Jeffersonian science.

FITCH THE FOUNDER

Jefferson's preference for agricultural production and his suspicion of artisan skill is well known to any reader of his famous manifesto against "manufactures" in *Notes on the State of Virginia*.[76] Jefferson's ambivalence about the rank and reality of mechanical production reflected the changing status of American craftsmen, who, more than any other social group, represented the inescapable connection between nation building and divided labor via the reorganization of artisan producers into American workers. In fact, Jefferson's distrust of American manufacturing coexisted with his deep admiration for mechanical skill as a version, in miniature, of the world-making power of the Maker: the founding or artisan deity of Enlightenment Deism. In "Productions, Animal, Vegetable and Mineral," for example, Jefferson lists human geniuses among the organic productions, or natural commodities, of North America. The context for this discussion is Jefferson's longstanding debate with French naturalists Buffon and the Abbé Raynal, who argued that nature was degenerate in the New World. Not only were American animals smaller and weaker, they claimed, but the continent "ha[d] produced not one able mathematician, one man of genius in any single art or a single science." Jefferson argued to the contrary that nature's laws were universal and brought forth genius in the New World as in the Old.[77] In fact, the genius of America was, like its animal species, not only equal to but potentially bigger and better than comparable European productions in nature or in culture. Just like the American mammoth, "the largest of all terrestrial beings," American genius (in the persons of Washington, Franklin, and Rittenhouse, in particular) "should have sufficed to have rescued the earth it inhabited, and the atmosphere it breathed from the imputation of impotence in the conception and nourishment of animal life on a large scale."[78]

> In war we have produced a Washington . . . whose name will triumph over time, and will in future ages assume its just station among the most celebrated worthies of the world, . . . In physics we have produced a Franklin. . . . We have supposed Mr. Rittenhouse second to no astronomer living: that in genius he must be the first, because he is self-taught. As an artist he has exhibited as great a proof of mechanical genius as the world has ever produced. He has not indeed made a world; but he has by imitation approached nearer its Maker than any man who has lived from the creation to this day.[79]

In this passage, it is the mechanical artist, David Rittenhouse, who is Jefferson's central example of American genius per se: Rittenhouse, the clockmaker-astronomer, is most demonstrably a genius because he is "self-taught." And, in keeping with the theological creationism—or Deism—

of Jefferson's *Notes*, the most compelling evidence of his genius is that Rittenhouse has, like the Creator, "made a world" by building the "Orrery," a working model of the solar system, displayed in Philadelphia.

Fitch, too, admired Rittenhouse and the men of science gathered in Philadelphia, and he aimed, like them, to "make a world." In 1791, near the end of his steamboat career, he and his partner, Voight, founded a "Deist Society" that openly "denied Jesus" while advancing a technocratic theology that explicitly mingled millenialist fervor with economic and territorial ambition and the representational practices of natural science. "I had two Views" in it, he writes of the founding of his Society. "The first was for the benefit of mankind and support of Civil Government and 2dly was stimulated by Pride and determined to let the world know as contemptable as I was and despised by all ranks of People from the first Officers of Government down to the Blacburry garls that I would call in all the world into my doctrines the Jews with the fullness of the Gentile Nations and establish one Area throughout the World."[80]

With his steamboat career a shambles, Fitch began to take the possibility of natural law so seriously that he patterned himself literally on the artisan God of Jeffersonian Deism. But he also went further than the civic religion of the Enlightenment when, at times, his literal-minded identification of mechanical genius with the power of world making led him to abandon the principle of deity altogether. Down at the docks Fitch and Voight found themselves "getting mildly glad in Liquor" and engaging with their visitors in open discussions of "Mechanical Philosophical or Religious Sentiments." Both men were "Deists by Profession" and, though it was "an unpopular sentiment," they found "large bodies of people were of [their] belieff altho too delicate to confess it." Founded for "that body of people," Fitch patterned his Society explicitly on the "classes" of "Wistly" and the Methodists and in part on the egalitarian Society of Friends (the Quakers). But Fitch's Deists went beyond these as well, decreeing "that all questions should be freely discoursed even to the denial of the divinity of Moses Jesus Christ or Mahomet."[81]

Evangelical in their investment in learned inquiry, the religious questions raised by Fitch and his friends shaded directly into questions of physical and mechanical science. In this, then, the Deist Society also resembled scientific and learned organizations such as the American Philosophical Society. Indeed, Fitch's Deist Society formed itself by adopting "a generious Constitution" and undertook to publish volumes of "Essays" (like the *Transactions* of the American Philosophical Society), in which "every man could place his Ideas."[82] But these were never published and, like his various steamboat companies, Fitch's Deist Society was never large; at its height it attracted over forty participants—many of whom also subscribed to Fitch's steamboat company. But among his writings, Fitch kept a "file" of the questions they compiled for debate, noting in some cases the member who posed the question:

—Is a Plurality of Wives Right or Wrong . . .

—Is there any such thing as conscience; or does not what we call Con[s]cience arise altogether from Education . . .

—Are there any Punishments or rewards after this life—unknown but bclicvc Mr. Voight

—Did all mankind proceed from one man & woman . . .

—Can Suicide be a noble act in any case whatever . . .

—Are not men and other animals composed of the same kind of matter—Voight . . .

—What was the Passion of Envy given to men for or what use could it be of in this World . . .

—Do not all men injoy an equal Share of happiness in this World . . .

—Why are the human Race more than some others of the Animal Species at all seasons ready for Coition? Mr. Muninger . . .

—Why have the females of the human Specie a menstrual Flux and not those of other Animals—Mr. Muninger . . .

—What is matter—unknown . . .

—Should a magnetick needle made with two points [at one pole and] with a Brass Pointer between the two points be less liable to Variation than that in present use—Mr. Voig[h]t . . .

—Is gratitude due from the young to the parents for their care and protection in raiseing and nursing them when not able to protect themselves.[83]

These queries engage religious and moral topics pursued by the American Philosophical Society in lectures, papers, and publication; they also recall the more surveylike "Queries" of Marbois, to which Jefferson responded in *Notes on the State of Virginia*. But the most salient difference between Fitch's questions and those asked by either liberal and evangelical Protestants or the American Philosophical Society is that Fitch's Deists envision an unmediated use of the representational apparatus of the Enlightenment—not merely to understand and describe, but to directly appropriate and transform, social and sexual relations. As illustrated by the queries posed by Fitch's Deist Society, for example, the concern with nature shades explicitly into an unsystematic materialism. The materialist fusion in the Society's queries between "nature" and radical social change is most obvious where human nature is compared with that of "other animals" and where questions about social feelings of "Envy" and gratitude—the feelings specific to social inequality—are juxtaposed with questions of whether all men are "equal" in "happiness." Within the "organic order" scrutinized by the Deist Society, then, any area became accessible to human inquiry: no topic was taboo, or too local and specific, or too general.

With the founding of his Deist Society in the early years of the French Revolution, Fitch found a point of connection with a wider, more radical, European Enlightenment. The Deist Society's mechanistic materialism was precisely what federalism and its circuits of self-production and self-display were designed to diffuse and exclude. In its explicit fantasy of a total revolution in the order of things, Fitch's Deism partook of the bureaucratic creationism of Linnaean science, but it also connected him with what Henry May and Margaret Jacob have, in different contexts, called "the radical Enlightenment."[84] Following the example of French revolutionaries, Fitch's Deists aimed to reorganize the structure of time as well as space. They began history itself over again by reestablishing the calendar, voting to begin the new era on the day of the Deist Society's first meeting, 25 February 1790 (although Fitch had "strenuously urged" that the new era begin on 1 February, "because it was my Birth Day," a suggestion that led his fellow Deists to think "that my Ideas were all as wild as Steam Boat building").[85]

By 1792, the Deist Society had begun to fall apart, but Fitch's hopes for it were revitalized by the arrival in Philadelphia of a famous radical Deist named Elihu Palmer. Like Fitch, Palmer was a former Presbyterian from rural Connecticut. While liberal Deism (carefully couched) was at the time a relatively acceptable accommodation to Enlightenment and Revolution, Palmer's aggressive and evangelical Deism was far less acceptable. He openly advocated a purely secular and rational ethics that finally excluded theism altogether. What most set Palmer apart was his rejection of "natural religion" and the accommodation it forged between reason and scripture.[86] Palmer is often identified with the radical Thomas Paine of *The Age of Reason*, but even Paine allowed that Jesus "was a virtuous and an amiable man [whose] morality . . . has not been exceeded by any." Palmer, by contrast, criticized anyone—including Joseph Priestley or William Godwin—who tried in any way to accommodate rational morality to Scripture, and by the late 1790s he was enthusiastically preaching the organic materialism of d'Holbach.[87]

When Fitch heard of Palmer's arrival in the city, he immediately "resolved to make a nois in the World and do the greatest good." Going "directly home," he siezed upon the manuscripts he had been writing for years:

> [I] got this Book and waited upon him and gave my Ideas verbally as well as what is here written. When I found that he was as well established in my beliefs as I was myself . . . I told him that I had been prepairing the Way in

the Wilderness for him thro' unbeaten Paths and could bring in 40 generious clever fellows into his Society in a lump and mentioned near 20 More whome I had great confidence in if he would take the Helm.[88]

By "this Book" Fitch means his "Life" (and presumably the "Steamboat History" as well), which now also contained the files of the Deist Society. Remarkably, Fitch offered his manuscript to Palmer as a how-to guide for seizing power on a global scale. But even with the support of Fitch's Deists, whose number at the time were "dwindling," Palmer failed to find a foothold in Philadelphia. His first act was to hire "a large roome . . . in Church ally," where he preached from the Book of Malachi and "publicly denied the divinity of Jesus Christ." Following the success of this meeting, Palmer advertised a second meeting, confidently "publish[ing] in the public papers that he [w]ould the sunday following preach against the divinity of Jesus Christ." But this time, when Palmer arrived he was opposed by a large crowd, led by William White, bishop of the Philadelphia diocese of the Episcopal Church, who closed the doors of the meeting room against him. Palmer quickly left town. Fitch had "urged his takeing the field but he not being such a Veteran as myself was conquered on the first repulse."[89]

In this episode of confrontation, which occurred not long before the deposit of his manuscripts in the Library Company, Fitch's faith in writing as a powerful social device is clearly evident. Throughout his discussions of the Deist Society, Fitch had associated publication and authorship with public punishment, not unlike being displayed in the stocks. For example, in a discussion of the disciplining of miscreant children, Fitch recommends shaming them by publishing their names in an annual list. By having "their Expultion and Certificates annually Published," reward and punishment would be "held up to them in more strikeing colours than a future state of Heaven or Hell."[90] Adults, likewise, who engaged in "improper conduct" would be treated with "greater severities . . . and not only expelled but to have their names published in some public paper their expultion and what expelled for. Which I though would be more Terror to them than all the Tormants of Damnation preached by the ablest divines."[91] The projected "volumes of Essays," however, were to be protected places, where a member could publish "without having his name known or becoming an Author."[92]

It is, clearly, in part because Fitch saw the appearance or display of himself in print as a form of discipline and punishment that he "sealed" rather than published his writings. But he also stopped short of publication because he identified with his writings so completely: he was unable to detach himself from his words or constitute them as an object (or book), and himself as their disembodied author. There are other reasons, of course, for his failure to produce his life in print. With his steamboat dreams collapsing, Fitch began to rely heavily upon the possibility that, where his invention had failed, his "Book" might hold the secret to universal power. He fantasized that if he failed to make a world he might at least proclaim in the wilderness the coming of a new genius—a new Maker of men—in the technological millenium. As a revelation of this coming, however, such a proclamation was unpublishable; neither objective nor subjective, it was, if anything, somewhat "lunatic." His "Life" and its fragmentary addenda told secrets that could not pass as projects for the public good. His writings could not inhabit the nation-making lines between public and private life that were reframing the world of things even as he wrote.

BETWEEN SECRECY AND SUBJECTIVITY: FITCH'S
"POSTSCRIPTS" OF 1790–1792

In the wake of the Patent Commission's decision of 1790 to issue a joint patent to both Fitch and Rumsey, Fitch penned seven short "confessions or postscripts," which are found in the manuscripts in between the "Life" and "Steamboat History."[93] Fitch's postscripts refer to the present of the manuscript's writing in the early 1790s, a period of poverty and breakdown. They fit fully into neither the "Life" nor the " Steamboat History" and speak, instead, to the meaning his "Book" had for Fitch when he sealed and deposited it in the Library Company and left for France (specifically, Nantes) in the year of the Terror. Transcribed by editor Frank Prager, the seven fragments deal, in contrapuntal fashion, with one or the other of two remarkable events: Fitch's cofounding (with his steamboat partner Voight) of the Deist Society and Fitch's "marriage" to his landlady, Mary Krafft, sometime in 1789, after she had become pregnant by Voight.

Fitch considered himself fortunate to have joined up with Henry Voight, the German metalworker who would later be appointed "Chief Coiner" at the federal mint in Philadelphia. Fitch described Voight as "the first Mechanical genius that I ever met with in the course of my life and I do believe his superior [in] Mechanical genius is not to be found."[94] Voight seems to have compensated for some of Fitch's deficits. While both Fitch and Voight were inspired with key ideas for making the steamboat work, their persons represented structural opposites: "[M]y despicable appearance and uncouth way of speaking and holding up extravigant Ideas and so bad an address must ever make me unpopular," Fitch writes, but Voight was "a handsome man and a man of good address and farmiliar friendly and sociable to all and a truely honest man in his Trade." In fact, the alternating opposition of their "dispositions" was dynamically productive, making their friendship itself an engine of steamboat production. Not only was Fitch "unpopular" where Voight was "farmiliar friendly and sociable to all" but, when Voight was given to "high Passions," Fitch was "more cool." As Fitch describes their complementarity, Voight was "confident in his own abilities," "flushed to excess with the prospect of success and equally depressed with a Disappointment. I esteem myself to be more cool and dispassionate. And it absolutely required two men of the same dispositions of ours to compleat the great undertakeing unless we had funds of our own."[95]

On the one hand, Fitch's partnership with Voight testifies to the degree to which the two men performed the act of steamboat invention upon a stage framed by cultural representations of the mechanical genius. On the other hand, Fitch's postscript accounts of the process of invention and assembly are far more complicated than contemporary print representations of genius ever allowed. In Fitch's account, invention and innovation are never accomplished or subsumed by detached, disinterested, and solitary mental effort. Nor does the act of invention entail any radical departures from the rank of mechanic. Rather, Fitch's experience demonstrates that the process of invention, in its functioning and breakdowns, was inseparable from the inventor's collaborative and emotional attachments in the face of the uneven but extreme pressure (to change and to produce) that was put upon the rank of artisan in late-eighteenth-century North America. In Fitch's case, the most central of these attachments was with his coworker, Voight, and another member of the mechanic class, their mutual friend and landlady, Mary Krafft. "[I]n the Steam Boat," Fitch writes of Voight, "I took him by the hand and kept him even pace with me ... and made all the Citizens believe he was the Principle man. ... And in the case of the Woman [I] served him even to madeness. Which no man would have done who was in his right senses but myself and I now much doubt that I was in my Right senses at the time."[96]

When Fitch suppressed his manuscript in 1792, he did so not only because he feared offending the first officers of government but because of the incoherent details of a confusing sexual triangle that involved Fitch, Voight, and Krafft. In the fall of 1790, Voight and Fitch's last steamboat company had disbanded. Fitch was again broke, and Krafft had let him board for free for many months.[97] Both Krafft and Voight already had "Valuable Families of Childeren of six or seven Each." For these reasons Fitch "strictly forbid" the "whole truth [of their affair] to be made public in less than 30 years but in the most delicate and Tender way. In which time probably they will be dead and their Childern married."[98]

Krafft gave birth to two children during her marriage to Fitch; yet Fitch claimed that he never had and never would have sex with her. ("[N]ot being a very handsome man and one of very indifferent address and of no flattery[,] . . . I Sir for Twentytwo years have never sought after woman but rather chose to avoid them . . . I have in this time kept a solemn Lent for more than seven years together. Which Sir I look upon to be scrupulously unreasonable in either sex.")[99] When Krafft became pregnant with her first child by Voight, Fitch offered to "Marry the woman and pledge my word of honor never to bed with her."[100] He did so, he claimed, out of disinterest and love of virtue: not only because of his "friendship" with Voight but because the idea of "the destruction of those families . . . wrecked [his] Tortured Soul to the centre." At first Voight "seemed to be posses[s]ed . . . with that degree of gratitude as was due for such a generious offer." Indeed, Fitch assured Voight that he meant to treat Krafft as the "Wife of your Friend ought to be treated. And believe me to be Base if I do not use her the same as I would my Old Friend Harry."[101]

In Fitch's manuscript the details of this triangle are murky at best. But what is clear is that Fitch's "love" for his "two best friends" overlapped disastrously with his partnership with Voight. In his manuscripts, both friendship and partnership collapse in wild verbal oscillations between the representational dichotomies of suppression versus publication, concealment versus "candour," the practice of secrecy versus the republican performance of subjective interiority. In one passage Fitch declares that the story must be suppressed for thirty years, while in another he says that he will "publish" it: "I think myself not bound to secrecy any further," Fitch writes, since Voight "has published it himself in order to make me despicable in the eyes of the World for indevouring to save Mrs. Krafft and her family from destruction."[102] Elsewhere, however, he describes his relationship with Krafft via an extended metaphor of Loyalism and defection that, in accord with his own failure to identify as a national subject, casts him in the role of "the British" and Krafft as Benedict Arnold: "And if she had as false a heart as an Arnold and trusted to my friendship and honor and have thrown herself on me for protection I should have acted as the British did and never betray or give up the Traitor."[103]

Although Fitch calls Krafft "a woman of forturne and a fortune in herselfe," he also viewed marriage to a woman as "the worst of ills." ("I know of nothing so perplexing and vexatious to a man of feelings, as a turbulent Wife and Steam Boat building.")[104] At the end of the Revolution, he had left a wife and two children in New Jersey and, as he claimed, "for Twenty-two years have never sought after woman but rather chose to avoid them and have in that time frequently treated the sex unbecoming a man. For which I ask their Pardon." By the late 1780s, however, he had become so "entangled" with Voight and Krafft that "if she had been the Devil himself [I] was determined to make the best of it."[105] At the same time, however, Fitch adhered to his view of his behavior as virtuous devotion: "On the

Whole I ackno[w]ledge Sir that I have far Exceeded Quixot in releaving Destressed Ladies but hope that the imputations of Windmills may not be laid to my Charge."[106]

Fitch repeatedly sought aid from federal sources, but his "friendships" with Voight and Krafft argue that the framing of the steamboat cannot be reduced to any unitary act of creation. Although editor Prager calls the postscripts "confessions" and Fitch suppresses them with his manuscript as a "secret," these fragments reveal, in fact, that Fitch had no "private" life, even while a (sexualized and gendered) natural history of privacy was emerging all around him, via the arts and technologies of republican publicity, and particularly through Jeffersonian science and the language of the affections, or "feeling." In the end, the episode with Krafft reveals the mechanic as an author struggling—but unable—to figure a sphere of privacy in a world in which the cultural creation of private "interiors" was rearranging the furniture of social life in such as way as to exclude John Fitch, and those like him, who figure neither (as subjects) in the republican lists of fame nor (as objects) in the ranks of a working class supposedly coming to historical or history-making consciousness.

As Fitch's "apology" suggests ("I have frequently treated the sex . . ."), heterosexual "dimorphism" represents another emerging, early-industrial category articulated and imploded by Fitch's "Life." As Denise Riley argues, the category of "Woman" emerged hand in hand with the secular humanist category of "Man."[107] The late-eighteenth-century discourses of anatomy, physiology, medicine, and the natural sciences were all quite clearly involved in the articulation of man and woman as the sexed and gendered objects of knowledge and production.[108] In failing to bring into view a subjective, or "private," interior of his own, then, Fitch likewise failed to participate in this sexualization of character, a sexualization that generated and gendered the culturally productive, nation-building dichotomy between private life and public order.

Patent Endings

The federal Constitution of 1787 had included a patent clause that gave Congress the power "To promote the progress of Science and useful Arts by securing for limited Time to Authors and Inventors the exclusive Right to their respective Writings and Discoveries."[109] Linking authorship with invention, the federal patent was a limited monopoly that allowed an inventor rights of ownership to the products of his mind for a period of time (usually fourteen years), at the end of which his inventions became public property. The creation of intellectual property through patent law was a way of encouraging the interests of an author or inventor—such as Fitch—

while at the same time serving the public good by eventually making knowledge public and "free" rather than monopolized and secretive.[110] Copyright paralleled the patent by defining writing, like machinery, as property, on the Lockean grounds of the author's "mental labor."[111]

On the one hand, throughout his "Life" Fitch acknowledged the continuing existence of preindustrial "secrecy" within a changing artisan culture (as when Timothy Cheany refused to teach him the "secrets" of clockmaking). But, as his battle with Rumsey over federal patent priority demonstrates, he also acknowledged (though he could not effectively practice) the very different, commodity-producing, nation-building dialectic of secrecy-versus-display that was being articulated by investors and inventors in fights over new machinery and patent rights. Fitch's peculiar kind of openness was primarily, then, a failure to orchestrate the keeping of secrets by way of a property-producing separation of private face from public power (or, vice versa, public face from private power). This is why Fitch called himself a "Blockhead" rather than a visible candidate for worthiness—and portraiture.[112]

As just one more "organic conception" that joined privacy to publicity on the grounds of production, the patent clause analogized authorship to mechanical invention and words to machines, or designs for machines. As the autobiographical writing of an inventor, John Fitch's "Life" and "Steamboat History" would seem to be another such federalist juncture of authorship with invention, private with public interest. But, where the two-part manuscript never becomes one work, Fitch's failure to make himself a representative producer and author articulates a countercultural relationship of mechanical genius to the federalist order of the patent system and its world-making equation of lives with works.

In 1935, Thomas Boyd analyzed the repetitive failures of Fitch's life from a socialist point of view. Boyd attributed Fitch's frustrations to a failure of social analysis on Fitch's part: "he could perceive no connection between private ownership and the increasing burdens of the poor."[113] While true, this analysis is somewhat reductive: it seems particularly inaccurate to attribute Fitch's painful life to his "own" failure of analysis— helpful though a Marxist insight would have been to him. Nevertheless, reconsidering Fitch's "Life" from the point of view of cultural history (where culture means the production of history itself as a performance of production) should not so much obviate Boyd's point as assimilate, complicate, and reorient it. In fact, Fitch cannot be blamed for the failure to see or to incorporate the multiple new technologies of visibility and legibility. The larger explanation for the disproportioned shapes of his "Life" and "Steamboat History" lies in his inability to hide and display himself so as to float on the innumerable backwaters of a social order in which secrecy and display were being *culturally* reorganized as powerful new modes of social reproduction.[114] Fitch could not see culturally and, so, it was at the level of culture building that he failed to accomplish the stable, pyramidal "balance of powers" that constitute the shalls and shall-nots of liberal/republican character. By 1788, the ability to organize one's "own" privacy had become a cultural requirement, a mark of cultural literacy. And Fitch had never organized an interior, private place of his own, separate from—and a repository for and representation of—his hunger for the transparency of belonging.

It is from this point of view that the texts with which Fitch surrounded his own death become understandable. In 1792, Fitch was penniless and his steamboat venture was at an end; he was worried about his sanity and convinced that he was going to die. He called in three friends to witness a will, which prescribed the "sealing" of his "Life" and "Steamboat History," as well as future disbursements from the small estate he expected would come from the land he had surveyed in Kentucky.[115] Apart from this, Fitch had only two dollars, one of which was to be given to the man "who wheals me to the place of interment, the other who shall dig the hole to lay me and cover me up." His then-landlady, Mrs. Hannah Lavering, was requested (without pay) to prepare his body: "I also give an Indian Blanket, in the hands of Mrs. Lavering to tie my body up instead of a coffin."[116] Fitch was particularly concerned that his body be kept out of "a Christian burying ground":

> My will and Pleasure is that I should be buried under ground or sunk with weights to the Bottom of some Waters, that I do not become more obnoxious to the living than I am now, but if buried, that I may be layed on some public highway or place of the greatest resort of the living—such as the State house yard, Gray's Gardens or some Public House that I could hear the Song of the Brown jug on the first day of February every year.[117]

In his request, Fitch rejects the monuments of the graveyard and positions himself again at a crossroads (a public highway) or in "places of resort." His list of such "resorts" crisscrosses and brings together (in its crossing of the political with the recreational) a range of topographies, from the political-turned-recreational State House yard, to the more purely recreational Gray's Gardens, to the "public house" or pub, where mechanics—and federalists—might retire to view and criticize the spectacle of the emerging republic. Boyd reprints the "Song of the Brown Jug" in his biography of Fitch. As a song, it is ephemeral; as a drinking song, it sets itself against the cares, demands, and representational forms of "my Nation." Even in print, it emits a distinctly antimonumental spirit:

With my jug in one hand and my pipe in the other
I'll drink to my neighbor and friend.
All my cares in a whiff of Tobacco I'll smother,
My life I know shortly must end.
While Ceres most kindly refills my brown jug
With brown ale I will make myself mellow
In my old wicar chair I'll set myself snug
Like a jolly and true hearted fellow.
I'll ne'er trouble myself with the cares of my Nation
I've enough of my own for to mind.
All we see in this world is but grief and vexation
To Death I am shortly resigned.
So we'll drink, laugh and smoke and leave nothing to care
And drop like a pear ripe and mellow.
When cold in my coffin, I'll leave them to say
"He's gone, what a True hearted fellow."[118]

PART II

The Mammoth State

Figure 6. Charles Willson Peale, *The Exhumation of the Mastodon* (1806–8).
(Courtesy of the Baltimore City Life Museums.)

CHAPTER THREE

Peale's Mammoth

IN THE summer of 1801, four months after Thomas Jefferson's inauguration, Charles Willson Peale (1741–1827) led a scientific expedition to the marshy farmland of southeastern New York. Some bones of the mammoth, or the "enormous nondescript of North America," had been unearthed by farmers digging marl, a claylike peat, for manure. Equipped and funded by President Jefferson and the American Philosophical Society, Peale traveled by carriage from Philadelphia and by boat from New York City to Shawangunk, a farming community near West Point. There he contrived a huge wooden pump to drain the excavation site and, hiring local men as wage laborers, exhumed the fragmentary remains of three mastodons. Enough bones were excavated to reconstruct two nearly complete skeletons. With the help of his son Rembrandt Peale and the Philadelphia wood sculptor William Rush, Peale manufactured the parts that were missing from one skeleton on the pattern of their counterparts in the others, carving them from wood or fashioning them from papier-mâché. He commemorated his "immense labor"[1] in a painting titled *The Exhumation of the Mastodon*, which he hung in the Mammoth Room of his natural history museum, next to one of the skeletons. Unveiled in Philadelphia on Christmas Eve, Peale's mammoth brought him popular and scientific acclaim, doubling the museum's revenues and proving the case Jefferson had made to Buffon that the "Great American Incognitum" was not simply a version of the African elephant or the Siberian mammoth but a species "peculiar to America."[2]

American mammoth bones had circulated in Europe and North America since the days of Cotton Mather. A hundred years before Peale's expedition, Mather identified huge leg bones and teeth unearthed near Albany, New York, as the remains of the Nephilim, the half-human, half-divine giants destroyed by God in the biblical flood.[3] Prior to the Peales' reconstruction of two skeletons in 1801, American anatomists named the American bones after those of the Siberian mammoth, a Russian derivation of the biblical Behemoth. The name "mastodon," which Peale adopted, was coined by Georges Cuvier in reference to the breastlike bumps on the animal's teeth. As Jefferson recounts in a letter to Peale, the French naturalist had named the remains "Mastodonte"—or "bubby-toothed"—because of the "protuberances on the grinding surface of [its] teeth, somewhat in the shape of the mamma mastos, or breast of a woman."[4] Peale's expedition to Shawangunk proved the mammoth to be a mastodon, an enormous, extinct American quadruped. But the mythical "mammoth" also lived on in the bubby-toothed mastodon: the skeleton continued to be referred to as a mammoth, even by Peale, and, with the recreation of a whole mastodon from mammoth parts in the first year of Jefferson's presidency, the word "mammoth" entered the political lexicon of the time, in association with the social and economic policies of Jefferson and his supporters, the Jeffersonian-Republicans.

At the end of the American Revolution, Thomas Jefferson envisioned an extended republic of husbandmen that would reach one day to the Pacific Ocean. His model of an agrarian state, cultivating and consuming its collective independence while exporting its surplus, was designed to retard the "natural progress of the arts" toward commercial luxury on the one hand and the growth of an urban working class on the other. Jefferson's political economy was opposed to Britain's example of empire through commerce and manufacturing, yet it was nevertheless itself a vehicle of empire. In theory and in practice, an agrarian republic was necessarily expansionist. As its population grew, its agricultural character could be preserved only by continual access to new land:

> In Europe the lands are either cultivated, or locked up against the cultivator. Manufacture must therefore be resorted to of necessity, not of choice, to support the surplus of their people. But we have an immensity of land courting the industry of the husbandman. Is it best then that all our citizens should be employed in its improvement, or that one half should be called off from that to exercise manufactures and handicraft arts for the other? . . . Corruption of morals in the mass of cultivators is a phaenomenon of which no age nor nation has furnished an example. It is the mark set on those, who not looking up to heaven, to their own soil and industry . . . for their subsistence, depend for it on the casualties and caprice of customers. While we have land to labour then, let us never wish to see our citizens occupied at a workbench, or twirling a distaff. Carpenters, masons, smiths, are wanting in husbandry: but, for the general operations of manufacture, let our workshops remain in Europe.[5]

Despite its hostility to manufacturing, by century's end Jeffersonian political economy had come to embrace not only the farmer in the countryside but urban artisans and self-supporting workers in general. In the course of the social and political conflict that accompanied the French Revolution, many artisans who supported Jefferson in urban seaports such as New York and Philadelphia expressed his production-based agrarianism as economic self-sufficiency generally.[6] During the late 1790s, Jefferson's supporters began to assert his model of a virtuous workingman's republic against Federalists such as Alexander Hamilton, who wished to pattern the United States on Britain's example of commercial development through the creation of banks, stock exchanges, and a national debt. Torn apart during Adams's presidency (1796–1800) by differing opinions over international events (revolution in France, counterrevolution in Britain, and war in Europe), the federalists of 1787–88 divided into two parties: the Jeffersonian-Republicans and the Federalists. Within the Federalist party itself an additional schism developed when Alexander Hamilton and his supporters set themselves against the comparatively moderate and pacific foreign and domestic policies of John Adams. By 1800, then, the word "federalist" had bifurcated into "*f*ederalists" (referring back to the nationalist centralizers of 1787) and "*F*ederalists," meaning the party of Washington and, especially, of Adams and Hamilton. It was this continual party division and political schism—as well as the death of Washington in December of 1799—that made it necessary for Jefferson to assert in his conciliatory 1801 inaugural address what would have been a redundancy in 1788: "we are all republicans; we are all federalists."[7]

Fought in the press, in street parades, and at the political meetings of Democratic-Republican clubs, this first national party division was intensified by revolution in France and war in Europe. Most Republicans remained sympathetic to the liberal social goals of the French Revolution even through the Reign of Terror and after Napoleon's rise to power; they called their Federalist antagonists "paper noblemen" and identified them (erroneously) with Europe's "ancien régime."[8] Federalists, by contrast, aligned themselves more closely with British reaction and sought in a variety of ways to pattern the United States on Britain's example of commercial development and cultural counterrevolution.[9] In the course of this war of words and images, urban artisans embraced the Jeffersonian ethic of virtuous self-production. In the process they implicated both Jefferson's agrarian political economy and the party division between Republicans and Federalists in the social and technological changes of early industrial, manufactory production, with its gradual, complex shift from colonial forms of artisanship to wage labor, from household and workshop to factory.[10]

Jefferson's agrarian political economy is sometimes understood as a reflection of actual economic and social reality, a transcript of the fact that a majority of late-eighteenth-century Anglo-Americans were, in fact, employed in agriculture. On the other hand, it is often viewed as ideology: a utopian and sentimental mask for class conflict, westward expansion, slaveholding, investment in manufacturing, and involvement in an international consumer market.[11] By focusing on Peale's museum exhibit of the first American mastodon, this chapter attends, by contrast, to the multiple and contingent structures of representation involved in the "framing," or raising, of production as the site of union reassembled by the rhetoric and representational practices of the Jeffersonian-Republican party. Between 1801 and 1809, the diverse textual and visual media of the mammoth exhibit in Peale's natural history museum took over, in effect, where the Grand Federal Procession left off. The static displays of Peale's collection (and, within it, the mammoth, at its summit and center) reiterate the nation-building, class-constituting technique of collective incorporation through production and its display, or the process of assembly itself preserved and restored as the grounds of *E pluribus unum*.

In 1800, Jefferson himself had tried to extract a mammoth from Shawangunk through the offices of Robert Livingston and the Philadelphia physician Caspar Wistar.[12] As Livingston informed Jefferson from New York, "I made some attempts to possess myself of [the bones], but found they were a kind of common property, the whole town having joined in digging for them till they were stopped by the autumnal rains."[13] Eight years later, William Clark would be more successful. At Jefferson's request, Clark, recently returned from his expedition (with Lewis) to the Pacific, employed local laborers to excavate more than three hundred mammoth bones from the Big Bone Lick in Kentucky. These bones were sent to the president in the White House, where he spread them out in the unfinished East Room and invited Caspar Wistar to come and study them.[14]

The Federalist press viewed Jefferson's preoccupation with natural history negatively, identifying it with his Deism, his French sympathies, and his commitment to western exploration.[15] In 1808, for example, William Cullen Bryant, a fierce thirteen-year-old Federalist, called upon Jefferson to resign and lampooned his fossilizing as impious and obscene:

> Go wretch, resign the presidential chair,
> Disclose thy secret measures foul or fair,
> Go, search, with curious eye, for horned frogs,
> Mongst the wastes of Louisianian bogs;
> Or where Ohio rolls his turbid stream
> Dig for huge bones, thy glory and thy theme.[16]

On the Republican side, however, a sympathetic public hailed Jefferson in 1801 as the Mammoth President and celebrated his election as a second American Revolution after years of Federalist fiscal, social, and foreign policy under Washington and Adams.[17] Delighted with his victory, Republican dairy farmers in Cheshire Town, Massachusetts, presented Jefferson with a two-hundred-pound cheese, dubbed the "mammoth cheese." The revolutionary motto stamped on its waxed surface read, "Rebellion against tyrants is obedience to God." With the mammoth cheese, the farmers of Cheshire Town opposed the virtue of agricultural productivity to the tyranny of Federalist fiscal and foreign policy and the party of Hamilton and

Adams. The mammoth cheese, however, was preserved rather than consumed. For years it remained on display in the rotunda of the House of Representatives, until it rotted and was thrown out early in Jefferson's second term.[18] After the excavation of 1801, Peale's mammoth (or "Boneyparts") likewise became the object of Federalist-party satire and Republican celebration in Philadelphia's partisan press.[19]

Within the museum itself, two exhibition texts and a painting directly accompanied the skeleton: Peale's *Exhumation of the Mastodon*, his son Rembrandt's *Historical Disquisition on the Mammoth* (1804), and the museum *Guide* of 1803. Each of these represented the assembled bones circularly, according to the logic of Jeffersonian-Republican political economy, as the source and summit, the means and end of Peale's own life of labor as artist and museum proprietor. By reconnecting the mastodon skeleton with the painting and pamphlet that framed it in the museum, this chapter displaces any single object—be it painting, skeleton, or *Disquisition*—from the center of focus and replaces it with the mammoth frame—here meaning not only the skeleton and its display but the larger federal framework of incorporation, which joined words with images and, in this case, with bones.[20]

By reconnecting Peale's *Exhumation of the Mastodon* with the other remains of the exhibit, including the *Disquisition* that was its print counterpart, the painting is repositioned within the representational framework of a museum that married image with word and "nature" with "culture" on the basis of productive labor. In 1803, the *Guide*'s description of the Mammoth Room represented the mastodon circularly as a skeleton within a skeleton: "Some bones of the Mammoth first gave rise to the Museum in 1785, which 16 years after possessed the first entire Skeleton."[21] Rembrandt's *Historical Disquisition* also identified the mammoth's rise and progress with the museum's, from its founding at the end of the American Revolution to its fulfillment during Jefferson's presidency. At the end of the Revolution, a small number of mammoth bones were brought to Peale's painting room in Philadelphia, where they were displayed as curiosities: "The bones of the MAMMOTH first produced the idea of a Museum, which, after eighteen years of rapid approach to maturity, under the unprecedented exertions of an individual, has in its turn enabled you to place among its treasures nearly a perfect skeleton of the MAMMOTH—the first of American animals, in the first of American Museums."[22]

Unlike such painters as John Trumbull or John Singleton Copley, Peale had seen battle during the Revolution and had participated in Revolutionary artisan politics. During his youth in Maryland, Peale worked as a saddlemaker's apprentice, an itinerant portrait painter, and a repairer of clocks, until, in 1763, a group of gentlemen planters sent him to London to study painting with Benjamin West. By 1776, a painter of portraits and miniatures in Philadelphia, he allied himself with the city's revolutionary artisan community. During the war, he fought as a captain in the city militia on the battlefields of Pennsylvania and New Jersey and served on the Committee of Safety that confiscated the estates of Loyalists in the city.[23] After the war, Peale remained a friend of Tom Paine and, during the 1780s, supported the radical Pennsylvania constitution whose unicameral legislature, until it was overturned in 1790, presented such a threat to more conservative republicans.[24] However, he quickly reached the limit of his tolerance for social and political conflict. After the tumultuous city elections of October 1780, he retired from Philadelphia politics, which, by its disruption of long-standing social connections, had caused him deep personal distress and threatened to deprive him of painting commissions.[25] He moved his family into the house of a Loyalist that had been confiscated during the war, where, in part of the house, he opened a portrait gallery.[26] Thereafter, in spite of his Jeffersonian allegiances, he claimed that his museum was above politics:

> I wish to be understood. This institution of a Museum can have no more to do with the politicks of a country, than with particular religious opinions. It has a much broader bottom. Facts and not theories, are the foundation on which the whole superstructure is built. Not on theoretical, speculative things, but on the objects of our sight and feelings— ... the production, preservation, and destruction of all material things deduced from facts.[27]

Illustrating Jefferson's principle of an all-inclusive social field—where (as Jefferson put it in his conciliatory inaugural address) "we are all republicans; we are all federalists"—Peale claimed that one day his museum would contain the entire world "in miniature." In 1802, Peale wrote to Jefferson that "my Museum, is [now] but part of an Establishment which in becoming national should embrace the exhibition of every article by which knowledge, in all its branches can possibly be communicated."[28] As a collection of every article by which knowledge might be communicated, the museum therefore represented a potentially infinite number of objects and an endless amount of work. Yet, Peale insisted: "I possess thousands of specimens, yet thousands are still wanting—in fact it ought to be[,] as a Museum, a collection of everything useful or curious—A world in miniature!"[29]

Peale meant "miniature" in the textual sense of an epitome, compendium, or digest. As the entire world in digest form, his museum was a "Book" of nature that represented the possibility of actual or literal representation in the language of science, if not in the realm of politics or government. The correlative of this was Peale's statement in 1800 that "the world itself is a Museum, in which all men are destined to be employed and amused."[30] Peale hoped that eventually his museum of the world would contain a specimen of every rock, insect, bird, fish, and quadruped produced by nature, brought together within a single "focus," and ordered according to the Linnaean system. As Peale never tired of repeating, Nature was a book whose structure was a display of both the original "Word" and the confining law of its Maker. As he inscribed it on a tablet at the museum's back door, facing out on the State House Garden:

> The book of Nature open
> _____ explore the wondrous work
> _____ an Institute
> of Laws eternal, whose unaltered page
> no time can change, no copier corrupt.[31]

Like his friends Jefferson and Franklin, Peale was a Deist: he regarded the world of nature as the work of a divine Maker, and his twenty-five-cent museum ticket bore the motto "Explore the Wondrous Work!"[32] The museum was an expression of natural theology: in Deist terms, the God of nature was not only the first cause, or unmoved mover, but an artisan extraordinaire, whose providential designs could be read in the leaves and stems or bones and muscle of his works. The Museum represented nature as creation, "work," and "book," and the deity as its Maker, Artist, or Author. At the same time, museum texts traced the museum's origin to Peale's own gargantuan labor of production. As he expressed it in a letter to Jefferson, the museum's success was the result "of my unremitted labours for years with the view of establishing a *PUBLIC MUSEUM*."[33] Jefferson, in turn, identified the museum with Peale's labor when, referring to the finished mastodon, he wrote, "I shall certainly pay your labours a visit, but when, heaven knows." Although Peale's museum never became officially national and remained a private, or proprietary, form of public enterprise, it was housed after 1802 in the old Pennsylvania State House, the building known today as Independence Hall. Prior to the expansion into the State House on Independence Square, Peale's collection was displayed next door in the Hall of the American Philosophical Society, where Peale and his family also lived, in separate living quarters.

Peale's museum never did contain the entire world in miniature. But it did display, among other things, "4000 insects in gilt frames, Minerals and Fossils in 4 large cases . . . a Marine Room of sundry Fishes, Lizards, Tortoises, Snakes, Shells, Corals, and sponges," 190 quadrupeds "mounted in their natural attitudes," and 760 birds, preserved by Peale's pioneering taxidermy techniques and posed in glass cases, the insides of which were painted by Peale and his sons "to represent appropriate scenery."[34] All these were catalogued according to Linnaeus, with their names written in Latin, English, and French, and displayed in gilt frames. After

the move to the State House, the Peale family continued to live in Philosophical Hall, where the museum's "Arts and Antiquities" were also
housed. This assemblage included new inventions, American Indian artifacts, plaster casts of Roman statues, a saltshaker belonging to Oliver
Cromwell, household gods from Pompeii, and wax figures of a Chinese
Labourer and Chinese Gentleman, an African, a Sandwich Islander, a
South American, and "Blue-Jacket and Red-pole, celebrated Sachems of
North America."[35] It was here that Peale's mastodon stood, on permanent
display in a Mammoth Room of its own, mounted next to the skeleton of
a mouse and accompanied by Rembrandt Peale's *Historical Disquisition* and
Peale's *Exhumation of the Mastodon*.

In a mammoth pun on the framing of the mammoth frame, each page
of Rembrandt's ninety-two-page *Disquisition* was framed separately and
strung, in ninety-two gilt frames, across the walls of the museum's Mammoth Room.[36] Peale's *Guide* of 1803 is not very specific about the exact
relation between the mammoth and the *Disquisition*. (Did the pages of the
pamphlet lead the museum visitor up to the skeleton, which stood as
ground and goal at *Disquisition*'s end?) But it does record an original juxta-
positioning of the pamphlet with the skeleton: "A particular account, by
Rembrandt Peale, of its discovery, with many interesting remarks on it, is
in 92 gilt frames, hung up in a convenient gallery for viewing the Skeleton."[37] In a manifestation of early national kitsch, scientific culture was
here reproduced democratically or diffused to the public through the
pamphlet's dismemberment and display. In the act of approaching and
reading each page of the *Disquisition* sequentially, in its frame, the museum's visitors were themselves constituted, in the public gaze of others in
the museum, as separate and separable subjects. At the same time, the
democratic diffusion of the pamphlet was accomplished by its elevation as
a collective object—in gilt frames that opened it to many eyes while preserving it from the wear and tear of human hands.

Like his son's pamphlet, Peale's painting was also produced specifically
for the mammoth exhibit, "to be placed," he wrote, "in the Museum near
the Mammoth skeleton."[38] In addition, the composition of the painting
can be traced to the pamphlet: in January of 1803 Peale sent an early
version of the *Disquisition* to President Jefferson, with a letter in which he
writes that the next edition of Rembrandt's pamphlet "probably will have
plates; he was just beginning a view of our last days work at Masten[']s in
which he introduces an American thunder-storm . . . it was in reallity the
most dreadful in appearance I had ever seen yet passed away with wind
only."[39] Proposed by Rembrandt Peale for the *Historical Disquisition* but
never executed, this scene is identical with the one pictured in *The Exhumation of the Mastodon*.

Both the painting and the pamphlet focus their narratives on a farm
belonging to a German immigrant named John Masten. Peale made an

initial expedition to Shawangunk in June of 1801, visited the flooded pit there, and examined the bones spread out in Masten's barn. At first, he was permitted only to study and sketch them, but finally Masten agreed to sell his collection, along with rights to the bones remaining in the pit, for three hundred dollars plus new clothes for his wife and a gun for his son.[40] Returning briefly to Philadelphia for money and supplies, Peale was ready for a second expedition to Masten's farm in July.[41] Back in Shawangunk, he hired "upwards of 25" men at "high wages" ($1.12/hour) to assist with the digging[42] and, with the help of a local carpenter, designed and built the pump that would keep the site from flooding. This is the pyramidal structure, vaguely resembling the frame of a teepee, that dominates the worksite in Peale's painting.

The mastodon is exactly what is missing from *The Exhumation of the Mastodon* (fig. 6); instead of the skeleton, a skeletal mechanism looms above the site. Supported by a complicated crisscross of boards and poles, Peale's pump reframes the scene within the scene, dividing and redividing the crowd of spectators who have come to witness the mammoth's second birth through the labor of excavation. Haphazardly (or, rather, in the style of documentary empiricism), Peale's mechanical contrivance cuts the scene into oddly fragmentary miniature scenes, partial paintings within the painting. It is the working of the pump as a visual frame, as much as the crowd of spectators or the labor of digging, that makes *The Exhumation of the Mastodon* "a busy scene," as Peale described it in 1806.[43] Rembrandt Peale's pamphlet likewise frames a "busy scene": both pamphlet and painting raise the skeleton as a wondrous work of labor and looking, or recreational spectatorship and laborious production, on the basis of which painted image and printed pamphlet may be connected with one another. According to the pamphlet,

> The attention of every traveller was arrested by the coaches, waggons, chaises, and horses, which animated the road, or were collected at the entrance of the field. Rich and poor, men, women, and children, all flocked to see the operation; and a swamp always noted as the solitary abode of snakes and frogs, became the active scene of curiosity and bustle: most of the spectators were astonished at the purpose which could prompt such vigorous and expensive exertions, in a manner so unprecedented, and so foreign to the pursuits for which they were noted. —But the amusement was not wholly on their side; and the variety of company not only amused us, but tended to encourage the workmen, each of whom, before so many spectators, was ambitious of signalizing himself by the number of his discoveries.[44]

Here, as in Hopkinson's and Rush's accounts of the Grand Federal Procession of 1788, the object of wonder and amusement is as much the crowd of spectators as the machinery or the labor of production—though here the spectators seem to assemble spontaneously. In Rembrandt Peale's account, the crowd virtually attracts itself to the excavation: passersby are drawn by the coaches and horses on the road or those already "collected" there. While the "foreignness" of "the operation" appeals to the crowd, the crowd's assembled "variety" amuses the Peales. But the diverting diversity of the crowd stands in marked contrast to, and is inversely reflected by, the laborers below them: the men in the pit are not differentiated by sex, age, or class but by the degree to which they can "signalize" themselves in the eyes of the crowd.

The Exhumation of the Mastodon likewise conjoins labor with looking. A random crowd of spectators, diversified by age, class, dress, and sex, is juxtaposed with a group of workmen in the pit, one of whom "signalizes" himself by raising a bone. In addition, however, the painting displays Peale's family, including eleven of his twelve children and two of his wives: both Betsy DePeyster Peale, who died in 1804, and Hannah Moore Peale, whom he married in 1806. (Notably, except for Rembrandt, Peale's family was not present at the excavation.) Grouped in a formal tableau in the right middle ground, the Peales of Philadelphia are set apart from both the laborers in the pit and the crowd around them. The visual field of the excavation site in the painting is complicated by the fact that both the crowd of spectators and the Peale family contain female as well as male subjects. The gendering of the scene intersects with the other divisions that structure both painting and pamphlet: the division between the farmers of Shawangunk and their urban employer; between the wage laborers in the pit and the Peale family above them; between the men who labor and the spectators who view them; and, finally, between the spectators who view the painting itself, from outside, and the spectators and workers within it.

The Exhumation of the Mastodon illustrates that Peale's museum was structured, on many different, intersecting levels, by a compulsion to rationalize labor's productive power.[45] But it also records the artist's encounter with the farmers and farmhands at Shawangunk, where his Jeffersonian-Republican model of independence came face to face with actual agricultural producers and, in the process, with its own self-divided relation with labor. One of the ways in which Peale's ambivalence toward his employees is manifested—and contained—is through the progressive frame that the painting imposes on the bodies of the laborers. In the painting, the men of Shawangunk stand on dry ground or on wooden steps, working knee-deep in water, digging with shovels or with their bare hands, or momentarily resting. But their labor is rationalized into an obvious historical progression: from the nearly naked man at the bottom of the pit, through the half-dressed men digging with their hands, to fully clothed and hatted men working with tools. On the one hand, the workmen in the pit represent the collective labor of digging depicted within a single moment and, more subtly, through history. On the other hand, Peale's rationalization of the labor into developmental stages has the effect of framing it as the labor of a single man, represented through time (as if in a time-frame sequence) at different moments in the progression.

Just as the painting rationalizes labor as a human product, Rembrandt Peale's *Disquisition* rationalizes the labor of production by drawing a negative contrast between Peale's "liberal plan" and the "vulgar" curiosity, poor work habits, and unenlightened customs of the men of Shawangunk.[46] In 1798, Masten and his neighbors had spent several days drinking grog and dragging bones from the marl pit—breaking many in the process—until the pit flooded and buried what remained. When Peale took over he carefully doled out the grog because, as he put it, "those who had drunk too much was not worth having."[47] Like Benjamin Rush's memorial "In Honour of American Beer and Cyder," Peale's mammoth exhibit frowned upon "spirituous liquors" misapplied. While rationalized labor was the groundwork of the mammoth framed in Peale's museum, unrationalized, disorderly labor was not part of the plan:

> unfortunately, the habits of the men requiring the use of spirits, it was afforded them in too great profusion, and they quickly became so impatient and unruly, that they had nearly destroyed the skeleton; and, in one or two instances, using oxen and chains to drag them from the clay and marle, the head, hips, and tusks were much broken; some parts being drawn out, and others left behind. So great a quantity of water, from copious springs, bursting from the bottom, rose upon the men, that it required several score of hands to lade it out with all the milk-pails, buckets, and bowls, they could collect in the neighbourhood.[48]

In addition to employing themselves unproductively, the men of Shawangunk were motivated by profit. For farmer Masten, in particular, Rembrandt's *Disquisition* recounts, the hope of gain "was everything"; while for his neighbors "curiosity did much, but rum did more, and some little was owing to certain prospects which they had of sharing in the future possible profit."[49] They would be disappointed, however, because Masten ultimately refused to share with them "the price of any thing his land might happen to produce."[50] By contrast, Peale's reorganization and partial mechanization of the excavation translates the divisiveness and disorder of the farmhands into his own success. Contrasting the farmer's failure with his father's "liberal plan," the *Disquisition* is dedicated to Peale's "persevering zeal," which reconstructed a mammoth in Philadelphia, "without any intermixture of foreign bones. . . . where it will remain a monument, not only of stupendous creation, and some wonderful revolution in nature, but of the scientific zeal, and indefatigable perseverance, of a man from whose private exertions a museum has been founded, surpassed by few in Europe, and likely to become a national establishment, on the most liberal plan."[51]

Among the farmers and farmhands of Shawangunk, the German immigrant Masten is distinguished by the mammoth exhibit as a special object of redemption and preservation. In the painting, Masten is the dark figure near the bottom center of the painting, where he stands on a ladder. Halfway in and halfway out of the pit, he marks the limit and ground of the museum's field of visibility. Looking back from the extreme foreground, Masten most closely approximates the position of the viewer outside the painting's frame: alone and disconnected from the human groups in the painting, he seems in the process of leaving the site. Yet his gaze has been arrested by the figure of Peale, as it was not arrested by the bones in his marl pit. The *Disquisition* introduces its description of Masten as "an anecdote not uninteresting to the moralist," recounting that Masten "[spoke] the language of his fathers better than that of his country" and would have preferred to let the bones "rot as manure."[52] Unlike Peale, Masten regarded both farming and mammoth bones from an "illiterate" point of view, or so the Peales thought. But Masten was also a productive farmer. Born on his farm, he "was brought up" to farming "as a business,"

> and it continued to be his pleasure in old age; not because it was likely to free him from labour, but because profit, and the prospect of profit, cheered him in it until the ends were forgotten in the means. —Intent upon manuring his lands to increase its production (always laudable) he felt no interest in the fossil shells contained in his morass; and if it had not been for the men who dug with him, and those whose casual attention was arrested . . . for him the bones might have rotted in the hole which discovered them: this he confessed to me would have been his conduct, certain that after the surprise of the moment they were good for nothing but to rot as manure. But the learned physician, the reverend divine, to whom he had been accustomed to look upwards, gave importance to the objects which excited the vulgar stare of his more inquisitive neighbors: he therefore joined his exertions to theirs.[53]

What would Masten do if he were free from labor? The Peales clearly would have wanted him to pursue natural history or at least visit the Philadelphia museum, where he would learn to regard his farm and himself as living artifacts of aesthetic and scientific significance. At the same time, though, the *Disquisition* makes it clear that Masten belonged to a comparatively traditional community, one in which profit seeking was constrained and complicated by cooperative labor and a variety of deferential social forms. The farmer is moved less by his own "curiosity" than by the opinion of the "learned physician and the reverend divine." But being dependent upon learned authorities, to whom "he had been accustomed to look upwards," Masten has not learned to look for himself and has not, therefore, achieved the kind of independence the museum impressed upon its visitors. The moral of the story is that Masten's inability to see himself, his property, and his mammoth bones as significant (or historically narratable) objects is a result of his failure to "employ himself" in recreational activities such as museum going, which could have opened him to the arts of spectatorship and self-regard.

The mammoth exhibit does not simply dismiss Masten as a figure external to the museum's visual field. This is partly because Masten's marginality implied the separate state of independence. But he was also impossible to dismiss because, as a property-owning farmer, he embodied Jeffersonian principles. While his lack of interest or, rather, sheer interestedness in respect to the bones was disturbing to the Peales, Masten was a farmer concerned with increasing his farm's production, an ambition that was "always laudable."[54] As an agricultural producer upon whose labor Jefferson's political economy grounded itself, Masten was, theoretically, central to the picture. At the same time, though, both painting and pamphlet cast the non-English-speaking "foreigner" as a dark figure, against whom Peale's concern for public over private interest and scientific principle over local custom is foregrounded.

In the painting, Masten stands in an ambiguous, even faintly satanic position. Bryan J. Wolf has argued that the thunderstorm looming in the right background represents the threat of nature's retribution upon the technological domination of nature that is the painting's focus.[55] But the other dark place in the painting is the extreme foreground where Masten stands, half-integrated into the scene, with his eyes focused on Peale, the victor at the marl pit, which is Masten's property after all. In the mammoth exhibit, Charles Willson Peale, public ownership, and national good win out over Masten, localism, and private interest. However, while Peale was funded by President Jefferson and the American Philosophical Society, his museum and his expedition were also proprietary, that is, privately initiated and supported. The museum and the mastodon were assembled for the public good, but also in the private interest of Peale and his family. In this sense, as the shadowy other at the mastodon site, Masten represents Charles Willson Peale's alter ego. Masten had been the first collector of the mastodon bones. More important, he represents Peale's own "uncultivated" self, insofar as Peale, like Masten, identified virtue with the means-end logic of production, public good with private happiness, or the national interest with his own family's welfare.

Production grounded and unified the diverse fields in which Peale labored as museum proprietor and, in *The Exhumation of the Mastodon*, he represents himself as an exemplary producer: as the object of his own making, the artist of the museum articulates the connection between individual and collective self-production. The role of artist and man of science was also, of course, inherently in conflict with that of the laborer, and the painting distinguishes Peale as cultivated artist and museum proprietor from the workmen in the pit. Peale stands at the edge of the pit, illuminated by sunlight. Gesturing to the laborers below with his right hand, he holds in his left hand an enormous scroll on which a life-size sketch of a mastodon leg is displayed. Unrolled horizontally, the scroll unites the members of Peale's family behind it in a tableau. This includes his three eldest sons, Raphaelle, Rembrandt, and Rubens Peale: Raphaelle holds the opposite end of the scroll, while Rembrandt stands at its center, pointing down to the drawing of the mammoth bones in imitation of his father's role as public educator, artist, and restorer of the mastodon.[56] Rubens stands between them, with Peale's two youngest daughters in front of him.

Peale's gesture to the laborers digging in the pit below serves to identify them with himself and his own labors as founder and proprietor of the museum—labors that are the support of the family behind him. On the artist's scroll, "the Word" is bone: in a graphic representation of the museum's equation of image with word and word with natural structure, nature is articulated as work (wherein the Maker's design is inscribed and legible). The drawing on the scroll also serves as a kind of heraldic device for the Peales themselves,[57] punningly representing foundation as the bones of a leg, or as the support of both the mastodon and the Peale family. As an emblem for the Philadelphia Museum, which was also the Peale family home, the Word-as-bone reads, "Our support lies in the works of nature."

By introducing his family's portraits here, Peale celebrates the museum and its mammoth as the foundation and support of his family in Philadelphia. And, by opening this foundation of private support to the public gaze and identifying it with the men working in the pit, Peale connects the unity and support of the Peale family with the grounding of all society in productive labor. Of course, it was not only shared labor but also the wage relation that restored the bones and connected the museum family from Philadelphia with the people of Shawangunk. In the painting, the half-naked laborer at the bottom of the pit stands in an Adamic pose, raising the bone he has discovered. Considerably smaller than the leg on Peale's scroll, this bone approximates Peale's own arm in size and corresponds with the smallest bones in the diagram: it finds a place in the artist's sketch in a silent articulation of union, wherein the labor of the local farmers and the work of the urban artist are conjoined. But Peale's celebration of social harmony through an economic and cultural mechanism of production is also based on a productive disjunction between labor and its employment (and, correspondingly, between word and image, labor and work), whether that labor be Peale's own as museum proprietor or that of the workmen on whom the excavation also depended.

Standing between the men in the pit and the women and children grouped behind him, the figure of Peale not only mediates between the laborers and the members of his family, but separates them from each other: the Jeffersonian-Republican identification of private productivity with the national good is both the cause and the effect of a class distinction. While the painting celebrates both the Jeffersonian-Republican revelation of labor as the nation's productive base and Peale's own labors as museum proprietor, it also records the artist's cultivated reluctance to identify himself and his family with the cultivators of Shawangunk.

Surrounded by their older brothers, two little girls stand at the center of the Peale family group. These are the youngest daughters of Peale and his second wife, Elizabeth DePeyster Peale, who died in 1804, two years before Peale began the painting. (Peale's first wife, Rachel Brewer Peale, who died in 1789, was the mother of Rembrandt, Raphaelle, and Rubens.) Peale married a third time in 1805: in *The Exhumation of the Mastodon* his new wife, Hannah Moore, stands immediately behind him. However, Elizabeth DePeyster is also on the scene. Pictured at a distance from the family grouped behind Peale, she stands at left, in a miniature landscape, with a little boy (her son Titian Ramsay Peale II), pointing up toward the coming storm and directing him to the safety of the military tent in the background. Her gesture toward the storm in the far right corner is mirrored by Peale on the other side of the painting, who points down toward the laborers in the left foreground. The boy's body, in turn, mirrors in miniature the tripod arrangement of Peale's pump.

Pointing up to the clouds, Elizabeth DePeyster gives direct expression to anxiety at the worksite. In a terrible irony, given the significance of metaphors of size and birth to the mammoth exhibit, Elizabeth (or Betsy) Peale died on 19 February 1804, unable to deliver an overly large baby boy after a pregnancy of twelve months. She died following an operation performed by a Philadelphia doctor to extract the baby.[58] Framed by Peale's pump, Elizabeth DePeyster Peale looks down at the laborers below and, by pointing to the sky and to the tent, connects the labor of the excavation with the coming storm.[59] The white tent beneath the blue sky is a place of comparative security in the scene: Peale had begun his Philadelphia career as a painter of Revolutionary portraits, and the tent represents the Revolutionary past within the Jeffersonian present of the painting. In good Republican fashion, however, its military presence is relegated to the distance, and the machinery and labor of production dominate the site instead. Linking the storm with the rebirth of the mastodon through labor, Elizabeth Peale expresses, even more clearly than the figure of her husband, the anxieties that structure and confront the mechanics of Republican political economy: that the laboring body not only produces but also threatens fixity and independence and that, within the representational framework of the extended republic, progress is re-production, or repetition.

In September of 1806, Peale was just beginning *The Exhumation of the Mastodon* when he wrote to his eldest daughter Angelica, juxtaposing the uncertain outcome of his "labour" on the painting with the imminent birth of a grandchild (Angelica's sister, Sophonisba Peale Sellers, was awaiting the birth of her first child). In the painting, Sophonisba stands behind the Peale family, beneath an umbrella, with her husband.[60] Juxta-posing the precarious labor of childbirth with both the looming storm in the background of the painting and his own labors with the paintbrush, Peale writes,

> I have on hand a picture which requires all my attention, and greater exer-tions than any undertaking I have ever done. How I shall acquit myself on the finishing is yet doubtful in a great number of figures in a busy scene of taking up the Mammoth Bones in a Deep Pit with numbers of spectators as was actually the case during that great labour. I hope to make it a very interesting picture, the subject being grand, nay awful, by the appearance of [a] tremendous gust coming on. Sophonisba will shortly be confined, she looms large.[61]

The connection between a mother's relationship to her children and the laborious second birth of the mammoth is reiterated by Elizabeth De-Peyster's youngest daughter, Elizabeth. At the far right of the painting, the little girl points down to their father's sketch and looks up at her older sister Sybilla, who, in turn, points up to the storm and to the sky in general. Sybilla's gesture is the answer to a central query of American education during the antebellum period: Do you know who made you? As her sister's teacher, Sybilla indicates that her Maker is in heaven. Since Elizabeth is pointing down to the sketch of the mastodon leg, the question is extended to the mastodon as well: its Maker is also above. Sybilla's gesture also con-nects the mastodon leg with the frame of the pump above her head. Since Sybilla and Elizabeth are the children of Elizabeth DePeyster, Sybilla's an-swer to Elizabeth's query can also be construed as a statement about their mother's whereabouts: "She is in heaven." On the other side of Peale's machinery, Sybilla's gesture is replicated, in a less harmonious context, by Elizabeth DePeyster Peale.

As the expression of the Jeffersonian-Republican reunion of means and ends, parts and wholes, the mammoth in the Peale Museum brings into focus a national interior, in both the geographic sense of a continental interior and in the disciplinary sense of a subjective interiority that is in-separable from the production and display of objects. As the expression of Jeffersonian-Republican political economy and its continental empire, Peale's mammoth makes visible the framed frame/work of a collective national subject as the dominated object of its own making and the domi-nating subject of its own gaze. Jeffersonian-Republican political economy was not, then, a mechanism simply for producing landed properties but for deploying whole fields through the production and proliferation of visibly self-made subjects.

Within the framework of the Peale Museum, territorial expansion was inseparable from the celebration of wondrous "work." During Jefferson's presidency, the role that expansion as well as production played in his political economy was evidenced most literally by Lewis and Clark's expedition of 1803–6 and the purchase of the Louisiana territory from Napoleon in 1804. On Jefferson's orders, most of the animal specimens collected by Lewis and Clark—prairie dogs, bighorn sheep, prong-horned antelope, and numerous weasels and squirrels—were sent to Peale's museum in Philadelphia for preservation and display.[62] Peale's curatorial role in the Lewis and Clark expedition directly connected the exhibi-tionary framework of the Philadelphia Museum with expansion into the continental interior: the scientific practices of collecting, classifying, and exhibiting the artifacts of the interior employed an urban artist such as Peale in the service of an economic expansion the engine of which was productive labor. In turn, Peale's museum celebrated labor in general and Peale's own labor in particular as the productive source of collective independence.

Crucially, both expansion and production were suffused with a humani-tarian ethic of tolerance within the museum's discursive and visual Jeffer-sonian frame. As humanitarianism, Jefferson's political economy pre-scribed a self-regulating social order that lifted all external, coercive force from the human body, while widening and deepening, or democratizing and elevating, the social field by framing it as a visual field wherein all persons were free not only to appear but to become the independent ob-jects of their own production. Only in the open exhibitionary field of a society free from coercion could independence and stability appear. Only in such a field, further, would individuals be free to make, master, and contain themselves as living monuments to freedom. As articulated by Jef-ferson in his first inaugural address, this revolutionary freedom from coer-cion entailed a new disposition of power that was both the cause and the effect of an extended sphere of visibility. Both revolutionary and counter-revolutionary opponents of Jeffersonian-Republican self-production were to be regarded as monuments, untouched but safely contained in (the frame/work of) an open visual field. As Jefferson proclaimed at his first inauguration: "If there be any among us who wish to dissolve this union, or to change its republican form, let them stand undisturbed, as monu-ments of the safety with which error of opinion may be tolerated where reason is left free to combat it."[63]

Peale too had founded his museum in the act of distancing himself from political warfare. As a monument to Peale's dislike of social conflict, the museum constituted social control through the arts of exhibition and display. The museum and the mastodon that epitomized its recreational suspension of productive labor did not mean simply the retreat of the artist from political conflict to the solitary status of the observer. Instead, they were the products of the displacement and diffusion of social struggle and social control to and through other sites of representation.

If, in *The Exhumation of the Mastodon*, the figure of Elizabeth DePeyster points to the precarious nature of the pyramid's base in productive labor, the contemplative man behind her embodies the successful reproduction of production in the figure of the self-made man. Framed by the wooden shack in the left middle ground, this is Alexander Wilson, Scots immigrant, dialect poet, and the father of American ornithology.[64] Arms crossed, hat on, Wilson stands at the summit of the chain of laborers digging below: the rise and progress of the labor in the pit is contained and recapitulated in this spectatorial figure. With his shovel, the uppermost workman tosses away a load of clay and with it, potentially, the yoke of labor. But the physical motion of his labor is translated into Wilson's independent pose: the contained self-regard of the scientific observer and self-made man. Arms folded, Wilson displays the cultivated autonomy that, according to the Jeffersonian logic of production, history itself labors to produce. In 1808, the year the painting was completed, Wilson had just finished the first volume of his *American Ornithology*, which by 1814 would encompass more than five hundred bird species. A former handloom weaver and sometime pedlar, Wilson aspired to collect and classify every species of bird in the United States. While he worked on his collection, Wilson depended on Jefferson's patronage and on the bird collection in the Philadelphia Museum. Throughout the *Ornithology* Wilson repeatedly thanks Peale and refers to his museum. In turn, in *The Exhumation of the Mastodon* Peale placed Wilson in a position of honor, though, like Peale's family, Wilson was not present at the site. By including Wilson in the painting and placing him in a position of lonely eminence, Peale honors his example as self-made scientist, American author, and fellow laborer in the endless fields of natural history. Eventually filling nine volumes, Wilson's *Ornithology* brought familiar eastern species (such as the robin and the bluejay) together with new species collected by Lewis and Clark and by Wilson himself on journeys through Tennessee, Mississippi, and Louisiana. Charting the migratory ranges of each species, Wilson's mammoth *Ornithology* implicitly identified the United States with the continent of North America. In this respect, the *Ornithology* was, like Peale's museum, a Jeffersonian-Republican text and a monument to continental empire.

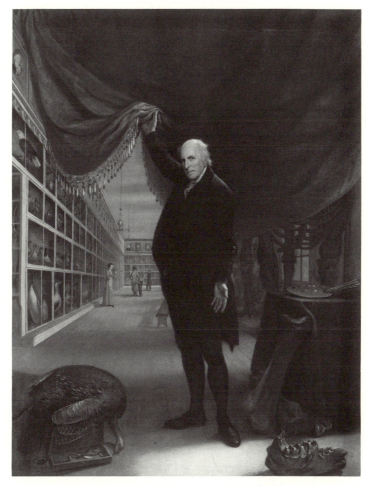

Figure 7. Charles Willson Peale, *The Artist in His Museum* (1822).
(Courtesy of the Pennsylvania Academy of Fine Arts.)

Long before the success of his mammoth exhibit, Peale had employed the mammoth and its bones as metonyms of the "rise and progress"[65] of his museum as a whole. In a museum lecture of 1799, Peale traced the origins of his museum to three objects assembled in the early 1780s: his collection of portraits of Revolutionary "worthies," a dried paddlefish, and the bones of the mammoth.[66] All three of these founding objects—paddle-fish, portraits, and mammoth—are represented in Peale's famous self-por-trait of 1822, *The Artist in His Museum* (fig. 7). But it is the mammoth leg beside the artist's leg that is the painting's punning frame and focus. Pictured between the mastodon skeleton, which is partly obscured against the window at right, and the hundreds of bird specimens that line the left wall, Peale has positioned himself as the point of integration between the mammoth One and the feathered Many, the gigantic and the miniature. As if he were one of the bird specimens in the cases at left, the artist in his museum is boxed in on three sides, with one end left open for viewing. The long upper room of the museum in Independence Hall serves as a single display case for the representative Man; expressing the art of self-production as self-containment, Peale is the biped on display. As the second creator of the world, in miniature, Peale has encased himself as a specimen in a museum of his own making.

With his left hand, he indicates his own leg and, beside it, the leg of the mastodon. Through this gesture, Peale puns once again on leg as foundation: just as the counterpart of this mastodon bone supports the mastodon skeleton behind the curtain, so Peale's leg supports him. Far more than in *The Exhumation of the Mastodon*, punning humor works here to contain the grandiosity of the artist's act of self-production and self-display. However, the joke is not very funny, because it is made at the expense of the single woman on the scene and masks domination as perfect openness, self-assertion as the withdrawal of self, and the presence of power as its absence, or extinction.

In fact, what Luce Irigaray has called the "re-mark" of gender is the primary source of amusement in *The Artist in His Museum*.[67] In Peale's painting, the two sides of the museum correspond with two ways of looking, which are represented, respectively, by the single woman, who stands in the left middle ground gazing up at the mammoth with her hands raised, and a man, pictured in profile in the far background, who looks down, in an attitude of distanced contemplation, at the birds on the left wall. This male figure exactly reproduces in profile the pose of the ornithologist Alexander Wilson in *The Exhumation of the Mastodon*. The woman, by contrast, stands with her back to the birds and looks up, in an attitude of wonder, at the mastodon on the other side of the room. The woman has a full view of the mammoth frame, in contrast to viewers outside the painting, for whom the red drapery (which serves as a backdrop for Peale's head) partly conceals the mastodon's. And since, with his left hand, Peale identifies the mastodon with his own body and its frame, the woman's wonder is also a joking mockery of the artist's grandiose self-display and of his identification of himself with the mammoth.

The woman's response to the gigantic skeleton finds its inverse in the self-containment of the independent young man at the rear of the museum, who studies the birds in their miniature worlds. Second only to the mammoth and perhaps to his collection of Revolutionary portraits, Peale's remarkably large bird collection was the pride of his museum. As a laborious technique of restoration and preservation taken to a graphic extreme, the museum practice of taxidermy epitomized a hyperreal fusion of nature with art, accomplished by the reproductive machinery of a production-based political economy: the birds' feathers and skin were preserved with arsenic and their bones and muscles replaced with statues carved from wood. The eyes, made of glass, were also cast by Peale. In an unpublished museum guide titled "A Walk Through the Philadelphia Museum," Peale describes his method of refitting his specimens with monumental new frames: "In fact they are statues of animals with real skin to cover them— a stupendous labor!" So precisely were the "mussils of the quadrupeds" represented by their replacements within "that Painters might take them for models"[68]—which was exactly what Wilson did when he used Peale's birds as models for his illustrated *Ornithology*.

The bird-watcher, miniaturized by distance in the painting's background, mirrors the stance of the viewer outside the painting's frame: just as the autonomous man in the rear of the museum contemplates the birds within it, so the museum visitor, standing before *The Artist in His Museum*, considers Peale, foregrounded in the enormous display case he has built for himself. However, unlike the birds in their cases with respect to the man who views them, Peale's eight-by-six-foot self-portrait is not miniature with respect to its viewer. Hung on the museum wall, it looms over the spectator who stands below. The spectator's position must also be identified, then, with the position of the woman with her back to the birds, who stands in awe before the enormous frame across the room.

There are two other figures on the scene: a man and a boy divide the single man in the background from the woman in the middle ground. This couple walks together, the boy holding a book between them or, more likely, a copy of the museum *Guide*. Roger Stein has suggested that the four figures in the background of *The Artist in His Museum* represent a recapitulation of Lockean/Linnaean epistemology, according to which they progressively emblematize, from background to foreground, sense perception, reason, and religious reverence or wonder: "The man sees, as the birds in the cases discover themselves to his sense; the father and son with a book reason justly upon the significance of the arrangement visually available in the cases and verbally ordered . . . in the catalogue in the child's hand, while the lady stands . . . with hands raised in wonder (her Quaker religion implies reverence)."[69] However, this reading reverses the developmental sequence of the figures, that is, from woman through dependent child to independent man. By not considering the thematization of dependence versus independence in its connection with the interplay between the gigantic and miniature elements in the painting, Stein does not see in the distanced man and the awestruck woman the reversibility of the left and right sides of the painting and their thematic integration in the pivotal figure of the artist. He therefore misses the amusing side of the rational(-ized) amusement offered by the painting, amusement that follows from the association of the almighty mammoth with the fore-grounded figure of Peale.

The woman, struck with wonder by the mastodon, and the young man, contemplating the bird families on display, recapitulate within the paint-ing the two poles that structure the viewer's own experience before *The Artist in His Museum*. According to the logic of viewership described by the figures in the painting, the awe of the viewer who herself stands beneath the huge painting is to be similarly framed and contained by an attitude of comparatively distanced, if not amused, contemplation (i.e., the attitude represented in the painting by the autonomous young man). Crucially, the ability to see the joke implies only amusement, not laughter. While the joke is at her expense, Peale is not holding the woman up to explicit ridi-cule. In fact, levity was a suspect category and one of the debilitating social vices his museum set out to cure.[70] Cultivated amusement was meant to produce knowing smiles rather than open laughter.

The man and the boy with their printed *Guide* represent Peale's own mediating relation, as educator, to the museum visitor standing before the painting. As Stein argues, the four background figures emblematize the ordering power of textuality. But, as demonstrated by the moment of com-munion between father and son, this ordering power of the text is marked as male. The educational goal of the museum was the cultivated indepen-dence represented by the man in the rear of the painting: the logic of education leads developmentally *back* to the position of the independent young man in the distance, rather than forward to the woman's amusing awe. As Peale put it in his "Epistle to a Friend" (1803), "What charming conversations will a knowledge of this science (of nature) afford between the father and his sons at the age when they become agreeable and useful companions to each other. How often in their morning or evening walks might the Infirmities of age be beguiled, while recounting their observa-tions and . . . the high-toned passions of the youthful nerve, might be re-strained until it gains maturity."[71] In a reflection of the museum's marriage of image and word, miniature and gigantic elements, the museum visitor who views the painting is positioned as simultaneously a male reader of Nature's Book and a female one. However, the seeming egalitarianism implied by this reversibility of gender masks and reproduces a relationship of subordination in which the female body, like the laboring bodies in *The Exhumation of the Mastodon*, is inscribed as both the prehistoric ground and an unincorporable part of Nature's Book.

In addition to the figure of the awestruck woman, Peale has included another humorous commentary on his mammoth act of self-display: the turkey specimen in the foreground. The head and neck of the turkey hang down, because the bird is dead; but the body is positioned so that the turkey bows obsequiously toward the artist, epitomizing, as farmer Masten did, the attitude of the uncultivated subject, who refuses to willingly look and actively construct the museum of the world for himself. As unenlightened Nature without Art, the turkey embodies traditional or prehistoric customs, not simply of "looking up" to figures of authority but of bowing down to kings, priests, and tyrants. Of course, all of this is Peale's own humorous self-commentary on the grandiose presumption of the artist who poses as the second Creator of the world, in miniature. But the humor is dark, even gothic in tone. Although the turkey serves as a joke, it is perched on a box of tools that is open to view. Just as the mechanics of the excavation were open to view in *The Exhumation of the Mastodon,* so here the drawer of the toolbox is open, and the viewer is invited to see the specimen of nature graphically, from the side of power—and to perform the part of the creator as well as the viewer of a (wondrous) work. The open drawer, with its scalpels and pincers, invites the painting's viewers to see and use the visual technology of the museum themselves in order to reproduce the independent pose of the artist and recreate the world, through their own collective effort, as a monument to independent selfhood.

CHAPTER FOUR

The American Lounger:
Figures of Failure and Fatigue in
the *Port Folio*, 1801–1809

In an unpublished pamphlet of 1805 titled "A Walk Through the Philadelphia Museum," Charles Willson Peale declared that "the work" of as-
sembling a museum was "so difficult that had he known what he was about
to undertake he would, perhaps, have rather put his hand into the fire."
Despite such acknowledgments of the painful effort of its assembly, however, Peale routinely denied that his collection's resulting dimensions
would present any difficulty to the comprehension or enjoyment of the
viewer. For Peale, a describable order lay behind the heaping up of things
in his museum, since his own labors of production and organization paralleled in miniature those of the Maker, or Creator, of all things. And he
believed that museum visitors would find this order not only obvious and
accessible but sublime as well: "such is the bewitching study of Nature,"
Peale writes, "that it expands the mind to embrace object after object, and
the desire is still fed in an endless magic and contemplation of the wondrous works of Creation."[1]

For at least one visitor, however, Peale's drive to re-create and classify
the entire world generated chaotic rather than sublime multiplicity. In his
"Walk," Peale records the opinion of one disgruntled visitor, "a country
man" who "complained" that on previous trips to the museum "he used
to be able to take it all in [in] one view—but now the Ideas were overrun
by the number of objects." "I want to see all," the man is quoted as saying,
"and thus I can see nothing satisfactory."[2] In his manuscript, Peale has
crossed out this last line—no doubt because it was explicit criticism, rather
than praise, of his museum. Like farmer Masten's unenlightened attitude
at the mammoth excavation, the comic haplessness of a man from "the
country" might be good advertising, but his irritation and fatigue were
not. The country man's declaration that, in the end, he could "see nothing
satisfactory" gave voice to precisely what Peale's museum denied: that the
taxonomizing impulse that had produced and displayed the world in miniature not only contained, but also proliferated, detail.

The country man who visited Peale's museum was not alone in his failure, or refusal, to enjoy an expanding world of things. In 1805, many
readers, writers, and viewers who had never visited the Philadelphia Mu-

seum shared the experience of being overwhelmed by the sheer number of particulars displayed around them. By the first decades of the nineteenth century, expressions of fatigue and failure could be experienced at a range of exhibitionary venues outside the natural history museum: in shops and shopping arcades, in newspapers and advertising and, perhaps most regularly and explicitly, in the early national "miscellany," or miscellaneous magazine.[3]

In 1788, Matthew Carey's *American Museum and Repository* had had few significant competitors, but the decades after the ratification of the Constitution would witness a growing flood of ephemeral miscellanies and literary "museums." Frank Luther Mott reports that at one time or another between 1794 and 1825 nearly every town of any size in the United States had a literary miscellany. Published weekly, quarto in size, and designed for entertainment, these miscellanies combined in varying proportions political news with literature, "original compositions" with poetry and prose liberally excerpted from European and American newspapers and periodicals. Highly eclectic, they "were quite free in the matter of helping themselves to whatever crumbs might fall from other literary tables." In 1824, the *Cincinnati Literary Gazette* acknowledged the proliferation of these short-lived *Museums* and *Repositories*, most of which "flourished for only two or three years and then resigned themselves to oblivion":

> *Museums, Mirrors, Monthlys* strike
> Our view in crowds and dozens:
> And so much do they look alike
> We see they all are cousins.
> Their phizzes seem so thin and wan,
> So hopeless their conditions
> They all must go to shades below
> In spite of their physicians.[4]

Presented as failed and unhealthy "crowds" rather than robust and productive individuals, miscellaneous magazines were neither encyclopedic nor permanent (as Peale hoped his museum would be) but pastiche-like and ephemeral. They sketched transient scenery, gathering the world in the form of fading souvenirs and fugitive fragments that parodied rather than imitated the endless effort of trying to reproduce it whole.

The longest running and most successful of these miscellanies was the *Port Folio* (fig. 8). Printed in Philadelphia from 1801 to 1824, under a string of editors and publishers, the *Port Folio* was initially edited by a Harvard-educated New Englander named Joseph Dennie, during the two terms of Jefferson's presidency.[5] A belated Connecticut wit writing in the satiric and didactic Anglo-American literary tradition of John Trumbull, Timothy Dwight, David Humphreys, and Royall Tyler, Dennie moved to

THE PORT FOLIO.

BY OLIVER OLDSCHOOL, ESQ.

".................................." VARIOUS, THAT THE MIND
OF DESULTORY MAN, STUDIOUS OF CHANGE,
AND PLEAS'D WITH NOVELTY, MAY BE INDULGED."
COWPER.

VOL. I.]   [No. 26.

PHILADELPHIA, SATURDAY, JUNE 27th, 1801.

TRAVELS.

FOR THE PORT FOLIO.

JOURNAL OF A TOUR THROUGH SILESIA.

LETTER XXVI.

Breslau, 2d September, 1800.

The church and other buildings, belonging to the college of jesuits, are among the most remarkable objects of curiosity at Breslau. The university was founded in the year 1702, by the emperor Leopold, and the buildings were begun upon so large and expensive a plan, that they were not completed in 1740, at the period of the Prussian conquest; and as a great part of the funds, appropriated to the works then ceased, they have remained unfinished. One of their houses, the government took away from them, and at the time when the order of jesuits was abolished, in the year 1774, the university here was continued under the title of a royal school institution. The principal apartments are two churches, one large, and magnificently decorated; the other a small one, where, occasionally, sermons are preached to the students in Latin—the Leopoldine hall, where all the public disputations are held, and an astronomical observatory at the top of the building, which has been erected within these few years. The philosophical and astronomical apparatus is small. The only instruments we saw, were Newtonian telescopes, caustic mirrors, a micrometer for measuring the distance of the stars, a quadrant with a meridian line, an air pump, and a couple of electrical machines. From the observatory, there is a very fine view of the vast plain, in which Breslau is situated, and of the distant mountains by which it is bounded, all which we saw with double advantage through their excellent perspective glasses. The number of students at this college are about six hundred. That of the professors is seventeen. Their course of studies, comprehends a period of eleven years, five of which are devoted to the ancient languages, three to philosophy, and three to theology; but under the term philosophy, they embrace almost every object of human science. The professors are all paid from the appropriated funds, and the instruction is given free from all expence.

There are public schools, likewise, connected with the churches of St. Elizabeth and Mary Magdalen, the first of which has about twenty professors, and teachers, and three hundred students. The instruction here is only preparatory to that of an university.

About an English mile out of the town, are the country-seat and gardens of prince Hohenlohe, the governor of Breslau. The place is called Scheidnich. The gardens are spacious and agreeable, and always open to the public. They contain various small monuments erected by the prince, in honour of Frederic the second,

the late and present kings. Last week he gave the king and queen, upon their visit here, a splendid entertainment, at which the gardens were finely illuminated.

Breslau is a place of considerable trade, and has much more an appearance of business and activity, than Berlin. The most essential articles of its exportation, are broad-cloths and linen; the latter of which, however, the merchants here all draw from the mountain-towns. Nor do they manufacture, themselves, a quarter part of the broad-cloths which they send abroad. Their situation, watered by the river Oder, which gives them an immediate communication with Hamburg and Stettin, naturally makes them the centre of the commerce of the province. They have likewise some trade over land, with the east, which is carried on by Russian caravans; from the description that has been made to us of which, we regret not staying here long enough to see one of them.

There are no manufactures of importance in the town. The sugar-refinery is indeed very large; and having to supply the greatest part of the province, refines sugar to the amount of several millions annually. Like that of Hirschberg, it belongs to a company; the property being divided into shares, originally of seven hundred dollars, but which are now worth more than three thousand.

We have visited two other manufactures, which had been mentioned to us. One, of what they call Turkish yarn, because it was formerly made only in Turkey; and the other, of sewing needles. The yarn is spun from cotton, imported by the Russian caravans from the east, and dyed red. The difficulty consists in the dying, an operation, of which cotton requires much preparation, to be made susceptible, not having, like wool, a natural oil, which imbibes the colouring particles, and facilitates the work. This yarn, when dyed, is used to weave in a mixture with linen. I mentioned having seen one such a manufacture at Schwiedeberg.

The needle manufactory is principally remarkable, as it is one of those in which the division of labour is carried to the greatest extent. Every needle must pass through seventy-seven hands before it is fit for use. But the needles made here, are much inferior to those of the low countries; of Munster and Aix-la-Chapelle, and bear no comparison with the English.

The most common ornaments of the rooms and chambers, in this country, are busts, portraits and imitations of antique basso-relievos, in stucco, or plaister of Paris. We have scarcely entered a house in Silesia, without meeting more or less of these, and we have here been to the work-shop of a man who makes them. He takes good likenesses, and the work is very cheap.

There is cannon foundery here; but the works are all for the account of the king; and for the

last two years they have had nothing to do. It resembles, in every respect, that which you saw at the Hague.

I have dined once in a society founded upon the same principles with the Casino, at Berlin. Here it goes by the name of the *Resource*, and consists of more than two hundred members. The company at dinner was mixed, as is usual at such places, chiefly officers of the army. I was seated next to a general Lentken, who told me he had been forty-eight years in the service, and in the seven years war, had received a wound for each year. The scars upon his face and hands testified to the truth of what he said. You will readily conceive that when you have once entered upon the topic of the seven year's war, and Frederic the second, with a Prussian general, you are in no danger of lacking materials for conversation. I found that of the general, of course, very amusing, though his circle of ideas, and of information, appeared to have been extremely cautious of spreading beyond the line of his business;

" And little of this great world could he speak,
" More than pertains to feats of broil and battle."

Yours affectionately.

MISCELLANY.

FOR THE PORT FOLIO.

LETTERS FROM AN AMERICAN, RESIDENT ABROAD, ON VARIOUS TOPICS OF FOREIGN LITERATURE.

No. IV.

DEAR SIR,

You will remember, that in the year 1793, while the government of the French republic was in the hands of Robespierre, a collection of papers, found among those of Louis the sixteenth, was published, under the title of *Politics of all the Cabinets of Europe*. The most important of these papers, and that from which the title was given to the whole collection, was a work, written by Mr. Favier, a person employed in Louis the fifteenth's secret ministry for foreign affairs; and the great object of this work was to prove, from a consideration of the political situation and views of all the European powers, that a great, an essential, a total change in the military, the federal, and the fiscal system of France, was indispensably necessary to restore her preponderance in the scale of nations. It was written in the year 1773, and had been presented to Louis fifteen, a short time before his death; but the editor of the collection justly observes, in the preface to it, that, in these conjectures of Favier, is to be found the germ of every thing that had since happened in France, without excepting the revolution.

In the course of the last autumn, was published, at Paris, a volume, *upon the state of France at the close of the eighth republical year*; written

Philadelphia in 1799 and soon after founded the *Port Folio*. His miscellany was immediately caught up in the partisan political struggles of the late 1790s that pitted the Federalist party of Adams and Hamilton against the Republican supporters of Jefferson. Between 1801 and 1807, Dennie's *Port Folio* articulated a distinctly anti-Jeffersonian, Anglophilic, and even at times counterfederal view of the "New Roof" of a republican Union, which had, in Dennie's view, clearly "fallen" with the election of Jefferson in 1801.

Because Dennie's *Port Folio* debuted as a "politico-literary miscellany," it is remembered today, and not without reason, primarily as an organ of Federalist attacks on Jeffersonian-Republican political culture. Speaking for and to a readership of gentlemen, Dennie's miscellany was distinguished by overt and explicit elitism and an air of restricted access. Whereas Peale's Jeffersonian museum extended and diffused the collector's gaze to anyone with twenty-five cents, the *Port Folio* appealed frankly to "Men of Affluence, Men of Liberality, and Men of Letters" and did so with immediate success.[6] By the end of 1801 it would achieve a circulation of two thousand subscribers, at a subscription rate of five dollars a year—a price that put it out of the reach of most mechanics and laborers.[7] Dennie's "Prospectus of 1801" addressed its appeals for subscribers primarily to clergymen and gentlemen of the bar and secondarily to merchants, manufacturers, and country gentlemen, who were directed to the "essays on commerce, and the useful arts which would interest them."[8] It spoke not at all, by contrast, to the artisan, unskilled laborer, farmer, or nameless "country man."[9]

In its address to an elite readership Dennie's *Port Folio* was not only aggressively anti-Jeffersonian in ideological content but ostentatiously counterproductive and anti-labor in the politics of its format. As Lewis Simpson observes, its editors, reviewers, and anthologists made a conscious effort to promote an aura of aristocratic dissipation, attempting to make themselves legendary for laziness rather than hard work; praising literary conversation, companionship, and good food; and preferring "partridge over politics."[10] The miscellany's fragmentary motto, furthermore, stressed neither useful knowledge nor civic virtue, but proclaimed the *Port Folio* "various" and "indulgent":

> . . . . "various that the mind
> Of desultory man, studious of change,
> And pleas'd with novelty, may be indulged."

In the pursuit of "novelty," then, the *Port Folio* was a digressive pastiche of almost anything short, moral, or entertaining. Advertised as a "portable repository" of fugitive papers that "retired leisure may read on Sunday,"[11] it printed weekly a random assemblage of fragmentary literary specimens excerpted largely from the works of eighteenth-century British authors. Dennie's *Port Folio* opposed both length and effort in reading and writing; "belles lettres" was its specialty and brevity its lodestar. The editor warned his contributors against "the dangers of "*prolixity*" as "a *deadly* sin" and, in keeping with Federalist-party hostility to the trades, condemned lengthy literary works as mechanical—or "wire drawn": "It is for the *interest* of all, who wish to contribute . . . to be as *succinct* and *brief*, as possible. Authors of fugitive papers may be assured . . . that the public eye always surveys, with the coldest indifference, those tedious, and wire-drawn essays, so aptly and classically characterized by the beautiful American word—*lengthy!*"[12] The *Port Folio*'s "Prospectus of 1801" called for contributions in over sixty genres and subgenres, requesting writing that was brief and witty rather than extended or sublime: the sketch over the wide historical canvas, the lyric over the epic, and protean change over the "constancy" of daily work.[13] Printed in large typeface, on a single folio page, and in no special order, Dennie's list of divided and subdivided genres seems randomly and almost infinitely divisible:

> . . . Sketches of tours and journies, either through our own or foreign territories.
> Journals of voyages.
> Articles of American biography or memoir writing.
> Moral Allegories, Tales, and Romances.
> Original Poetry.
> Scenes of original plays . . .
> Original letters
> Faithful translations from valuable French, Spanish, or German books, pamphlets or papers.
> Humourous and satiric ballads, in the style of John Gilpin.
> Essays on rural economy.
> Parodies of poets, particularly of Shakespeare.
> Ship news extraordinary.
> Scientific papers . . .
> Mock odes, imitations in the manner of *The Rolliad*.
> Hudibrastic poetry.
> Detections of Jacobinical forgery, falsehood, and misrepresentations.
> Dramatic Sketches of Characters.
> Descriptions of the fashionable dresses of the season . . .
> Articles for an obituary of remarkable, or distinguished persons, accompanied by anecdotes, after the model in "*The Gentleman's Magazine*."
> Meteorological diaries.
> Epigrams . . .
> and The various tribes of gay and useful miscellany; and in this pleasant and

flowery walk, the Editor will assume the freedom to particularize the objects, he wishes should be attended to.[14]

In its fragmented, openly elitist format, then, Dennie's *Port Folio* articulated an explicit alternative to the "mammoth state" imagined by Jeffersonian-Republicans. Aiming to take the mechanics, so to speak, out of "federal mechanics," his miscellany was faux-aristocratic and bric-à-brac— a cabinet of curiosities rather than a Linnaean museum.

In fact, the *Port Folio*'s Federalist-party pose was only one of its protean faces; to argue that the *Port Folio* represents Federalist opposition to Jeffersonian-Republican political economy is, in fact, to say nothing new. Unlike the Grand Federal Procession, Fitch's "Life," or Peale's mammoth, the *Port Folio* has a fairly extensive history of critical commentary. The dominant tendency of this commentary has been to read the *Port Folio* accurately but narrowly as a mouthpiece for the anti-Jacobin economic, foreign, and cultural policies of the Federalist party of Adams and Hamilton.[15] Such a reading finds support not only in the aristocratic pose of the *Port Folio* but in the moral and didactic aspects of its periodical essays (which ally Dennie rather distantly with the tradition of New England literary republicanism represented by Trumbull and Humphreys and the more Calvinist federalism of Jedediah Morse and Timothy Dwight). But, while its party fervor is demonstrable, the *Port Folio* was also outrageously "sprightly, various and vivacious" in ways that made it more than an organ of Federalist literary and political opinion. Literary criticism too, however, has been reductive in its reading of the *Port Folio*, arguing that, as an imitative compilation, its Anglophilic potpourri of excerpted poetry and prose represents an essentially unincorporable negative space in early national literary history, against which a more identifiably American national literature would define itself by the mid-nineteenth century.[16] Taken together these readings collapse the specificity of the *Port Folio* by assimilating it to the emergence of a two-party system and by representing it as an essentially irrelevant, even plagiaristic, moment of proto-national literary prehistory.

In fact, the significance and historical specificity of Dennie's *Port Folio* lies neither in its explicitly anti-Jacobin politics and patent Federalist-party federalism nor in its negative relation to a later, supposedly more original American national literary tradition. Rather, when the *Port Folio* is read alongside the exhibitionary performances, collections, and texts of early industrial Philadelphia, its reading and writing subject presents a flickering and temporary but unmistakable alternative to both Jeffersonian political economy and to the larger framework of federalism itself (its Union of persons with objects, words with things), which the Jeffersonian Revolution of 1801 had, by its own account, simply reconstituted and reproduced.

Partisan rhetoric aside, the "New Roof" of 1788 had not, in fact, fallen with the partisan conflict of the 1790s, because the new republic was not located in the consensus of a ruling elite (which could be and was rup-tured by party division). The federal state was located, instead, in the mul-tiple media, arts, professions, and occupations that raised themselves into view by constituting and dividing themselves as the artifacts of representa-tive self-production. The federal house divided by party conflict was, in other words, always already a museum, a mammoth framework, an assem-blage of representational practices grounded upon (representations of) productive labor as the unifying focus of their collective legitimacy.

As a locus of resistance to federalism in the mammoth form of the Jeffer-sonian state, the *Port Folio* became a place where, in effect, the fatigue and irritation of the "countryman" who objected to "the heap" of things in the Peale Museum found a persona, a politics, and a name. This politics was more than merely partisan, however, and its persona never achieved even the specificity of Peale's backcountry visitor. Criticizing the mammoth state from the point of view of neither the mechanical artist nor the ag-ricultural producer, the *Port Folio* projected, instead, a discontinuous and scattered, altogether fatigued and overwhelmed, reading and writing sub-ject: the dilatory consumer and "looker-on," known to "a select few" as "the lounger." This lounger was a randomly learned idler, rambler, and spectatorial shambler, whose reading, writing, and viewing activities consti-tuted a "various and desultory" form of diversion rather than productive enterprise, of voyeuristic viewing rather than creative composition. Some-times ridiculous and sometimes hateful in his affected air of elevation, the lounger nevertheless challenged the federalist and republican—and the Federalist and Republican—projects of collective self-making.

Elitist and Anglophilic, the *Port Folio* lounger never criticized class divi-sion or the cultural mechanics of industrialization from the point of view of production. Nevertheless, wherever he recorded his own, counterpro-ductive experiences of fatigue and failure, the lounging subject of the *Port Folio* stood, in his disintegrated way, for the inherent brokenness of—the need to take "a break" from—the continual making of meaning, the end-less performance of production in a universe of things. In his sporadic and inconsistent self-positionings, the lounger figured, in ways not unlike John Fitch's life-in-letters, a revelatory failure to accomplish the Union of the particular with the general view, or words with things, persons with (their) objects, federal mechanics with republican architecture. Neither maker nor made, neither mechanic nor republican architect, he lounges somewhere outside the federal loop, among other unmechanical people without "character": unskilled or immigrant laborers, enslaved laborers, women, children, or anyone else outside the Grand Federal Edifice or republican museum. This is not to say that the *Port Folio* lounger ever spoke explicitly for such groups. Reveling in imitation and parody, and failing at most forms of productive self-representation, the lounger would almost certainly have rejected (often in racist and misogynist terms) any attempt to identify him with degraded, excluded groups. But in his refusal to be identified with any collectivity and in his antimechanical rejection of self-making, the subject of the *Port Folio* gestures toward another illumination, casting a flickering light upon an unrepresentable crowd of spectators, consumers, and aspiring producers surrounding the pyramid of extended republicanism.

Although he failed as a producer, the lounger was, however, a virtuoso consumer, who mirrored the rage to "be made" as a phenomenon of fashion. In its "Lesson for Loungers," for example, the *Port Folio* advises, "Whenever you call a hackney-coach, order the driver to stop his horses, as nearly as possible to the foot-way. This will naturally occasion a number of people to stop, and give you an opportunity, of shewing your person, or a new coat, made by Watson."[17] Here, the lounger, like a kind of "fashion museum," displays production and personhood in the form of a brand name. In the process, though, he marks a connection denied by Peale, between the spectator and the consumer, between the mammoth framework of the natural history museum and the market stalls in the streets of Philadelphia.[18] As a consumer, the lounger's chameleon-like and meandering movements follow precisely the path spurned by Peale and Jefferson, tracing the connection between the market or shop, the Linnaean museum, and the representational practices of the corporate state itself, whose productive powers exist only within the context of global commerce, of an internationalizing network of customers and commodities.

The following pages offer a tour of some of the particular loungers who can be distinguished within (without adding up to) the lounging subject of the *Port Folio*. Well-dressed pedants, unhappy students, aimless former Whigs, failed professionals, and eccentric autodidacts, these American loungers recall and call into question not only the principle of *E pluribus unum* but the idealized republican architect of the federal state. In their faux aristocratic detachment and air of distinction, the *Port Folio* lounger mirrors something that none of the historians of American federalism have fully acknowledged, namely, that the republican worthies of the founding period (Washington, Franklin, Rittenhouse, Wilson, Peale, Adams) were themselves curious characters tossed up by an international trade in human products, that they walked and talked upon the extended stage of a global industrial market, in the light of multiform complexes of representative self-display. In the borrowed light of lounging, the federalist scene of representative self-production disintegrates, together with the fantasy of republican worth.

Ultimately the lounging subject of the *Port Folio* articulates a direct, though dilatory, challenge to the virtuous public man of the Pocockian republican tradition in American historiography, wherever that tradition has been used to explain the American Revolution, the writing of the Constitution, or national consolidation in the early national period.[19] Contrary to the histories of Bernard Bailyn and Gordon Wood, for example, the American lounger suggests that, in the the United States in the first decade of the nineteenth century, republican disinterest and detachment cannot be understood apart from the expansion and proliferation of an early-industrial commodity market that produced, individuated, organized, and classified persons as things. It is this market—international, incomprehensible, imperial, disintegrating, disorganizing—that is brought flickeringly into view by the meandering man of the early-industrial crowd: the lounger.

FROM THE TOP OF VAST STORES

Technically speaking, "The American Lounger" was a periodical essay series published irregularly in 103 numbers of the *Port Folio* between 1802 and 1804.[20] Edited by a pseudonymous lounger named "Samuel Saunter," this series consisted of fictional letters critical of contemporary morals and manners—while the letter writers themselves came in for moralizing commentary by "Mr. Saunter." But it is not this "American Lounger," the essay series, that epitomizes the lounging subject of the *Port Folio*. Discontinuous and protean to the point of formlessness, this other (larger) lounger was projected by the overall format of the miscellany and its praise of the desultory, the various and broken, the fragmentary and failed. Particularized by the *Port Folio* under a variety of names and descriptors, this lounger includes not only Samuel Saunter but "The Lay Preacher," "Meander," "Papyrius Cursor," and "Charles Chameleon" among its countless "literary virtuoso[s] and laborious annalist[s]."[21]

Timothy Dwight once referred to Joseph Dennie as the "American Addison" and the comparison has stuck, in part because of Dennie's own description of the *Port Folio* as a miscellany that "combin[es], in the manner of the *Tatler*, Politics with Essays and disquisitions on topics scientific, moral, humourous and literary."[22] Nevertheless, although the *Port Folio* was edited and published within the tradition of eighteenth-century British periodical literature, it is inaccurate to identify it with the *Tatler* (1709–11) or the *Spectator* (1711–15). For one thing, the genre of the periodical essay was at least a century old when Dennie began the *Port Folio*; by 1801, more than 214 essay periodicals had been published on the pattern of the *Tatler* or the *Spectator*, including Samuel Johnson's *Rambler*

(10 March 1750–14 March 1752) and *Idler* (15 April 1758–5 April 1760) as well as Henry Mackenzie's *The Lounger* (5 February 1785–6 January 1787).[23] Certainly, many issues of the *Port Folio* opened with a pseudonymous essay in the style of the British periodical essay: Steele's *Tatler* had been authored by "Isaac Bickerstaff," the humorous bachelor and wry observer of "manners" who would spawn hundreds of descendants in North America, from Benjamin Franklin's "Silence Dogood" to Francis Hopkinson's "Old Bachelor" to Washington Irving's "Launcelot Langstaff." But, despite Dennie's own comparisons of the *Port Folio* to the *Tatler* or the *Spectator*, the crucial difference between the *Port Folio* lounger and Addison's spectatorial subject is this: the miscellaneous, lounging subject of the *Port Folio* as a whole cannot control or bring within the scope of a single focus the multiplicity that the (more or less happily bourgeois) literary persona of the centered but rambling *Spectator* was, initially, invoked to control.[24] This failure to organize is where lounging begins. Lounging marks, in fact, the disintegration of the comparatively unified editorial personae of the British essay tradition and its replacement by the more diffuse reading, viewing, and consuming subject of the miscellaneous "gentleman's" magazine.

In fact, as a "repository," the *Port Folio*'s primary problem was the expanding world of literary artifacts. It sat on the top of a centuries-long outpouring of English literature, to which it referred loosely as "the store" or "the storehouse," as in the following description of Sterne: "The romances of RABELAIS and the Anatomy of Melancholy, by BURTON, appear to be the literary store-house, which he [Sterne] has broken open. . . .If a virtuoso had leisure or phlegm enough to ransack the volumes produced in the reigns of Elizabeth, and the first James, he would find a clue to many of Sterne's labyrinths."[25] Of the "volumes produced in the reigns of Elizabeth and . . . James," the works of Shakespeare alone represent a huge floating "storehouse," awaiting literary robberies by plagiaristic geniuses such as Sterne:

> Like the ark too, [Shakespeare] carries within him all the rich and various stores of nature, and from him the world of genius has been peopled. It would be an amazing task to examine the productions of wit since the publication of the works of Shakspeare [sic], and observe how many pretty poems and plays have been garnished with scraps from this great original; how many little hillocks of fame have been raised, on robberies from this immense mass."[26]

Peale had likewise referred to the vast "stores" of nature represented by his museum, describing it as a Noah's Ark, a place of preservation and unity, riding high above (and upon) the waves of revolution and counterrevolution. But the stores of literature surveyed by the *Port Folio* were contained by no organizational ark; the lounger found himself at the top of a vast literary heap, where, like Peale's country man, he could "see nothing satisfactory." The lounging subject of the *Port Folio* faced an enormous crowd of commodified objects—books, words, authors, producers, workers—that had been produced, advertised, celebrated, displayed, and cast up as detritus by American commercial expansion, as well as by the long history of British and European imperialism generally. His tone, therefore, is one of complaint in the face of surplus. For the lounger, such surplus was not stimulating but overwhelming: "The public repositories, the shop of the bookseller, and the ready loan of obliging friends, supply such varieties of literature, that plodding labour might tire to review, and the keenest glances be insufficient to comprehend."[27] In fact, fatigue was so central to the character of lounging that, in 1809, when Dennie had become ill and decided to retire as the editor of the *Port Folio*, a new prospectus was printed that explained his illness as exhaustion. "Variety," it seems, had finally overwhelmed him: "no individual," the anonymous editor writes, "might presumptuously hope to conduct, without assistance, a work whose essence consists in endless variety. . . . If Edward CAVE [editor of the London *Gentleman's Magazine*], had been the lone Editor of this Magazine, it never would have reached its twelfth number."[28]

Like late-eighteenth-century miscellanies such as the *Gentleman's Magazine* (edited by Cave from 1731 to 1754 and by David Henry and Richard Cave from 1754 to 1766), the *Port Folio* relied heavily upon the serialized periodical essay. But, unlike the *Tatler* or *Spectator*, none of the *Port Folio*'s pseudonymous authors gave his name to the magazine as a whole. Instead the principle of "Variety" itself was substituted for the comparatively self-identical "Spectator" or "Bickerstaff." In this sense, then, the *Port Folio* did resemble Cave's *Gentleman's Magazine*—the motto of which was (rather ironically, considering its adoption by the United States) *E pluribus unum*. At the same time, however, the title page of the *Port Folio* displayed the following attribution: "BY OLIVER OLDSCHOOL, ESQ." But the word "by" in this attribution was unstable, indicating both "authored" and "edited/assembled." And "Oliver Oldschool" made no consistent appearance in the *Port Folio*, nor did he author any single, discrete essay series. Although letters and complaints to the *Port Folio* were generally addressed to "Mr. Oldschool," the miscellaneous subject of the magazine was clearly not Oliver Oldschool but the ethos of miscellaneousness that shaped its lounging subject. Sometimes parodied, sometimes celebrated, the lounger does periodically try to present himself as a center of political efficacy and integrative insight, in the British Whig tradition of the *Spectator* of 1712. But no matter how didactic or moral any particular lounger pretends to be, the reading and writing subject of the *Port Folio* never equals the sum of its lounging parts. From Oliver Oldschool to "The Lay Preacher," no single lounger ever manages to figure the Author or Maker of all representations—or that Lounger in the sky who can contain and read all the books of the world.

In the case of "The Lay Preacher: Short Sermons for Idle Readers," the lounger dispenses Whig-like didactic advice, admonishing women on proper dress and men on the niceties of polite and polished behavior. Originally written by Dennie in New Hampshire and then reprinted in the *Port Folio*, "The Lay Preacher" articulates a comparatively Whiggish and leisured form of lounging. But, in the end, even this "Preacher" represents only an early-industrial kind of "fashion police," weighing in heavily on behalf of polished manners and agreeable behavior rather than a puritanical rigidity in moral questions. While each number of "The Lay Preacher" opens with a biblical verse, these treat the prophets of the Old Testament and the apostles of the New as models of courtier-like breeding: Moses is celebrated, rather weirdly, only for his well-bred courtesy toward women gathered at a crowded well, while the apostle Paul is praised for spreading Christianity by dint of his courtly politeness and his "pleasing" ability to be all things to all people.[29] On one hand, the Lay Preacher tries to represent himself as a center of political efficacy and moral insight (at least on questions of manners) by becoming a "watchman" of the streets, as well a lounger. But, while he may aim for a pyramidal, Whig-like equilibrium, his self-divided balance collapses into a chaos of diversion. The Preacher insists, for example, that when "I traverse [the city's] *streets*, or its *broad ways*, the utility of such a ramble, need not long be doubted. It will enable me, to variegate my speculations, to discern all the hues of 'many colour'd life,' to turn gay subjects to moral purposes, and furnish copious materials for rebuke."[30] On the other hand, the moral profit of his sermons evaporates into entertaining pleasure (and their elevated point of view disperses itself in distraction) in homilies that declare that "pleasure and piety, like the Hermia and Helena of the poet, may be harmonized." The Lay Preacher even declares that visits to "fane and chapel" may be replaced by the works of Laurence Sterne or "a retired walk" through sublime and beautiful scenery.[31]

If, within the lounging spectrum of the *Port Folio*, the comparatively bourgeois Lay Preacher marks one extreme, then the explicitly decadent, purely entertaining, and "giddy" lounger stands at the other extreme. This lounger never sermonizes, cannot or will not work, read, or write systematically, and avoids all forms of "church"—including even such mildly improving literature as "The Lay Preacher." Entirely overwhelmed, the lounger sketched by "The Lounger's Diary" does nothing but sleep, dream, smoke, read magazines, observe the world of fashion, look from windows, and peruse belles lettres at random:

> *Sunday morning, half past nine.* Yawned;—execrably sleepy.
>
> *Ten.* Read half your bill.—Head-ach[e].
>
> *Half past ten.* Too cold for church.—Head-ach[e] increased by bell.—N.B. To change my apartment, that I may avoid that noise.
>
> *Eleven to Twelve.* Took my chocolate.—Read half a page of Henrietta Harville [a sentimental novel] . . .
>
> *Twelve.* Terrace—not a soul.—On my return saw a cocked hat with man under it.
>
> *Half past one.* Dinner.—No appetite . . .
>
> *Half past five.* Sipped my tea with Feather.—N.B. His silk stockings.—N.B. The pattern seen last winter in town.—N.B. Not to tell him till he has worn them.
>
> *Six to half past.* Yawned and rou'd.
>
> *Half past to seven.* Rou'd and yawned.
>
> *Seven to eight.* Got vapours by looking out Microcosm.
>
> *Eight to Nine.* Wrote my journal.—Buckled my shoe.
>
> *Nine to Ten.* Intolerable vapours.—N.B. vapours greatest bore in universe. . . .
>
> *Ten to half past.* Lounged to Dapper's room.—Caught him reading Latin. . . . —*O imitatores, ser, ser, ser,* Lud, my memory! Do you remember the line in Virgil, Greg?[32]

The characterless character of this lounger is formed through his relationship to food, fatigue, and forgetfulness. In place of productive "professional" labor, he substitutes dilatory reading; he knows Latin, but can't remember the books he's read. Here, the neoclassical value of imitation ("*O imitatores. . .*") has won out entirely over originality or the capacity of genius ("the line in Virgil") to stimulate reproductive effort. The obliteration of originality has, in turn, ruined memory, and the lounger oscillates haplessly between stimulants and depressants, coffee (or chocolate) and ennui, with no middle-ground appetite for meat. In contrast to the Lay Preacher, he is taken over by fatigue, or "vapours." He longs for sprightly, gay entertainment (such as that offered, in principle, by the *Port Folio*) but, in the end, only reproduces the lengthy and tedious forms he despises. Ennui is increased by "looking out [the] Microcosm"—in this case a toy, probably a kaleidoscope, for reproducing the world in jewellike fragments. Throughout the eighteenth century the word "microcosm" referred to one of any number of mechanical curiosities—sometimes actual models of the universe and sometimes automated figures representing the world in its "parts," where "parts" meant human activities or occupations.[33] By the first decade of the nineteenth century, the word "microcosm" had accrued multiple meanings and was used as the title of encyclopedic reference works and of magazines and miscellanies (such as Ackerman's *A Microcosm of London; or, London in Miniature* [1808]). For Peale, of course, his museum was a "microcosm," a wondrous work of creation that generated an endless desire to see more. For the lounger, by contrast, any panoramic or microcosmic display, however toylike, produced "vapours": overstimulation and fatigue without intervening excitement. And, foregrounding the fact that he cannot enjoy or remember what he has read and cannot make himself do his prescribed professional duty, the lounger is compulsively addicted to the memorandum format.[34] In the case of Meander, however, the memorandum is only a record of the constant making and breaking of resolutions to use time more productively.

Meander is a law student, one of the many early American men of letters for whom, as Robert Ferguson recounts, the ideal of the liberally learned lawyer/statesman was a continual torment.[35] In his "Journal," Meander resolves to rise at dawn, "to study law with plodding diligence," and "to make my profession, and a course of history, my capital objects." In contrast to the utterly dilatory lounger of "The Lounger's Diary," Meander declares that "belles lettres" must be considered "a subaltern pursuit." But it is by "belles lettres," nevertheless, that he is continually diverted:

> Overslept myself, did not rise till nine. Dressed, and went out, intending to go to the office; but, as the morning was uncommonly beautiful, I recollected an aphorism of Dr. Cheyne's, that exercise should form part of a student's religion. Accordingly, I rambled through the woods for two hours . . . Did *nothing* very busily till four. Seized with a lethargic yawn, which lasted till seven, when a dish of coffee restored animation. . . . Slept but little, last night. . . . Dreamed that lord Coke threw his "Institute" [of Law] at me. Rose at nine, looked abroad; and the atmosphere being dusky . . . felt unqualified for reading. For several days there has been a succession of gloomy skies. The best writers affirm such weather is unfriendly to mental labour. The poet says:
>
> > "While these dull fogs invade the head,
> > Memory minds not what is read."
>
> Took up a magazine, which I carefully skimmed, but obtained no cream.[36]

Notably, Meander's world and its random decisions are "by the book." They are not determined, in other words, by productive labor but by quotations, allusions, and learned references assembled and deployed without productive result—as in Meander's evocation of "Dr. Cheyne," who advises literary-medical self-manipulation for a physiological subject whose desires can be briefly stimulated only by coffee or printed reminders to exercise.

In the end Meander fails, of course, to "effect an entire revolution in [his] conduct, to form a new plan of study," and his solution is to become, *Port Folio*–style, a traveler. Leaving home on horseback, with a company of "jocund travellers," he is heard to shout in farewell the following "well known anacreontic": "*Dull thinking will make a man crazy.*"[37] According to the *Port Folio*, the moral of this story is "in the name of prudence, [to] avoid eccentricity; expand not your *fluttering* pinions; trudge the foot-way path of life; dethrone Fancy, and crown Common Sense. Let each one, seek and fulfill his daily task; 'one to his farm and another to his merchandize.' "[38] But this bourgeois moral is utterly ironic, since it is the productivist or mechanic commitment to "farm and merchandize" that the lounging subject of the *Port Folio* repeatedly rejects. In the lounging state, in other words, it is precisely the middle-ground, Whiggish ideal of a productive equilibrium—a tidy balance of work and leisure, farming, selling, reading, and travel—that cannot and does not hold, despite constant reminders that it must.

In one of the best brief discussions of the *Port Folio*, William Gilmore calls its editor Joseph Dennie a "fop," a "founder of the genteel tradition of American literature," and "a precious version of the Romantic flaneur . . . like a forerunner of Edgar Allan Poe or Charles Baudelaire."[39] Dennie has been viewed variously, by Gilmore and others, as degenerate, derivative, transitional, Romantic, gentlemanly, genteel, an ideologue, a flaneur, and a fop—as well as simply a poorly disguised extension of New England Federalism or, as previously discussed, an imitation of the British periodical subject. Certainly, the long-standing difficulty of classifying Dennie indicates a need to attend more carefully to the specificity of the *Port Folio* and its subject. It is only by assuming that the lounger of the *Port Folio* is a specific social subject—rather than a foppish Addison, a Connecticut Federalist, or a forerunner of the flaneur—that his in-between or manufactory-era status illuminates the constitution of labor in early industrial Philadelphia and the relationship of literary work to the transformation of the mechanical arts.

To respond to Gilmore first, the early American lounger projected by the *Port Folio* under Dennie was not a flaneur like Baudelaire (as described by Walter Benjamin), although he bears some relation to the desultory crowd of later European dandies, flaneurs, aesthetes, and decadents.[40] The crucial distinction between the European flaneur and the American lounger lies in this: the lounging subject of the *Port Folio* engages the extended representational field of the American republic rather than the urban political and social sites of, say, London or Paris. It is at the edge of the federal stage (or outside the Grand Federal Edifice) that the lounger—neither Philadelphian nor citizen of the world—attempts haplessly, fitfully, parodically, and plagiaristically to act as a representatively national character. Because he is a creature of early industrial capitalism, furthermore, the *Port Folio* lounger does not recognize the word "class." As opposed to "rank," class identities are not visible to him, as they would be, implicitly or explicitly, to the 1840s flaneur. Although he spends much of his time in the city streets, the lounger scans a crowd that does not include "the eyes of the poor" (as they emerge in the poem of that title by Baudelaire).[41]

The question of the lounger's relationship to both an earlier British periodical tradition and the later phenomenon of *flânerie* raises the question of the *Port Folio*'s relationship to the literary-political tradition of New England. Where does Dennie's lounger fit in the spectrum of the New England literary federalism represented by comic satirists and would-be epic poets from Trumbull to Barlow? Certainly, even in his more moral and admonishing moments, the lounger could never serve as a grand federal republican—a George Washington, a Ciceronian orator, an Edmund Burke. But his characterless character does retain a confused trace of the republican ideals of civic virtue and the public good. The lounger could be described, then—although only in a very limited sense—as another American heir of the British republican or "Countrymen" tradition of Bolingbroke and Burgh, Trenchard and Gordon,[42] as that tradition has been traced by, among others J.G.A. Pocock, Isaac Kramnick, Bernard Bailyn, and (for New England poetry), William C. Dowling.[43] In his recovery of a Connecticut tradition of literary republicanism extending from John Trumbull, David Humphreys, and Timothy Dwight to Joel Barlow, Dowling redefines the neoclassical—often antimodern, antimarket, and intensely nostalgic—ideology of republican virtue as an operation of social critique that repeatedly unmasks ideological positions, including, finally, its own. Dowling argues that, in Barlow's *Columbiad* in particular, this unmasking of unmaskings eventually transcends its own revelatory operation (through a kind of negative dialectics) to articulate a utopian vision, a truly revolutionary historical criticism. While one might be tempted to see in the dilatory movements of lounging a form of progressive unmasking, in fact, in the case of the lounger, the point of view from which economic interest and moral corruption can be repeatedly unmasked is stymied, displayed as static, frozen. The republican tradition articulated by Dennie's *Port Folio* is not the unmasking of ideology but the endlessly reproducible zigzag of a consumer in the crowd. Lounging is not a potentially utopian flânerie that rewrites history; it instead reflects a process of idle viewing, an endless passage between the stimulation and waning of desire for things-as-

persons and for persons-as-things. In Dennie's *Port Folio*, even the lounger's apparent center of resistance—his deeply reactionary, irritable, and
counterproductive political style—remains discontinuous and is never
traceable to any single lounging character. The *Port Folio* is finally undecid-
able on the question of "fashion" versus "substance," in politics as in all
representational forms. But, where the Federalist political partisan is lost
in the lounger, another meaning begins. Like a ghost in the machinery of
self-government, the lounger, hostile to progress and blind to class, con-
founds the divisions of party politics, marking both federalism and republicanism in the United States as class-constituting artifacts of early industrial development.

ALL THE LITTLE WORLD MAKERS: THE REPUBLICAN AS TOURIST

In March of 1801 John Quincy Adams was his father's ambassador to Prussia when he wrote from his post to urge the *Port Folio* to maintain the
kind of Whiggish balance dear to the representational tradition of the
extended republic. Adams was supportive of Dennie, who was loyal in the
struggle to protect President John Adams from the full force of increasingly organized Jeffersonian opposition. Dennie drew, in turn, upon the
prestige and literary contributions of John Quincy Adams, serializing the
younger Adams's "Journal of a Tour Through Silesia" in the first forty-five
issues of the *Port Folio*. But, even while he contributed to the *Port Folio*,
Adams was worried that the miscellany might veer too far from the federal
high ground, and he advised Dennie to pattern himself more carefully
after "his illustrious predecessor Addison," who, in times of political ran-
cor, "tempered his declaration for the whigs [in the] *Spectator* with so
much caution in the conduct of the work, that even the Tories were forced
to read and forgive."[44]

Hard at work negotiating a peace in Europe between Napoleon and the
enemies of France, Adams became concerned when, in the heat of partisan conflict, the *Port Folio* published political essays that openly advocated
an American alliance with Britain—to the point of bemoaning the American Revolution.[45] Urging the magazine "to coolness, nay, I will even say
to moderation upon political topics," Adams aimed to temper Dennie's
Anglophilia. Some may "talk," he writes, "of an offensive and defensive
alliance with Great Britain; but pray has she ever been more generous
than France? About as generous as [a] . . . miser was wont to be."[46] As a
diplomat, John Quincy Adams positioned himself as a kind of American
fulcrum between Britain and France. His commitment to an equilibrium
in Europe reveals his devotion to the federalist principle of a collective
"balance" of powers, a commitment to balance that would mark his performance as a statesman throughout his long career. It is his advocacy of

equilibrium that makes the disequilibriums of his literary work for the *Port Folio* so significant.

Like the meandering of any other lounger, Adams's vacation in Silesia maps the outline of republican, federalist, and Jeffersonian world making. But Adams's travel writing for the *Port Folio* reveals that it is not only the mechanical artist or the American farmer but also the quintessential republican statesman himself who is a product of an international commodity market and its arts of production and of production displayed. Even as a tourist, Adams represents himself in the elevated position of the true republican, gazing down upon an expanding world of things and of world-making persons. But, in the end, despite all his taxonomizing impulses, he too becomes a lounger in his inability to collect, contain, control, or bring into focus everything he surveys—no matter how he tries, or admonishes, or fantasizes in an international context about a new, Napoleonic cum federalist center.

John Quincy Adams on Manufacturing

As the name "Meander" suggests, the lounging subject of the *Port Folio* was a quixotic creature of travel literature, a follower of the literary wanderings and wanderers of the world. Whenever, therefore, an issue of the *Port Folio* did not open with a periodical essay (or a biographical sketch of literary or political genius), it opened with a serialized work of travel literature, such as Adams's "Journal of a Tour Through Silesia." Adams described the meandering, desultory character of his writings for the *Port Folio* as "miscellaneous . . . suitable to the character of the paper itself": "They will be the result of my studies at leisure hours, and as my habits in this particular are changeful and capricious, I must reserve to myself an entire liberty of sending what I please, and in a manner as irregular as I please."[47] In fact, in keeping with the lounging character of the *Port Folio*, Adams's "Tour Through Silesia" is both tedious and difficult to categorize. At least one commentator has described the text as remarkably dull.[48] Rambling, sprawling, all-incorporative, Adams's letters from Silesia display a variety of genres, from amusing anecdotes, short poems of his own composition, useful information, biographies of famous (German) writers and statesmen, natural history, and sketches of curious characters and places. And, in typical *Port Folio* style, each of Adams's travel letters aims to be brief and entertaining (even while they tire the reader with detail).[49]

Adams claimed that the broadcloth (coat material) industry of Silesia justified his tour of Prussia's most valuable province—a manufacturing province, "the only part of the Prussian dominions, the commerce of which is important to the United States, and might furnish us with linens and broadcloths upon more advantageous terms than we receive them from England and Ireland."[50] Adams was particularly interested in the cottage industry of Silesia, a rural manufactory that successfully turned out woven goods via a domestic system of production, in contrast to the more mechanized and rationalized division of labor typical of British textile production. From Grünberg, Adams writes that, while he "cannot dispute the principles of Adam Smith respecting the division of labour," he nevertheless prefers the organization of the rural broadcloth industry of Silesia to the urban factory. In Grünberg, there "is no large capitalist at the head of an extensive manufacture, and employing at wages, which will scarcely keep soul and body together, a large number of workmen." Instead, some seven thousand rural weavers each perform, in their separate households, the whole process of broadcloth production, from shearing to selling: "the spinning, the carding, the dying, the weaving, the drying, the pressing, the napping." Only a few cooperative "fulling-mills" are used in common. Although Adams admits that this relatively undivided organization of labor may produce a slightly lower "quantity of work'd materials," it is preferable to the usual "system of subdividing labour, *ad infinitum*," so that "each individual workman is but an infinitesimal fragment of a vast body." For Adams, as for Jefferson at his most bucolic and egalitarian, a generalized rural "competence" is theoretically preferable to intensified industrial output. "[W]here all the operations for the production of a manufactured work can be performed by one man, or by a small number of men," Adams writes, "each single workman will be of more consequence in himself, more independent of his employer. . . . There will be less accumulation and more circulation of wealth."[51]

Making economic observations such as this, John Quincy Adams sounds more like a Jeffersonian than a Federalist. One might imagine that Adams's interest in a productivist domestic system reflects a distinction internal to the Federalist party, one that distinguished the economic policy of John Adams, say, from that of Alexander Hamilton. In fact, however, it primarily indicates that the two-party distinction between Jeffersonian and Federalist policy was a profoundly blurred, even irrelevant dichotomy within the larger productivist arts and proliferating sciences of federal self-making. Indeed, virtually every partisan spokesman—from John Adams and Alexander Hamilton to Jefferson and Albert Gallatin—supported improved manufactures and international commerce, with local variations on the theme.[52] This is not to say that individual policy debates were insignificant or inconsequential. But party politics and decision making took place within a shared, federalizing structure that constituted Union as the production and display of productive persons—not only on farms and in artisan shops but in all occupational venues.

In this context it will be remembered, furthermore, that with Jefferson's election and the collapse of Adams's presidency, a so-called Virginian dynasty of Republican presidents—Jefferson, Madison, and Monroe—inherited the mantle of federalism. It would not be until John Quincy Adams's election in 1824 that the United States would see another president from New England. And it has often been observed that, despite the Federalist-party roots he inherited from his father, John Quincy Adams rode into office in 1824 as a "National Republican," on the westward-looking, commercially expansionist coattails of Jeffersonian-Republicanism. As the next chapter's discussion of Alexander Wilson's *American Ornithology* will demonstrate, the long Jeffersonian victory implied the continuing domestic and imperial expansion of an already extended federal republic of things.[53]

In one sense, the election of Jefferson over John Adams is surprising: it would seem that as a Deist and Francophile from slaveholding Virginia Jefferson would be unable to represent national unity. But, as commentators from Eric Foner and Joyce Appleby to Alexander Saxton have explained, the Jeffersonians managed to succeed as a national party by bracketing the divisive issue of slavery while elevating the Republican-party, producer ethic of free labor, free trade, and free land.[54] What is less emphasized by historians, but which was, perhaps, more deeply material, were the arts, sciences, and technologies—the proliferating professions—of production that structured Jeffersonian-Republicanism as federalist culture building. When federalism is acknowledged to be, first and foremost, a dense tangle of representational structures, the commercial and technological commitments common to both Federalist and Jeffersonian parties become vividly evident—so much so that, even in conflict, their party positions mirror one another as class-constituting, nation-building displays of American manufacturing.

Adams the Tourist

As one might expect, while he was a tourist in pastoral/industrial Silesia, Adams stood in a relationship of profound ambivalence to the forms of travel writing. As a republican diplomat, he was continually in conflict with belles lettres. Upon commencing his "Tour," he wrote to his brother Thomas: "[I] hope I shall never sacrifice any of my public duties for it."[55] And, in a letter to fellow diplomat William Vans Murray, he justified his trip as a chance to gather useful information: "While my time has been given to sloth and enjoyment, yours has been employed in toil and usefulness. I should take great shame to myself from the comparison, were I not fully conscious that I could not have spent those months in a more beneficial manner."[56] As a republican statesman and his father's ambassador to Prussia, Adams was a young member of an international club of early industrial leaders. But on vacation in Silesia, Adams's stance of republican elevation was somewhat more vulnerable to the commercial and industrial framework that had raised him to his distinguished position. In Silesia, Adams began to see from the grand federal mountaintop that his point of view depended upon an array of representational technologies that were not specific to American federalism at all but made and sold all over the world. In fact, it seemed, anyone on earth could learn to reproduce production and to "raise" himself in the order of things.

For Adams, this slight shaking of his virtue and detachment occurred particularly when he was out viewing famous sights rather than when he was collecting useful information. As a tourist, the American found world-making persons everywhere, producing and displaying themselves like so many new and fashionable specimens. At every Silesian tourist site, for instance, be it mountain, castle, or waterfall, "a book" was kept in which any traveler could enter his name in "the lists of fame." After climbing the mountain "Kynast" to visit a castle, where "the commandant has coffee made . . . to refresh the traveller," Adams inspects the pages of the inevitable "book," in which all "who wish to record their ascension hither, inscribe their names, and those, who feel or think themselves inspired poetically by the keen air of the mountain add lines." In such books, "modest prose-men contented themselves with setting down some moral maxim," while others, the "humblest aspirants to this species of immortality, merely put down their names, which, at least, remain here, when they are forgotten every where else."[57]

Like all tourist writing, Adams's "Journal" is a collection of references to other travelers and their writing: everywhere Adams goes, another traveler and his travel book have preceded him. In the "Giant Mountains" near Schriebershau, Adams describes a traveler named Zollner who had also published an account of a tour through these mountains in 1791. In his book, Zollner had named his tour guide: one "Siegmund Seidler, jun. originally a poor shoe-maker from Schriebershau," who has since become "the most widely celebrated of all the guides upon the Giant Mountains." Because the "indefatigable" Seidler was "brought forward" by Zollner "in the list of fame," he was ever after "celebrated by all the German tourists on this route. . . . so far superior is he deemed to all his brother trudgers." There is "not so much as a foot-path," Adams concludes, "[but] is a kind of profession."[58]

Wherever Adams goes, he notes similar instances of the exhibitionary frameworks he himself deploys. At every tourist sight, he creates and projects the stable representational framework of collection, classification, and display that not only makes every footpath a profession but structures national culture as a museum and manufactory of the world. In the process, however, Adams finds himself in a revealing position: he is forced to recognize that the seemingly exceptional republican virtues of American federalism are, in fact, part of an international machinery of nation building. Even in pastoral Grünberg, the equality of condition generated by a "domestic," rural organization of production belie ongoing mechanization: in Grünberg, Adams visits a manufacturer named Mr. Förster, who "possesses and uses [only] the machines for spinning and carding the wool." Upon going to "see these machines work'd," Adams observed that they resembled those "which are employed in the English manufactures, and are well known in America."[59] Adams's account of Silesian manufacturing suggests that the world of things and of world-making persons is indeed a world and not a unitary invention traceable to New England—or even to Philadelphia. It is at this juncture that Adams (like Peale's "country man") becomes unable to organize the innumerable things of the world multiplying around him. And it is here that he becomes—in spite of his rigidly virtuous, unbendingly stable voice—just another lounging subject of the *Port Folio*. No longer positioned securely at the peak of the republican pyramid, he sits slightly to one side, gazing about distractedly, in the oddly absent position of the lounger. This is not an explicitly unhappy situation: Adams's tourist writings participate in a world-making drive to assimilate and assemble the fugitive fragments of mechanical reproduction in order to display them in the museums (and magazines) of man-making history. But these objects were overwhelming in number. In Bunzlau, for example, even the local pottery yards enter the lists of fame when Adams encounters a mammoth pot, "of prodigious size, made about half a century ago, which contains nearly fifty bushels": "It is about twelve feet high; is hooped like a barrel, which it resembles in form, and is kept in a house built on purpose for it—The Germans appear to have a particular predilection for things of enormous dimensions in their kind; . . . this pot serves as [an] example to shew how much *size* enters into their ideas of the sublime."[60] In this paragraph the single, outrageously gigantic pot stands out for the reader as well, as a parody of the author's practice of metonymy and of the mammoth state he tries to represent. The prodigious pot figures in miniature the even larger (manufactured) things that it contains: from industrializing Prussia, to the entire globe, to the hands of their Maker(s).

In the tradition of the Jeffersonian museum, curious artifacts stand side by side with curious persons in Adams's "Tour." In Bunzlau, Adams meets two men whom he describes as the greatest curiosities of all. These men are artisans—"mechanical geniuses, by the name of Jacob, and of Huttig, a carpenter, and a weaver." The carpenter Jacob has reconstructed the Passion of Jesus Christ in the form of a puppet show ("all accompanied by a mournful dirge of music"), but it is the weaver Huttig who is more interesting to Adams.[61] Huttig has transformed the rooms of his house into miniature replicas of the world, in part or in whole. Having never left home, due to "an infirm constitution," the walls of his rooms are "covered with maps and drawings." One wall represents Switzerland with all its mountains; another, "the course of the Oder, with all the towns and villages through which it runs"; and yet another, Silesia, with the mountains again distinguished. In two other rooms, Huttig has built astronomical machines, one "representing the Copernican system of the universe" and another "the various phases of the moon, and those of Jupiter's satellites." Like the orrery constructed in Philadelphia by David Rittenhouse (whose mechanical genius Jefferson praised for having "approached nearer the Maker than any man"),[62] Huttig's "whole firmament of fixed stars moves round our solar system once in every twenty-four hours, and thus always exhibits the stars, in the exact position, relative to our earth in which they really stand."

But this is not all. The tedious reconstruction continues. In "his garret," Huttig displays the oceans of the world. "Very small ropes" are "drawn over the surface" of these oceans "in such a manner as to describe the tracks of all the celebrated circumnavigators of the globe," including Columbus, Anson and Cook—whose journeys are marked with little model ships "bearing their names" and "placed upon the surface of his ocean." Having re-created this world of travelers, Huttig then interpolates his visitors into it, telling them that now, if only a traveler from Africa would visit him, he could "boast of having had visitors from all the four quarters of the globe." Finally, near the end of the tour, Huttig shows Adams two tables, upon which are ranged "all the towns and remarkable places of Germany, and, on the other of all Europe," their names "written on a small square piece of paper, and fixed in a slit on the top of a peg," the mountains marked "by small pyramidic black stones, [and] little white pyramids . . . stationed at all the spots which have been distinguished by any great battle or other remarkable incident." Huttig is full of amusing anecdotes at this juncture: in particular he points to Switzerland, where "the French army of reserve so lately passed, and where Buonaparte so fortunately escaped being taken by an Austrian officer." The weaver concludes his tour with an extensive comment upon "the character . . . of the first consul." Standing over his reproductions of Germany and Switzerland, Huttig himself is a Napoleon in miniature: a framer of little worlds, displayed as souvenirs to his own powers of world making.[63]

Napoleonic Federalism

Napoleon fascinated Adams as well as Huttig. To the American, Napoleon represented the possibility of balance through a division of powers—or the representational principles of federalism reiterated worldwide. Perhaps, Adams fantasized, Bonaparte could serve, from his elevated position on the stage of international power, as a fulcrum, or a point of stability, in the world. The *Port Folio* likewise admired Napoleon's political and military "genius" and reflected occasionally on the still open question of whether he would fulfill the hopes of the Enlightenment in Europe (doing battle on behalf of the universal laws of republican political and natural science) or cast it all back into the darkness of Jacobin revolution or monarchical reaction. "[A]s citizens of the world," the *Port Folio* intoned, "we believe it to be desirable that an EQUILIBRIUM should exist between [Great Britain and France] and serve mutually to bridle their ambition":

> As to France . . . what shall we say? Who will undertake to fortell the future fortunes of a nation, which . . . exhibits all the varieties of the human character? Who will attempt to explore the heights, or fathom the depths of the resplendent and profound genius of Buonaparte? . . . The temporary destiny of France seems to hang upon the life of this extraordinary man. Remove him, and all is probably once more afloat in that country. It certainly has no safe political constitution . . . [and] unless it shall shortly acquire one, its fortunes are precarious, its advantages evanescent . . . they will flit away, like the painted forms of a magic lanthern.[64]

In this passage the *Port Folio* explicitly articulates the hope that the "resplendent genius" of Napoleon can somehow substitute for the lack of a French constitution. Without a world-making individual or federal structures of representation to unify and integrate its parts, France's varied character threatened to dissolve into the flickering and insubstantial forms of a kaleidoscope—a world "afloat," without an Ark or a Napoleon-Noah to keep it all in focus. In negotiations with France, both Adams and his father supported an engaged but wary neutrality in relations with France and Britain, viewing both nations as dangerous powers essentially opposed to American independence and American commercial development. For John Quincy Adams, the great desideratum of 1801 was to prevent war, through an international balance of powers. It was this republican faith in a federal pyramid made international that led him to hope that, in the end, Napoleon would choose a federalist and republican middle ground, a moderate but dynamic position somewhere between the theater of European monarchy and the "Jacobinism" that "served his ambition." "*In the name of the French people,*" Adams writes to his mother in March of 1801, "[Napoleon] takes the sceptered despots by the hand, and, as he looks at the gold and jewels of their crowns, feels a mysterious sympathetic itching play round his temples. Yet if the crown were offered him tomorrow, he would refuse it as Caesar and Cromwell did before."[65] Like the *Port Folio*, Adams imagined that Napoleon could substitute for the lack of a French constitution. However, such a substitution was, in fact, only imaginable within a global culture of representative self-production,

a nation-building repertoire of representational frameworks that Napoleon made use of (as did "Huttig" and the American federalists): the parades and publications, museums, new inventions—all the myriad exhibitions of productive power that shaped both national "manufactories" and
an international working class.

Even American republicans like John Quincy Adams and his father
found themselves performing virtue within an early industrial exhibitionary complex. The younger Adams, for example, was deeply identified
with the oratorical ideal of Ciceronian eloquence: "[I]n my opinion," he
writes, even "a traveller who presumes to give the result of his observations
to the public, ought to be versed in every art and every science, as much as
Cicero requires in an orator."[66] American republicanism of the mid-1790s
presumed Roman examples. As Garry Wills has shown, George Washington was widely and repeatedly compared to the virtuous Roman farmer/
soldier Cincinnatus; and, as both Jay Fliegelman and Robert Ferguson
have demonstrated, in oratorical practice and in learned or literary circles,
the Roman orator Cicero represented the republican ideal of civic virtue
united with liberal, if not global, learning.[67] Ultimately, the lounging format of the *Port Folio* simply extended the neoclassical figure of oratorical
virtuosity and virtuous republicanism to any and all grand exemplars of
liberal learning in every field or profession. On the grounds of mechanical
production, in other words, republican virtuosity meant creative literary
and artistic production, or genius of any stripe. Pan-learned republicans
or "public men" in the *Port Folio* included Shakespeare, Sir Joshua Reyn-
olds, Samuel Johnson, Edward Gibbon, Laurence Sterne, and Edmund
Burke as well as innumerable, lesser-known writers, historians, and painters, patterned upon them like so many plaster-of-Paris busts. And where
the virtuous republican is revealed to be an artifact of mechanical production—as he was already, of course, in 1788—there the lounger (Meander)
steps in.

> Evening. Lounged to my book-shelf, with an intent to open Blackstone, but
> made a mistake, and took down a volume of Hume's History of England.
> Attention became quite engrossed by his narrative of . . . Henry I. A versa-
> tile, brilliant genius, who blended in one bright assemblage, ambition, pru-
> dence, eloquence and enterprize. . . . The formidable folios, which stood
> before me, seemed frowningly to ask, why I did not link to my ambition, that
> prudence, which formed part of Henry's fame? The remorseful blush of a
> moment tinged my cheek . . . but, straightway recollecting, that I had re-
> cently supped, and that, after a full meal, application was pernicious to
> health, I adjourned the cause, Prudence versus Meander, till morning.[68]

Nostalgic, perhaps, for the person of Washington, the lounging subject
of the *Port Folio* generated multiple substitute figures of representative in-

corporation—but without deciding finally for any one of them. In its lounging indifference, however, the *Port Folio* itself resembled a kaleidoscopic nation, a collectivity without (a) constitution. Lounging disintegrated the republican ideal of representative manhood in all of its American incarnations: be it federal mechanic and architect, Jeffersonian husbandman, virtuous statesman, or literary "genius." Within the lounger's distracted gaze, all four of these republican characters become interchangeable versions of one another upon a stage—or screen—for the display of American productions. Within the pages of the *Port Folio*, Ciceronian public men such as Adams appear (like Francis Hopkinson) to be federal "arrangers," or virtuosos, who can integrate all "the parts" (*E pluribus unum*) in any field, be it music, oratory, literature, history painting, natural or world history. But in the bric-a-brac assemblage of the *Port Folio*, the "museum" of the world has become a vast, miscellaneous, and unsortable "store," in which even the most sublime virtuoso, or genius of union, becomes (in his "off" hours) a lounger, a virtuoso viewer of fugitive fragments—of the carapaces of bugs, or the feathers of birds, or the innumerable other miniature and irrelevant productions of political, literary, and natural history.

In *The Fall of Public Man*, Richard Sennett argues that, by the early nineteenth century, "public behavior" was increasingly transformed into "a matter of observation, of passive participation, of a certain kind of voyeurism."[69] Prior to his "fall," Sennett's public man performed public service on a stage that isolated and elevated him above the multiply mediated processes of economic production—above, that is, the cultural reproduction, rationalization, and mechanization of labor. According to this narrative, civic virtue and republican disinterest begin to disintegrate precisely where the representative public man comes into contact with economic production and consumption: that is, with the manufactories of an expanding consumer market. What such narratives of the "fall" of public, or republican, man ignore, however, is what Adams's "Tour Through Silesia" foregrounds: by 1800, even the "unfallen" republican was a character of international industry, of a global commodity market, its manufactories, and its creation and division of labor.

Sennett's psychoanalytically inflected writings are not formally or politically comparable to the wide-ranging histories of ideas, the dense archival work, and the gigantic moral canvases of such republican historians as Pocock, Bailyn, or Wood. However, in spite and perhaps because of its narrower and more populist argument, Sennett's narrative of the fall of public man brings into relief the essentially nostalgic and masculine (i.e., man-making, character-building) face of the republican school of American historiography represented by Bailyn or Wood. This is also what John Quincy Adams's vacation writings accomplish in the *Port Folio*, although by a different route. Indulging, without naming, the character of the lounger, Adams's "Tour" operates like a kind of de-constituting "magic lantern," revealing even the most exemplary republican personality to be an artifact of mechanical production and its display. On vacation in industrializing Silesia, the republican federalist practices tourism, encounters open-ended variety, and meets other aspiring "mountain-climbers" who mirror his own elevated situation. In Silesia, John Adams's son discovers that little world-making Napoleons are floating everywhere in the world of things. Assembled and displayed in the *Port Folio*, this crowd of aspiring persons directly challenges the privileged and specifically masculine (and adult) liberties of action and virtue described by republican political theory. In the end, one might say, Adams's "Tour" explains why, some twenty years later, P. T. Barnum's little star, the dwarf Tom Thumb, was most popular and successful when he was dressed in the costume of Napoleon.

But where did the lounger go after 1810? A literary historian might observe that the counterproductive idleness of the *Port Folio* lounger of 1801 was simply raised to the level of cultural representativeness in the writings of Washington Irving (with, perhaps, the single, rather unrepresentative exception of Irving's best work, in *Salmagundi*). Or, perhaps, the peculiar possibilities of difference introduced by lounging were lost in the mirror of party politics. The early years of Dennie's editorship corresponded with years of particularly vociferous partisan debate between Federalists and Jeffersonian-Republicans. It was, in fact, during a period of strident political conflict that the lounger emerged, to engage (without becoming representative of) this nation-building party dimorphism. This, certainly, is precisely what Irving's preindustrial idler "Rip Van Winkle" figures, among other things: the (lounging) difference lost in the mirror of nation building, where party politics is another device of American manufacturing and where the preindustrial worker "awakens" to find himself just another early national curio or museum artifact. The title of Irving's famous collection *The Sketch Book* is particularly telling in light of the lounger's (imaginary) disappearance into it. Until 1809, the *Port Folio* entirely lacked illustrations or visual art. The *Port Folio* had begun to lose money after 1807, and in 1809 the Philadelphia publisher Samuel F. Bradford purchased the magazine. Dennie continued on as its pseudonymous editor until his death in 1812, and many of the same "Confederacy of Gentlemen" continued to write for it. But with its purchase by Bradford, the magazine's format was changed to radically broaden its appeal, making it less partisan and polemical and more entertaining in general. The long, untranslated Latin poems that were a hallmark of the *Port Folio* under Dennie's editorship began to disappear. Bradford emphasized instead the graphic connection between words and images (which had always sustained the edifice of federalism) by introducing at least one engraving into every issue. These included portraits of famous men, new inventions, and picturesque views, while at least one issue for 1809 included women's fashion plates. With these changes, the lounger faded from the pages of the *Port Folio* in spirit and in fact. Already a shadow in the increasingly hard-working world of American productivity, perhaps the lounger migrated to Europe after 1809—only to reappear some thirty years later in the company of dandies and flaneurs, on the streets of London and Paris. In the end, the American lounger was a shadowy figure of Napoleonic federalism; he appeared, at any rate, at the moment when the grand federal tradition saw itself mirrored in the world-making figure of Napoleon. In the pyramidal fantasy of a continental empire, made, mastered, and "balanced" by a single man, federalism recognized itself as a man-making culture of production, projecting and inhabiting a global stage of representative (self-)productions. In Napoleon, you might say, the republican architect saw "the maker" and, in the process, saw himself as architecture. From this point of view, the lounger is "the magic lanthern" of the American manufactory, a short-lived moving image cast by a confluence of representational technologies, emerging and in transition. Without being either one, the lounger thereby illuminates the deep connection between republican virtue and representational virtuosity—between the federal republican and his dissolution in the figures of mechanical artistry.

PART III

The Strong Box

Figure 9. Alexander Wilson. Detail from Charles Willson
Peale, *The Exhumation of the Mastodon* (1806–8).
(Courtesy of the Baltimore City Life Museums.)

CHAPTER FIVE

Feathered Federalism: Alexander Wilson's
American Ornithology, 1807–1814

I spent nearly the whole of Saturday in Newark, where my book attracted as many starers as a bear or a mammoth would have done."

Alexander Wilson, 10 October 1808

IN 1807, Charles Willson Peale included a portrait of Alexander Wilson in his painting *The Exhumation of the Mastodon*. Wilson is the contemplative figure in the middle ground of the painting, posed against a wooden shack, his arms crossed, at the top of the line of laborers digging for bones below (fig. 6). In a painting full of pyramidal structures, from the tent in the background, to the shack in the middle ground, to the machine looming in the foreground, Wilson stands at the pinnacle of the laborers' collective work. Among the artifacts of the excavation, it seems, are not only the restored bones of the mastodon but also this lonely figure: Alexander Wilson, the author of the first *American Ornithology*. The summa of productive labor, or so Peale's painting reads, is this representative man, in whose reflective pose work is harmonized with leisure, and labor with spectatorship: in him, as in the turning wheel of the foregrounded pump, the re-productive energies of the Jeffersonian "Revolution" are summarized and contained.

This chapter considers the enormous labor of literary production that Peale so admired: Wilson's *American Ornithology*, published in nine volumes by Bradford and Inskeep of Philadelphia between 1807 and 1814.[1] Like Peale's museum, Wilson's collection of some five hundred bird species was a Jeffersonian artifact of productive labor earnestly and eagerly performed. It was also, however, an artifact of westward expansion and exploration. Like Lewis and Clark, Wilson took the exhibitionary practices of Jeffersonian science on the road, bringing the representational devices of the Peale Museum to the fields and streams of the interior, with which they were already articulated but which had not emerged fully into view under the "new roof" of the federal state.

As an agent of federalism's expansion, Wilson's *Ornithology* displays new western species from the continental interior (Tennessee, Mississippi, and the Louisiana territory) as well as familiar eastern birds (Blue Jay, Robin,

Oriole, Bluebird). But *American Ornithology* represents another kind of interiority as well. In his essay "On Manufacturing" in *Notes on the State of Virginia*, Thomas Jefferson celebrated the American husbandman or independent farmer as the source of collective independence and virtue. It is not the mechanical artist but the "husbandman," Jefferson writes, who "keeps alive th[e] sacred fire" of virtue, "which otherwise might escape from the face of the Earth." Relying upon his own labor rather than upon "the caprice of customers," the farmer is the privileged producer of Jefferson's landscape: "Corruption of morals in the mass of cultivators is a phaenomenon of which no age nor nation has furnished an example."[2] In this classic statement Jefferson grounds independent nationhood on the virtuous labor of the husbandman, but in fact his yeoman republican never lived alone in the landscape of agrarian capitalism. As works of natural science from Peale's museum to Wilson's *Ornithology* demonstrate, Jefferson's manly cultivator was always accompanied by the whole farm—a family farm—fully equipped (in the discourse of natural history at least) with mother, children, and an attendant network of affective familial connections already installed. In fact, when Jefferson's husbandman is restored to the nexus of natural history collections, lectures, and sentimental anecdotes that surrounded him in the late eighteenth century, he emerges as a figure inseparable from the affective interior of the industrial-era bourgeois family.[3] In the anecdotes of natural history, the agrarian producer of Jeffersonian political economy is both federal mechanic and family man, inseparable from the class-divided culture of customers and commodities that Jefferson claimed to reject ("as for the general operations of manufacture, let our work-shops remain in Europe").

Certainly, literary critics and historians have recognized that narratives of family versus sexual feeling structure the novels of the early republic (from *Charlotte Temple* to *Wieland*).[4] That the rhetoric of sentiment or feeling is also present in the discourses of early-industrial science is of equal, if not more broadly revelatory, significance. In 1799, for example, Peale summarized the affective philosophy of his museum in a series of lectures delivered at the University of Pennsylvania. The 1790s had been a period of counterrevolution and reaction in Philadelphia, as well as Paris. Peale is concerned, therefore, to argue that his museum is a deeply moral rather than libertine institution, a virtuous rather than prurient display of Mother Nature's "parts." From birds to bears, Peale declares, social harmony characterizes nature's nations. Contrasting the American Cuckoo to the European Cuckoo—a notorious libertine and the "prototype of cuckoldry"—he argues that the secrets of American nature support a peace-loving domestic order:

> "Here I feel gratification, nay, pleasure, that I am able to show this nest and Eggs belonging to these American Cuckoos. They build their own nest;

they foster their young; they chaunt their soft notes to sweeten the care of Incubation—and I am proud to believe that they are faithful and constant to each other."[5]

Although he was able to tell anecdotes such as this with some humor, Peale was completely serious about the social virtues he found in nature. In his museum, the heterosexual family circle is the stamen and pistil of social order: in drawings, dioramas, paintings, and printed texts, Peale displayed Nature clothed—as affectionate, familial, and ultimately sociable.

In Peale's anecdotes and in Wilson's *Ornithology*, however, "constancy and parental care" coexisted with a remarkably aggressive individualism. In another lecture of the late 1790s, Peale located domestic harmony even at the outer reaches of market expansion. As our "traders to the Faulkland and other Isles on the coast of Patagonia and Chili" report,

> Sea-Lyons, Sea-Wolves, and other such animals, are often found so numerous, as to cover the shores; so thickly are they inhabited, that a man with a short bludgeon, may kill hundreds of them before breakfast! —yet among this immense number of creatures a perfect harmony prevails! —Suppose we descend, and view the smaller animals, —here, myriads of insects present themselves to our view. They are far more numerous than any other class of animals, and yet behold among them also, a perfect harmony. This is a serious comparative view of animated creation. . . . And if we study the manners of such animals in general, we shall find amongst them, most excellent models of friendship, constancy, parental care and other social virtues."[6]

Here Peale juxtaposes a violent foreground (the "man with a short bludgeon") with the harmonious background of animal family life—a reminder that, in fact, Peale himself shot and stuffed the majority of birds in his museum. (Peale's letters and diaries document countless shooting expeditions undertaken to harvest bird specimens for his collection and for exchange with institutions in Europe.)[7] What Peale's representations of animal community illustrate is that a migratory domestic ideology was indispensable to the opening of new sites of commercial investment. Such fantasies of nature's familial character led, however, neither to a coherent environmentalism in relations between human and animal "communities" nor to a usable humanitarianism in cross-cultural or race relations nor to egalitarianism between sexes and sexualities. Instead, in the bird dioramas of Peale's museum and in Wilson's *American Ornithology*, natural science articulates a dynamic link between independence as a form of manly productive activity and the heterosexualized family circle as the site of that manhood's reproduction, naturalization, and display. When it is recognized, furthermore, that federalist political culture was inseparable from American manufacturing and its extension, it is clear that Jeffersonian narratives of animal sociability articulate two kinds of interiority together. From the beginning, national existence involved an elastic structure of territorial expansion enabled by the mobile ideological construction of a family circle—or nest—wherein the family itself was a "farm," a site of cultivation, a scene set for the elaboration of affective interiority. The sentimental education of the late-eighteenth-century male republican was coextensive, then, with a separate, sex-based educational and biological trajectory of development for "woman." And these sex-specific developmental careers were articulated not only by the novel but by the anecdotal discourses of natural science.

The word interior is worth emphasizing here. As Mary Pratt demonstrates so memorably in *Imperial Eyes*, the practices of Linnaean science mark a distinct epoch in the long process of European colonial enterprise in Africa and the Americas. In natural history and travel literature, Linnaean nomenclature structured the shift from the exploratory mapping of continental edges, or seaboards, to the infinitely more detailed appropriation of continental interiors. Certainly, the practice of natural science in federal Philadelphia fits Pratt's description of this turn to continental interiors—even if one considers only the expeditions of William Bartram or Merriwether Lewis and William Clark, or the Louisiana Purchase of 1803 (through which the huge Louisiana territory was literally bought by Jefferson from France). But foregrounding the word "interior" means highlighting the word's double meaning, the link it articulates between territorial expansion and the creation of affective subjects, or feeling states. From Crèvecoeur to Alexander Wilson, the scientific narratives of bird love in particular and animal sociability in general indicate quite clearly that the territorial expansion of the United States was dynamically coextensive with the creation and circulation of a domestic family scene, in more discourses than one.

Nowhere is this more evident than in Wilson's mammoth collection. Despite the Linnaean context of this work, Wilson refused to order the species presented in *American Ornithology* according to a systematic classification that would require opening, for example, with "Acciperes" ("Rapacious" birds) and "proceed regularly through the orders and genera," that is, from "Picae ('Pies,') to Passerines, Columbe, etc." He rejected a top-down taxonomic organization because "it is highly probable that numerous species at present unknown would come into our possession . . . interrupting the regularity of the above arrangement."[8] As a result, *American Ornithology* is a list of species arranged in no systematic order other than that in which they came into the "possession" of the collector. On the one hand, this mode of organization makes Wilson's bird books a loose record of his travels. Moving from east to west, the collection opens with species familiar in the original thirteen colonies, turning, by volume

3, to new or lesser-known species of Louisiana, Kentucky, and Tennessee (including specimens collected by Lewis and Clark). But it also allowed Wilson to present his birds according to other, thematic and subjective, criteria, emphasizing and dramatizing certain birds over others according to their size or novelty, the interest they held as American "characters," or the amount of literary or anecdotal data surrounding them. Each volume contains, then, between thirty and fifty illustrated species, described in essays that mix anatomy with anecdote and, sometimes, poetry with prose. These essays vary radically in length, according to the characterological or emblematic significance, the peculiarities, or the familiarity of the species under description. Small birds, such as the Maryland Yellow-Throat, the Small Blue-Gray Flycatcher, and Warblers are given very cursory empirical descriptions, while larger or more famous birds, such as the King Bird, the Gold-Winged Woodpecker, the Mocking Bird, the Parrot, and the Ivory-Billed Woodpecker, are occasions for extended meditation upon that species' collective character and its implications for the character of American nature generally.

Wilson's specimens appear, then, as a series of separable, randomly organized tableaux where, as in so many display cases, each species performs some aspect of a republican personality construed affectively and socially, within a diverse and migratory (even rapacious) but still sociable and domestic collectivity. Gendered and heterosexualized, Wilson's birds are feeling subjects. As type specimens, or "feathered tribes," living in bird families or leaving home (only to start families of their own), they give voice—or song—to the possibility of a native national "nest," whose federalizing representational practices will adopt and contain the cultural differences of all collectivities. It is this culture-constituting juncture of nation-state and family form that makes Wilson's bird books not only a work of Jeffersonian natural science but of early-national ethnography and sociology.

In a 1786 letter, Jefferson himself had described the thirteen former colonies as a "nest" from which the entire continent would be peopled. By the mid-1780s, emigration west (to Kentucky and Ohio in particular) had raised fears that the confederation was growing too fast and would simply fragment as its political authority extended over too great an area. In his letter, Jefferson tries to counter these fears by figuring the Anglo-American emigration to Kentucky as natural extensions of the national "nest" through a peaceful diffusion of settlement comparable to a migration of birds:

> Our present federal limits are not too large for good government, nor will the increase of votes in Congress produce any ill effect. . . . Our confederacy must be viewed as the nest from which all America, North and South, is to

be peopled. We should take care not to think it for the interest of that great continent to press too soon on the Spaniards. Those countries cannot be in better hands. My fear is that they are too feeble to hold them till our population can be sufficiently advanced to gain it from them piece by piece.[9]

Here, bird migration is a metaphor for the peaceful and gradual replacement of a "feeble" Spanish empire by settlers moving west in the form, presumably, of Anglo-American freeholders or husbandmen. Together with his idealized yeoman farmer, Jefferson's metonym of the former colonies as a nest is his most telling figure for United States territorial expansion. The nest harmonizes a familial subject with agricultural production, naturalizing human settlement as an endlessly reproducible form of property formation. Certainly, the husbandman was always an agent of expansion (as Jefferson puts it, "we have an immensity of land courting the industry of the husbandman.").[10] But the western diffusion of (this state of) cultivation was simultaneously a family form—a mobile ideological farm—structured internally by the reproductive distinctions of the nest: age, sex, and gender. It is this metonym of the nest—of union as a phenomenon of production and its migratory reproduction—that Wilson's bird books carry to its logical republican extension. Hauling his sample volume of *American Ornithology* from city to city, from settlement to settlement, in search of new subscribers and new bird specimens, Wilson traveled through virtually every city "from the shores of St. Laurence, to the mouths of the Mississippi," from the Atlantic ocean to the interior of Louisiana. He described his journeys through the United States and the territories of the interior as a "zigzag" from "one country to another."[11] As a result, however, his nine-volume collection of the "manners and migrations" of American birds is something more than an oversized field guide. It is, instead, a fragmentary kind of panorama, unrolling the expansionist inner state of production's reproduction during the years of Jefferson's and Madison's presidencies (1801–16).

THE NEST GOES WEST

> I have laboured with the zeal of a knight errant in exhibiting this book of mine, wherever I went, traveling with it, like a beggar with his bantling, from town to town, and from one country to another. I have been loaded with praises . . . shaken almost to pieces in stage coaches; have wandered among strangers, hearing the O's and Ah's, and telling the same story a thousand times over.
>
> Alexander Wilson to Daniel Miller, 26 October 1808

It was because of Wilson's journeys on behalf of *American Ornithology* that, some seventy years after his death, Henry Adams used Wilson's travel writings to help introduce his own nine-volume *History of the United States of*

America during the First Administration of Thomas Jefferson to the Second Administration of James Madison. Specifically, Adams used Wilson's letters to support his contention that the sprawling Jeffersonian state was without adequate transportation, largely impenetrable, and—particularly in its far-flung interiors—an unenlightened and backward, even medieval, domain.[12] By Adams's account Wilson himself was a cultivated but somewhat eccentric specimen—an "ornithologist, a Pennsylvania Scotchman, a confirmed grumbler, [and] a shrewd judge," but "the most thorough of American travellers."[13] What Adams fails to note, however, is that Wilson traveled not simply because he wished to but also because he had to. The compulsion derived in part from the literary market; for example, in his struggle to complete his huge collection, Wilson explicitly emulated the work of other celebrated literary travelers, particularly his friend William Bartram, whom he met in 1803, and Lewis and Clark, who left for the Pacific in the same year. On the heels of Lewis and Clark's departure, Wilson had written to President Jefferson, hoping to be appointed to another government-sponsored western expedition up the Red River.[14] Neither this expedition nor Wilson's appointment would materialize, but Wilson continued to aspire to the status of the celebrated traveler and to identify himself with Lewis and Clark. Conveniently for Wilson, Jefferson ordered the animal specimens collected by the Corps of Discovery to be sent to Peale's museum in Philadelphia: volume 3 of *American Ornithology*, therefore, exhibits some of the new western species gathered by Lewis and Clark—Lewis's Woodpecker, for example, and Clark's Crow—together with western species collected by Wilson on his own solitary expeditions, including the Louisiana Tanager, Swamp Sparrow, Savannah Sparrow, Water Thrush, Painted Bunting, Mississippi Kite, Tennessee Warbler, Kentucky Warbler, Prairie Warbler, Carolina Parrot, and Nashville Warbler.[15]

But if Wilson traveled in pursuit of literary celebrity, he also traveled on behalf of his publishers, Bradford and Inskeep, in an effort to gather book subscriptions—and money to publish—his expensive collection. *American Ornithology* was in every sense a luxury commodity. Its price of $120 (or $12 per volume) was prohibitive for all but library companies, learned societies, colleges, and the wealthiest of individuals. Demographically elite, geographically far-flung, and crossing partisan lines, Wilson's subscription list displayed the names of Jedediah Morse and Josiah Quincy, Thomas Jefferson and James Madison, Thomas Pinckney, Nicholas Biddle, Benjamin Smith Barton, Rufus King, Robert Livingston, and Gouverneur Morris.[16] (Widening this elite list slightly, its 448 names also include eleven city libraries, five learned societies, six universities, an agricultural society, a state legislature, a hospital, and a Scottish museum.)

Prior to the 1820s, American publishing was generally an intensely local affair, in which only Philadelphia and New York could claim a centralized book trade with the ambition (as yet unfulfilled) of a national distribution embracing the southern and western interior.[17] The years in which Wilson assembled his *Ornithology* would be noteworthy for the number of enormously ambitious, expensive, multivolume publishing projects undertaken in Philadelphia, of which Wilson's was only one. In 1790, Thomas Dobson began to print the first American edition of the *Encyclopedia Britannica*, which by 1803 would be completed, in twenty-one volumes with six hundred copperplate engravings. Between 1795 and 1796, Bioren and Madan of Philadelphia published, in eight volumes, the first complete American edition of Shakespeare (probably edited by Joseph Hopkinson). And in 1798 William and Thomas Birch began to engrave their series of twenty-eight *Views of Philadelphia*, published in 1800 for subscribers in Philadelphia, New York, and Baltimore. In an address to the new Pennsylvania Academy of Fine Arts in 1810, Joseph Hopkinson (the son of federalist poet Francis Hopkinson) summarized the stunning expansion of Philadelphia publishing in terms of the number of engravers employed on these projects. According to Hopkinson, the number of engravers in the city had grown from three to sixty since the American Revolution due to a postwar boom in bookmaking.[18] By 1810, every engraver active in the United States had been employed by one or another of the multivolume publishing projects underway in Philadelphia.

But even these ambitious projects were somewhat dwarfed in 1798, when Samuel F. Bradford undertook—with Alexander Wilson's help—an American edition of Abraham Rees's *Cyclopedia or Universal Dictionary*. Published in forty-seven volumes with over fourteen hundred engravings, the huge undertaking of Rees's *Cyclopedia* (1810–27) made possible the publication of *American Ornithology* when Bradford and his New York partner, Inskeep, hired Wilson to work on the *Cyclopedia* as their book agent and assistant editor, at a salary of nine dollars a year.[19] By hiring Wilson, Bradford and Inskeep piggybacked the publication of Wilson's *American Ornithology* onto the larger project of the *Cyclopedia*, enabling Wilson to travel across the continent in search of subscribers and information not only for the one work but for the other as well. Travel was critical to the completion of both projects: specimens and data had to be collected, local book retailers contacted, and the continent scoured for subscribers wealthy enough to capitalize such oversized commodities and willing to do so. Throughout the federalist period, as Trish Loughran has argued, national union was irreducibly "virtual"—a matter of rhetoric, fantasy, and visual art—at a time when the United States embraced a geography of communities so profoundly local and specific, so intensely diverse and disjunct, as to be actually unrepresentable.[20] Given its demographically elite but geographically extensive range, Wilson's *Ornithology* was, then, like Peale's museum, not only Jeffersonian but also federal, and federalizing.

It was within these contexts of book production, then, that Wilson would make two extended expeditions, in addition to numerous shorter ones.

In 1808, he traveled alone from New England to Charleston and Savannah and, in 1810, from Pittsburgh to Lexington, Natchez, and New Orleans. As a result, his subscription list represents subscribers from Mississippi and Louisiana, as well as the eastern seaboard states: Pennsylvania (with 114 names), New York (60), Connecticut (3), Massachusetts (14), New Hampshire (8), Maryland (16), District of Columbia (20), Virginia (34), North Carolina (11), South Carolina (36), Georgia (21), Kentucky (15), Mississippi Territory (23), Louisiana (60), and finally "Europe" (15; from Russia, Scotland, London and Liverpool).[21] In a letter home to relatives in Scotland in 1811, Wilson dramatized his solitary effort, attributing his struggle to a longtime "ambition of being distinguished in the literary world":

[A] wish to reach the glorious rock of *Independence* . . . has engaged me in an undertaking more laborious and expensive than you are aware of and has occupied almost every moment of my time these several years. I have since Feby. 1810 slept for weeks in the wilderness alone in an Indian country with my gun and pistols in my bosom, have found myself so reduced by sickness as to be scarcely able to stand . . . have by resolution surmounted all these and other obstacles in my way to my object and I now begin to see the blue sky open around me and Independence slowly descending to give me a wag of her fist.[22]

Wilson's reference in this passage to "Indian country" is to the territories around Nashville and near Natchez, where he relied upon the hospitality of Chickasaw villagers—and heard the tale of Merriwether Lewis's madness and suicide at the cabin of Mrs. Grinder:

[S]he listened to him walking backwards and forwards . . . for several hours, and talking aloud, as she said, like a lawyer. She then heard the report of a pistol. . . . [Two hours later], on going in they found him lying on the bed; he uncovered his side, and showed them where the bullet had entered; a piece of the forehead was blown off, and had exposed the brains, without having bled much. . . . He begged the servant not to be afraid of him.[23]

Wilson narrates the sensational story of Lewis's suicide in one of several travel letters sent back to Philadelphia for publication in the *Port Folio* (now also owned by Bradford and Inskeep). But Wilson's retelling of the famous anecdote anticipates an irony at the heart of his own travels on behalf of Jeffersonian science. By 1813, Wilson himself was dead of illness aggravated, if not caused, by overwork: "heart palpitations," chronic dysentery, and chronic poverty. In just six years, between 1807 and 1813, Wilson had assembled a remarkable seven volumes of *American Ornithology*, collecting, describing, classifying, and illustrating more than three hundred species. Eventually illustrated with almost one hundred plates, drawn by

Wilson, engraved by Alexander Lawson, and hand-colored by men and women employed by Wilson, the work was enormous, underpaid, and exhausting. When Peale included Wilson's portrait in *The Exhumation of the Mastodon* (1806–8), Wilson was at work on volume 1. By July of 1813, he would write to his father in Paisley, Scotland: "Intense application to study has hurt me much. My 8th volume is now in the press. . . . One volume more will complete the whole."[24] When Wilson died, he left almost nothing save two copies of his *Ornithology*, one bequeathed to his father in Paisley and the other to his nephew William Duncan. Bradford and Inskeep put a claim against his estate for $2,284.22, which was to be discharged with further sales of the *Ornithology*. Its eighth and ninth volumes were finally completed in Philadelphia by Charles Lucien Bonaparte, Napoleon Bonaparte's expatriate nephew.

The connection to Napoleon is more than coincidental. If the collections of Italian and German art brought back to Paris by Napoleon's armies were mementos of empire in Europe (and if Alexander Von Humboldt was only the latest colonialist voice of centuries of imperial investment in South America), then Wilson's *Ornithology* is the peculiar expression of Jeffersonian empire in North America. Despite its rural or pastoral aspect as a field, the specificity of *American Ornithology*—its federalist stamp, so to speak—lies in its character as a performance of production, in its display of its author as both representative producer and celebrated employee of the federal state.

THE BIRDS OF NORTH AMERICA

Over and over again, the text of *American Ornithology* represents Wilson pursuing and shooting birds, observing and drawing specimens, writing and, sometimes, conversing. In such anecdotes, the collection displays its own production—and exhibits the author of *American Ornithology* as its central specimen. Wherever it represents its own making, furthermore, *American Ornithology* displays not only an author internally divided by production performed but an audience sharply divided along gender lines. Obsessively preoccupied with the gendering and sexualizing of production's reproduction, *American Ornithology* addresses both an anonymous and undifferentiated female audience positioned as spectator and consumer and a highly differentiated audience of productive male readers, the latter addressed individually by name or collectively as "professional gentlemen," "schoolboys," and "sportsmen." In his introduction, for example, Wilson's audience is a receptive and appreciative mother. Comparing himself to a schoolboy home for the holidays, Wilson describes his *Ornithology* as a "bouquet" of wildflowers, offered with these words: "Look my dear 'ma, what beautiful flowers I have found growing on our place. Why all the woods are full of them! red, orange, blue and 'most every color. O I can gather you a whole parcel . . . of them, much handsomer than these, all growing in our own woods!" Running out, "on the wings of ecstasy," to gather more specimens, Wilson concludes:

> Should my country receive with the same gracious indulgence the specimens which I here humbly present her, should she express a desire for me *to go and bring her more,* the highest wishes of my ambition will be gratified; for, in the language of my little friend, *our whole woods are full of them!* and I can collect hundreds more, *much handsomer than these.* —A. W."[25]

Here, where nature is "our place" and "our very own woods," ownership is presumed as a kind of natural title to animals and flowers. The labor of production, likewise, is natural and spontaneous, because it is rooted in a child's affective attachment to his mother—who is also, of course, "my country," a silent, receptive, and anonymous public. Presided over by this child-author and his affectionate mother, both home and nation can, it seems, be found anywhere, wherever specimens of natural history are gathered. With this introduction, *American Ornithology* projects an interior that is both a continental and a sentimental state: the nest goes west, Jeffersonian-style; its incomprehensibly diverse locales become "our place"; its migrations or extensions are advertised as natural, peacetime forms of organic growth.

Introduced by this figure of the collective "mother," Wilson's *Ornithology* nevertheless turns immediately to the sexual and social character of adult males, the topic that dominates virtually every entry. Beginning with the Blue Jay, the first entry in volume 1, the adult male bird serves as the type specimen of each species. The Blue Jay, for example, is an "apt scholar," who, with "education," can become "a notable example of mildness of disposition and sociability of manners." A "kind of beau among the feathered tenants of our woods," he is also a notorious thief and rapacious "tyrant," who plunders every nest he can find, "tearing up the callow young by piecemeal, and spreading alarm and sorrow around him."[26] Having captured a blue jay, Wilson places it in a cage with a female orchard oriole—whose behavior he compares to that of certain "Indians" in relation to white men: "after displaying various threatening gestures (like some of those Indians we read of in their first interviews with the whites), she began to make her approaches."[27] Eventually the oriole and jay begin "to roost and play together in perfect harmony and good humor." Their relationship, consisting of "attachment on the one part and mild condescension on the other," demonstrates, Wilson concludes, that "the disposition of the Blue Jay may be humanized, and rendered susceptible of affectionate impressions, even for those birds which, in a state of nature, he would have no hesitation in making a meal of."[28]

If the reader wonders why Wilson opens *American Ornithology* with this particular species, an explanation comes at the end of his twelve-page essay: the Jay is virtually ubiquitous in North America. Like Peale's mastodon, it is representative of both nation and continent, belonging "exclusively to North America": "I cannot find it mentioned by any writer or traveller among the birds of Guiana, Brazil . . . Africa . . . Europe, and even in the eastern parts of Asia."[29] Being educable, furthermore, the Jay also epitomizes the softening and civilizing function that Wilson claimed for *American Ornithology* as a whole. Wilson anticipated that the "peaceful, unassuming pages of AMERICAN ORNITHOLOGY" would have an effect identical to that produced upon rapacious birds by "adoption"—and upon uncultivated people (be they Anglo-American men or "Indian" women) by the sight of birds displayed in a cage.[30] From the opening pages, then, the cage is the counterpart to the nest. Gendered, sexualized, and racialized anecdotes like the narrative of the oriole and the jay abound in Wilson's collection and, in each, the affective dynamic of "bird love" is an artifact of the exhibitionary cage of American manufacturing.

Wilson advertised his *Ornithology* as an all-American production, a display of the materials, technologies, and productive power of the United States: the "engravings are a monument to the merits of Messr's Lawson, Murray and Warnicke, the elegance of the letter press a high honor to the taste of the founders Binney and Ronaldson . . . while the paper, from the manufactory of Mr. Ames, proves what American ingenuity is capable of producing when properly encouraged."[31] Although the "materials and mechanical parts" are "the production of the United States," Wilson admitted that he was "principally indebted to Europe" for the colors of his plates, except for the "beautiful native ochres" mixed in "the laboratory of Messr's (Charles Willson) Peale and Son." Nevertheless, "the spirit for manufactories, every day rising around us" gives hope that the American artist will soon be "completely independent of all foreign aid" and able to "exhibit the native hues of his subjects in colors of our own . . . equal . . . to any other."[32] Mechanical production, alone, however, was not enough. From the beginning, of course, the mechanics of nation building had required that production be displayed: federalism founded itself upon labor divided through representation. Throughout *American Ornithology*, then, the visual and aural enjoyment of nature's "works," constituted an awkward and incomplete pastoral aesthetic that aimed to legitimate territorial extensions of the young republic through displays of cultivated feeling.

As it had in Peale's museum, however, the aesthetic and performative politics of domestic expansion presented its own difficulties: what was to be done, in particular, with the agricultural or mechanical producer who refuses to view himself as a "husbandman"? How could the uncultivated cultivator (continue to) serve as the grounds of republican representation? Peale had raised these questions with regard to Masten, the German-speaking farmer who viewed the mammoth bones exhumed from his field as just another form of produce, like grain or marl, harvested for profit. Just as Peale had criticized Masten for failing to "see" or adequately frame the world of nature around him, including the bones emerging from his marl pit, so *American Ornithology* addresses the uncultivated farmers of North America, exhorting them to see, recognize, protect, and represent the feathered tribes surrounding their fields: to cease simply slaughtering birds as "vermin," or for food, pleasure, "revenge," or no reason at all. By bringing nature into view, Wilson aimed to elevate—by raising into view—the mechanics of production. He advocated, in fact, the practice of raising birds in cages: "[T]he innocent and agreeable amusement of keeping and rearing birds in this manner will become more general than it is at present . . . [w]hen the employments of the people of the United States become more sedentary, like those of Europe."[33]

In the same vein, Wilson argues that the "Gold-Winged Woodpecker" exhibits a cultured, or cultivated, character rather than the "repetitive" life of degrading labor describd by the French naturalist Buffon: "Constrained to drag out an insipid existence in boring the bark and hard fibres of trees," the woodpecker reminded Buffon of the lives of "European peasants and mechanics," and illustrated the degraded or degenerate character of American nature generally. But woodpeckers were not only maligned; they were also shot by the score by American farmers: "At present our farmers and junior sportsmen . . . take every opportunity of destroying him . . . for the trifle he will bring in market; . . . for the mere pleasure of destruction, and perhaps for the flavour of his flesh."[34] At harvest time, in particular, farmers wreak their vengeance on the bird: motivated by "the impious wish of extermination," "the farmer . . . steals among the rows with his gun, bent on vengeance.").[35] Defending the "innocent amusements" of the Gold-Winged Woodpecker against both Buffon and the American farmer, Wilson asks his reader to take a closer look at the Woodpecker—and his looks (fig. 10). "The abject and degraded character which the Count de Buffon . . . has drawn of the whole tribe of woodpeckers, belongs not to the elegant and sprightly bird now before us."

> *He* cannot be said to "lead a mean and gloomy life, without an intermission of labour," who usually feasts by the first peep of dawn, and spends the early and sweetest hours of morning on the highest peaks of the tallest trees. . . .
>
> Can it be said . . . that "the narrow circumference of a tree circumscribes his dull round of life," who as seasons and inclination inspire, roams from the frigid to the torrid zone, feasting on the abundance of various regions? Or is it a proof that "his appetite is never softened by delicacy of taste," because he so often varies his bill of fare, occasionally preferring to animal

Figure 10. Alexander Wilson, "Gold winged Woodpecker. Black throated Bunting. Blue Bird." *American Ornithology*, vol. 1 (Philadelphia: Bradford and Inskeep, 1807).

Figure 11. Alexander Wilson, "Ivory billed Woodpecker. Pileated Woodpecker. Red headed Woodpecker." *American Ornithology*, vol. 4 (Philadelphia: Bradford and Inskeep, 1811).

food the rich milkiness of young Indian corn . . .? Let the reader turn to the faithful representation of him given in the plate, and say whether his looks be "sad and melancholy."[36]

Displayed in a handsome engraving and described in vivid prose, this specimen is no mere "mechanic," Wilson argues, but, rather, a citizen of the world, "roam[ing] from the frigid to the torrid zone" and capable of enjoying the varied diversions of "taste"—diversions that correspond, finally, with the "sportive, elegant," and (above all) varied pleasures of *American Ornithology*.[37] Wilson directs the reader to a plate, furthermore, where, in a compositional arrangement common to European fashion and travel illustration, the position of the viewer is represented within the engraving by another, smaller bird, who looks up admiringly at the large, handsome, and "happy" woodpecker above.[38] This simple lesson in good looks—in learning to see and emulate the personhood of others (and to become aware of their looks, in turn)—epitomizes *American Ornithology*'s project of cultivating a domestic subject: in birds, so in human beings, the aesthetic capacity for enjoying oneself in nature, preserving rather than destroying its productions, validates the right to possession. But the farmers represented by *American Ornithology* were, in fact, generally uncultivated, much less versed in the arts of poetry, painting, and music than they were "acquainted with the value of corn, from the hard labour requisite in raising it."[39] When, in "The King Bird, or Tyrant Flycatcher," another bird is shot dead by a farmer, the episode figures, therefore, the end of poetry—as well as the overthrow of sexual and economic virtue.

Unlike a professional textbook of twentieth-century biological science, *American Ornithology* is full of poems and fragments of poems, many of which are of Wilson's own composition.[40] The discussion of the King Bird, for example, includes a poetic "epitome," composed by Wilson, that narrates the tragedy of the King Bird's murder in the form of a political allegory. A species long familiar to readers of eighteenth-century natural history, the King Bird, or Tyrant Flycatcher, was known for his curious propensity for raiding beehives and eating bees.[41] Wilson argues, however, that the Tyrant Flycatcher is not, in fact, a tyrant but a truly noble specimen, inspired to aggression only by love of his nest ("When the speck'd eggs within his nest appear, / Then glows affection, ardent and sincere; / No discord sours him when his mate he meets; / But each warm heart with mutual kindness beats.").[42] Furthermore, like the Gold-Winged Woodpecker, the King Bird vacations in the "torrid zone" ("Where vast Maragnon flows"), only to return home, to his nest, at the end of his travels:

> With Spring's return the king bird hither hastes;
> Coasts the famed Gulf, and, from his height, explores

> Its thousand streams, its long indented shores,
> Its plains immense, wide opening on the day,
> Its lakes and isles, where feathered millions play:
> All tempt not him; till gazing from on high,
> COLUMBIA's regions wide below him lie;
> There end his wanderings and his wish to roam,
> There lie his native woods, his fields, his *home*,
> Down circling, he descends, from azure heights,
> And on a full-blown sassafras alights.[43]

An icon for "the temperate zone," the sassafras identifies the bird's northern "home," while, foregrounded on his perch at the poem's end, the King Bird himself is stilled and framed—an image suitable for any parlor wall. In *American Ornithology*, it is the "homing" impulse that makes the King Bird iconic. Chasing away the plundering jay, the thieving cuckoo, and even the eagle from his nest, he embodies the spirit of 1776, by combining domestic sentiment with noble aggression:

> Come now, ye cowards! ye whom Heaven disdains,
> Who boast the happiest home—the richest plains;
> On whom, perchance, a wife, an infant's eye
> Hang as their hope, and on your arm rely;
> Yet, when the hour of danger and dismay
> Comes on your country, sneak in holes away,
> Shrink from the perils ye were bound to face,
> And leave those babes and country to disgrace;
> Come here (if such we have,) ye dastard herd!
> And kneel in dust before this noble bird.[44]

Ironically, however, by the poem's end, the American farmer himself becomes the enemy of this icon of the American Revolution. When he shoots the King Bird, the agricultural producer is the counterrevolutionary coward, or tyrant, in question; the husbandman becomes the enemy of husbandry, and Wilson's poem ends on a curiously tangled, even counterrevolutionary, note, with the tragic murder of "the rightful king":

> See where he skulks! and takes his gloomy stand,
> The deep-charged musket hanging in his hand;
> And, gaunt for blood, he leans it on a rest,
> Prepared, and pointed at thy snow-white breast.
>
> . . . .
>
> If e'er a family's griefs, a widow's woe,
> Have reached thy soul, in mercy let him go!
> Kill not thy friend, who thy whole harvest shields.

Some small return—some little right resign,
And spare his life whose services are thine!
—I plead in vain! Amid the bursting roar,
The poor lost king bird welters in his gore![45]

Wilson's graphic conclusion is marked by a convergence of nostalgia for the American Revolution and counterrevolutionary sympathy for the true "king." As an icon of husbandry husbanded and surplus cultivated, Wilson's poetic specimen also demonstrates that, while it is common to draw a line between the Enlightenment world of the federalists and the nineteenth-century culture of sentiment and sensation, in fact the parlor world of pianoforte and family pictures—together with the repressive hypothesis that naturalized the middle-class interiors of "Victorian" culture—was already being articulated by Jeffersonian science. And, as the conflicted and generically fragmented entry "King Bird" demonstrates, those interiors were also already in a state of breakdown.

SPECIMENS OF FAILURE

So fond are they of gum-berries, that, wherever there is one of these trees covered with fruit, and flocks of robins in the neighborhood, the sportsman need only take his stand near it, load, take aim, and fire; one flock succeeding another, with little interruption, almost the whole day: by this method, prodigious slaughter has been made among them with little fatigue. . . . In January, 1807, two young men, in one excursion after them, shot thirty dozen.

Wilson, *American Ornithology*, 1:31–32

Wilson's *Ornithology* does not focus on individual specimens alone, however; it is full of descriptions of huge flocks of birds: Red-Winged Blackbirds, Rice Birds, Grackles, Passenger Pigeons, Robins, Carolina Parrots, and others. In their overwhelming numbers—in flocks that sometimes take days to pass over a single point of observation—birds in huge groups represent a kind of living surplus, a surplus that seems to escape, or fly free of, the relations of production. On the one hand, then, the birds of America can be shot or harvested as food or as food for sale. On the other hand, insofar as birds, bird skin, or bird feathers are not of enormous market value, they also figure another, noneconomic kind of surplus, an aesthetic surplus that seems, at first glance, to escape the mechanics of exchange. It is as a living surplus, however, that American birds also represented the possibility of other kinds of investments. And Wilson repeatedly deploys the language and visual practices of "enjoyment" and "appreciation" as a way of recouping this second kind of surplus. Insofar as they are not particularly valuable economically, American birds—in flocks, in nests, and in cages—seemed to represent something above, or outside, commodity production and exchange. Like the distinction between flowers grown for pleasure and crops grown for market, birds would seem to offer a form of enjoyment that could ratify national growth as something other than merely productive, interested, commercial, or mechanical.[46] In his discussion of the Black-Throated Blue Warbler, Wilson explicitly distinguished the ornithological "taste" for birds from a Canadian taste for quadrupeds, and the virtues of the United States domestic economy from the British fur trade.

> [T]he feathered race is little known or attended to . . . on that part of the continent. . . . The habits of the bear, the deer, and beaver are much more interesting to those people, and for a good substantial reason too, because more lucrative; and unless there should arrive an order from England for a cargo of skins of warblers and flycatchers, sufficient to make them an object worth speculation, we are likely to know as little of them hereafter as at present.[47]

Unlike fur-bearing quadrupeds, but like the independent Jeffersonian republic, both the American "nest" and *American Ornithology* would seem to be aloof from a corrupt international nexus of trade and commerce: "I candidly declare," Wilson writes, "that lucrative views have nothing to do in the business. . . . [A] wish to draw the attention of my fellow-citizens from the jarrings of politics, to the contemplation of the grandeur, harmony, and wonderful variety of nature . . . are my principle . . . motives."[48] In his *Ornithology*, Wilson makes every effort to turn birds to the purpose of use or enjoyment, by instructing uncultivated people in the culturally reproductive uses of this feathered surplus. In *American Ornithology*, birdwatching is presented as a rural "sport," a leisure-time pursuit that cultivates surplus as visual enjoyment or aesthetic appreciation. But, at the same time, the pursuit of birds by the visual apparatus of *American Ornithology* produces a landscape of violence, contradiction, and rupture. Wilson himself, for example, shoots gratuitously at the huge flocks of birds he encounters. In such instances (where Wilson slaughters birds or where he seems unable to contain the remarkable surplus diversity he pursues), *American Ornithology* fails to ratify the representational mechanics of federalism. At such sites of rupture, furthermore, one finds that birds do, in fact, escape the net of use and enjoyment. There are many such sites of breakdown in *American Ornithology*, marking the limit and the failure of the Jeffersonian "nest." At the violent edges of *American Ornithology*, the representational mechanics of federalism cannot seamlessly contain ("as in a single focus") the mammoth state it projects: at such moments, the federal mechanic and the Jeffersonian husbandman break down together as representative producers and as the privileged figures of domestic expansion.

Not suprisingly, the most graphic episodes of breakdown correspond with those entries that describe birds of the Southwest, that is, the country inhabited by the Muskogee, Chactaw, and Chickasaw. In "Ivory-Billed Woodpecker," the entry that opens volume 4, for example, Wilson compares his specimen to both a "baby" and "an Indian." Adorned in miniature with "ivory" (the commodity that helped open Africa and India to European capital), Wilson declares the Ivory-Billed Woodpecker to be doomed to "extinction" and analogizes the species to Native Americans who reject adoption, assimilation, and the plough. A "royal hunter . . . the king or chief of his tribe, . . . ornamented with carmine crest and polished ivory," the bird is "ornamented like "the southern tribes" (i.e., Creek, Seminole, Chactaw, Chickasaw), who are said to ornament themselves, in turn, with the head and bill, skin or feathers, of birds: "Thus I have seen a coat made of the skins, heads and claws of the raven, and caps stuck round with heads of butcher birds, hawks and eagles."[49] In the swamps of North Carolina, Wilson captures a member of this species, and decides to keep it alive to use as a model for his drawing (fig. 11). The bird is inconsolable, however, and its screams in captivity "exactly resemble the violent crying of a young child." Carrying his miniature captive "under cover," Wilson soon arrives at Wilmington, North Carolina. As he enters town, the bird's "affecting cries surprised everyone within hearing, particularly the females, who hurried to the doors and windows with looks of alarm and anxiety."[50] When Wilson arrives at his "hotel," the landlord, "alarmed at what he heard, asked whether he could furnish me with accommodations for myself and my baby." The American ornithologist quickly relieves everyone's anxiety: he produces his "baby," withdrawing the bird "from under the cover," while "a general laugh [takes] place." But the Ivory-Billed Woodpecker himself comes to a less-than-humorous end. Left in Wilson's hotel room, the woodpecker wreaks havok, breaking a fifteen-inch hole through the wall, covering the bed with plaster, and nearly escaping. Wilson tries tying the bird to a mahogany table—upon which it likewise "wreaked his whole vengeance," nearly destroying it.[51] While taking drawings of him, Wilson reports, the woodpecker "cut me severely in several places" and "displayed such a noble and unconquerable spirit that I was frequently tempted to restore him to his native woods. . . . He lived with me nearly three days, but refused all sustenance, and I witnessed his death with regret."[52] The head and body of Wilson's woodpecker remain, of course, captured by Wilson's drawing; but, more centrally, as both feathered hunter and adopted infant, the Ivory-Billed Woodpecker lives on as an artifact of the national family, of its memories, jokes, and stories.

The principle of assimilation is familiar to historians of Jefferson and his administration. Many scholars have noted, for example, Jefferson's rejection of military force in favor of a policy that aimed to convert North

American Indians to commercial farming via education, example, and cross-cultural rituals of adoption.[53] Jefferson himself advocated the peaceable assimilation (through cultivation) not only of Native American people but of all "unproductive" tribes, including recent European immigrants and Anglo-American "squatters."[54] In attempts to convert a-federal people to federal land-use policy, Jefferson and his agents theoretically preferred a politics of example, or performance, to the overt violence of forced removal.[55] In "Carolina Parrot," the affecting spectacle of a bird in a cage serves explicitly as a mediator of contact, a softening agent of union, between Wilson and the Indians he encounters in the interior. The only species of parrot native to North America, Carolina Parrots (like the Ivory-Billed Woodpecker) are now extinct but, in the winter of 1810, Wilson observed huge flocks in Kentucky and Tennessee, and as far north as Marietta, Ohio, where even "in the month of February, along the banks of the Ohio, in a snow storm, [they were] flying about like pigeons, and in full cry."[56] Somewhere in Kentucky, Wilson manages to capture one of these birds. He names her Poll, and carries her with him for the remainder of his trip to New Orleans, even though, upon being "remitted to 'durance vile' . . . it paid me in kind for the wound I had inflicted and for depriving it of liberty, by cutting and almost disabling several of my fingers with its sharp and powerful bill."[57] Despite her aggression, Poll served as a useful traveling companion and a source of amusement until the end of Wilson's journey. With Poll's cage in hand, Wilson attracted numerous spectators as he traveled through Louisiana. The bird proved especially useful in Chickasaw and Chactaw country: "the Indians wherever I stopped to feed, collected around me, men, women, and children, laughing, and seemingly wonderfully amused with the novelty of my companion. Wherever I chanced to stop among these people, we soon became familiar with each other through the medium of Poll."[58] Curious, in turn, crowds of parrots also flocked "sympathetically" around Poll—"Numerous parties frequently alighted on the trees immediately above, keeping up a constant conversation with the prisoner."[59]

But, in the end, Wilson's anecdote of the parrot precisely replicates the violence of Peale's sealskin traders in Chile and Patagonia, who, while admiring nature's social virtues, kill hundreds of animals "before breakfast." One morning, Wilson reports, at the Big Bone Lick, near the mouth of the Kentucky River, a large flock of parrots came "screaming through the woods in the morning, about an hour after sunrise, to drink the salt water of which they . . . are remarkably fond. When they alighted on the ground, it appeared at a distance as if covered with a carpet of the richest green, orange, and yellow: they afterwards settled, in one body, on a neighboring tree which stood detached from any other, covering almost every twig of it, and the sun, shining strongly on their gay and glossy plumage produced a very beautiful and splendid appearance." Then, without explanation, Wilson begins to shoot:

> Having shot down a number, some of which were only wounded, the whole flock swept repeatedly around their prostrate companions, and again settled on a low tree, within twenty yards of the spot where I stood. At each successive discharge, though showers of them fell, yet the affection of the survivors seemed rather to increase; for after a few circuits around the place, they again alighted near me, looking down on their slaughtered companions with such manifest symptoms of sympathy and concern, as entirely disarmed me.[60]

As in Peale's reference to the "man with a short bludgeon," so here the absolute dissociation between aesthetic appreciation (of a colorful "carpet") and the act of slaughter (and between slaughter and the intervention of humanitarian sympathy) marks a place of breakdown in the Jeffersonian subject of *American Ornithology*. When Wilson shoots down showers of birds, only to be brought to heel by their affectionate "looks," his ornithological fantasy of cultivation cannot assimilate its own violence to its (adoption of a) cultivated tone. Throughout *American Ornithology* Wilson instructs his viewers and readers in a laissez-faire ethic of benevolence: look but don't touch; buy, read, or be visually absorbed, but don't shoot. At the same time, however, feathered death abounds. Wilson's pet Poll herself dies during the journey home to Philadelphia. Strangely gratuitous, this story also evades, without legitimating, *American Ornithology*. Upon reaching New Orleans, Wilson observes that his parrot has become "restless and inconsolable" after the death of a companion parrot that had been caged with her. In response, Wilson performs another experiment:

> I placed a looking glass beside the place where she usually sat, and the instant she perceived her image, all her former fondness seemed to return, so that she could scarcely absent herself from it for a moment. . . . It was evident that she was completely deceived. Always when evening drew on . . . she laid her head close to that of the image in the glass, and began to doze with great composure and satisfaction.[61]

Immediately after this experiment with the mirror (in which the parrot contentedly parrots a parrot), Poll plunges to her death. When Wilson boarded his ship in New Orleans for the ocean journey back to Philadelphia (there were no steamboats yet to ply the Mississippi upstream), he took Poll with him. Wilson was sleeping when Poll "wrought her way through the cage . . . flew overboard and perished in the Gulf of Mexico."[62] Like the slaughter of parrots at the Great Salt Lick, the anecdote of the Poll's plunge is gratuitous: after playing her part as a picturesque "character," she doesn't come home to roost, as do so many of Wilson's bird-men and bird-women; she ends, instead, in the wake of *American Ornithology*, a kind of illegible surplus, neither subject nor object in the mirror of production's reproduction. Wilson's experiment with the mirror might be chalked up to science, but Poll's little death cannot be absorbed by the ornithological project of cultivation—except where it foregrounds a representational framework that aims to let nothing escape its view.

The Producer *Célèbre*

Wilson's own ambition of emerging from obscurity as a celebrated literary character involved ventriloquizing and abandoning a remarkable series of literary celebrities who had preceded him in a transatlantic market. During his career, Wilson imitated, in succession, Robert Burns, Thomas ("Anacreon") Moore, and, finally, William Bartram. As a handloom weaver in Paisley, Scotland, in the 1780s and 90s, Wilson had begun his career by emulating the Scots dialect poetry of Burns. Like Burns, "the heaven-born ploughman of Ayreshire," Wilson hoped to appeal to a British literary market that advertised Scots dialect poetry—and poets—as the products of "native genius."[63] In 1786, the first 612 copies of Burns's *Poems, Chiefly in the Scottish Dialect* had been published in Kilmarnok; when the second edition was published in Edinburgh in 1787, there were ninety subscribers from Paisley, including Wilson, who subscribed for two copies.[64] Educated in the local schools of Paisley, Wilson then attempted, with great difficulty, to publish his own volume of dialect poetry. First printed in Paisley by James Neilson, Wilson's *Poems* of 1790 were republished with additions in Edinburgh in 1791, as *Poems, Humorous, Satirical and Serious.*[65]

Ten years later in the United States, however, it was not dialect poetry but travel literature that was helping to establish a literary market at the intersections of industry with empire. Wilson therefore made himself a literary traveler. He began, in 1804, by imitating Thomas Moore. Moore had visited Philadelphia and Niagara in 1803, describing both in verse.[66] Wilson, therefore, immediately made his own journey to Niagara, producing his own (much longer) travel poem,"The Foresters: A Pedestrian Journey to the Falls of Niagara in 1804." As Elizabeth McKinsey describes the literary history of Niagara, "Thomas Moore and Alexander Wilson inaugurated what would be a torrent of poetry about the Falls . . . soon there would be plays and tales . . . as well as countless magazine and occasional prose pieces that focused on the cataract."[67] After imitating Moore, Wilson turned to other forms of travel literature, emulating Alexander von Humboldt (who had visited Philadelphia in 1804), Lewis and Clark, and, of course, William Bartram, the celebrated literary traveler to the countries of the Creek, Chactaw, and Cherokee.[68] When Wilson was finally able to mount his own solitary western expedition in 1810, he did so in a self-consciously performative fashion, embarking from Pittsburgh, alone, in "a Batteau," which he self-consciously named the *Ornithologist.* Wilson claimed that the idea for sailing down the Ohio in 1810 had been suggested by the example of the Philadelphia typefounder Mr. Ronaldson, who in 1806 had traveled "with one companion in a small Batteau" to St. Louis, where they purchased "a quantity" of the lead needed for making type.[69]

In his earlier poem "The Foresters," however, Wilson and his companions had traveled to the falls in a skiff similarly dubbed the *Niagara.*[70] The boat inscribed the *Ornithologist* was part of Wilson's effort to emerge from obscurity as a literary "character," and it was precisely this performative side of Wilson's ornithological pose that would later appeal to Jean Jacques Audubon. In 1824, many years after Wilson's death, Audubon would quite literally follow in Wilson's footsteps, as his imitator and competitor. In 1823, Audubon was in search of literary celebrity when he made his own pilgrimage to Niagara Falls—after having visited Wilson's publishers, engraver, and editor in Philadelphia, where he was "coldly received." At Niagara, Audubon recalled Wilson's long employment by Bradford and Inskeep when, signing the register at his inn at the falls, he wrote after his name, "who, like Wilson, will ramble, but never like that great man die under the lash of a bookseller." Immediately after leaving Niagara for the Southwest, however, Audubon again emulated Wilson's performance of ornithological self-production by buying a skiff, or "batteau," in Pittsburgh to take him down the Ohio River.[71]

Despite the fact that Audubon imitated Wilson's way of negotiating an exhibitionary literary market, Audubon's *Birds of America* (London, 1827–38) has proved the more popularly known and reprinted work of the two. Audubon represented himself more successfully as an adventuring frontiersman of natural science: Audubon's birds have been viewed as a place where Romantic art meets natural science, where history painting meets book illustration, and even where artistic genius on a grand scale came into contact with (the supposedly mechanical truth of) particular details, elevating them, almost—but crucially, not quite—to the level of high art. Like Wilson, Audubon also wrote an ornithological text: his *Ornithological Biography* (Edinburgh: A. Black, 1831–39), a five-volume series of short sketches in which—as in Wilson's text—self-advertising merges fascinatingly with travel literature and anecdotes of natural history. The *Ornithological Biography* deserves more study than it has been given (least of all because it elaborates and complicates the myth of Audubon the Jacksonian frontiersman, the Crockett-like ornithologist in buckskin). But the text is little read or known in comparison with Audubon's famous prints, especially those in *Birds of America. Birds of America* is viewed primarily as visual art, as first and foremost a collection of beautiful pictures, produced in England for wealthy patrons on gigantic paper called "elephant folio" and then sold (separate from its ornithological/biographical text) in sets of five prints each. Overall, it has not been as a writer but as a great painter of birds (birds painted, moreover, in the grand style, by an artist who reportedly studied with the history painter David) that Audubon has come to represent "American ornithology," if not American natural history in general, in the minds of many North Americans; it is for Audubon, not Wilson, that the best-known ornithological society in America is named.

What this brief comparison should foreground is not that a hard-working Alexander Wilson has been treated unfairly by history in comparison to the more "flamboyant" Audubon, but that Wilson was, first of all (though not exclusively) a writer and, more particularly, a poet. In Wilson's *Ornithology*, the linguistic text is as crucial to, and as much a part of, the ornithological project as the engravings. Wilson learned to draw late in life, with help from William Bartram and Bartram's niece Anne; but from his youth he had aspired to literary celebrity. The *Ornithology* is a text written and illustrated by a man who saw himself as a "literary" traveler first, rather than as a visual artist or painter per se. It is in the tradition of Robert Burns and Thomas Moore (as well as Gilbert White, Thomas Bewick, and William Bartram), then, that his *Ornithology* should be read—and viewed.[72] Certainly, Wilson's drawings can be viewed or framed alone, but ultimately his *American Ornithology* must be considered as an illustrated *text*. Perhaps because they are so disjunctively combined, the visual and verbal forms of *American Ornithology* are not as easily separated as they have been in the case of Audubon's *Birds*—which is one reason that Wilson is less often studied, and reprinted, than Audubon.

Having begun his climb to authorship as a Scots dialect poet, Wilson includes his own English-language poems in the collection. Formally and stylistically, his *Ornithology* is, finally, a ragbag, resembling in its early-industrial architecture the birds' nests he describes: "formed of a little loose hay, feathers of a guinea fowl, some wool, hanks of thread, hog's bristles, skeins of silk, pieces of cast snake skins, and dog's hair . . . bits of rotten wood, fibres of dry stalks of weeds, pieces of paper, commonly newspapers . . . the whole tightly sewed through and through with long horse hairs, interwoven with the silk of caterpillars and the inside lined with fine dry grass."[73] Like this disjointed mix of manufactured and organic fragments, Wilson's *Ornithology* does not seamlessly ratify the natural history of American culture. His bird books are not the work of an artist who could successfully bury the mechanics of production in the rural pleasures of the husbandman. They fail to bridge the innumerable Jeffersonian passages they articulate—the passages between words and images, history and nature, domestic sentiment and territorial expansion, immigrant poet and American ornithologist. In fact, instead of a natural history of American culture, the gaps and ruptures of Wilson's ragbag collection force into view a cultural history of American nature[74]—a history articulated at the disjunctions rather than the union of visual with verbal representational forms, of home with work, of producers with their products.

CITIZEN BIRD

In 1890, Mabel Osgood Wright coauthored a four-hundred-page children's ornithology titled *Citizen Bird*. Wright was an early director of the Audubon Society and the author of *Bird-Craft*, one of the most popular field guides of the late nineteenth century. Like her fellow conservationists Anna Comstock and the novelist Gene Stratton-Porter, Wright opposed the killing of birds for feathers; she also helped to popularize bird-watching and educational techniques such as the schoolroom use of a brooding hen (or, today, eggs and incubators).[75] More explicitly than Wilson's *Ornithology*, Wright's *Citizen Bird* is a pedagogical fiction, employing seven "Characters," listed on the opening page in the manner of the traditional dramatis personae. The ornithological plot opens as a "Dr. Roy Hunter" accompanies four children into a field where, in a series of encounters between "the Bird People" and "the House People," he teaches humanitarian ethics and natural morality by recounting "bird stories" and eliciting the children's own observations. The fiction unfolds on two levels, as the bird stories are framed and paralleled by encounters between the children and their instructor. *Citizen Bird* inculcates an ethic of humanitarianism in which preservation harmonizes with laissez-faire economics; Dr. Hunter tells the children that if the naturally industrious Bird People are allowed to work unmolested (eating bugs and distributing seeds), both human and animal economies will prosper. As the doctor says of Citizen Bird:

> [W]e must learn to love and protect this feathered neighbor of ours, who works for his own living as well as ours, pays his rent and taxes, and gives, besides, free concerts to the public, daily. He certainly deserves the name of Citizen Bird. His patriotism, which is simply love of the country where he was born, leads him to return to it whenever he thinks of settling down in life and making a nest-home, no matter how far he may have wandered away at any other time; and this patriotism makes him one of the greatest travellers on the face of the earth.
>
> Every time you children deny yourselves the pleasure of taking an egg from a nest, or think to spread a little food for hungry birds, when cold and snow almost force them to starve, you are adding to the food-supply of your

country. To be sure, it may be only a few grains of wheat here and an ear of corn there, but it all means bread-food of some sort, and the bread of a nation is its life.[76]

Here, ecology meets political economy in the recreational labor of spreading birdseed in backyards and schoolyards. While the single type specimen of bird citizenship is clearly male, the visual and verbal pedagogy of bird-watching extends virtual bird citizenship to an audience of children and "females" who watch, read about, support, buy, and imagine Citizen Birds, at home, at school, abroad, or in the field. Materialized in birdhouses and Bird People, ornithology conjoins daily life with a national imaginary, nature's reproductive unit[77] ("the nest") with industrious productivity, and economic laissez-faire with the interventions of "private" charity ("to spread a little food for hungry birds")—all in an effort to naturalize and unify the divisions of labor in a world of citizen-workers. Ultimately, the exhibitionary site of the bird house replicates in miniature, or in the interior of one's own backyard, the exhibitionary and performative technologies of the national nest that "the first" *American Ornithology* brought into view.

In the preface to volume 5, Wilson imagined the final days of national expansion. As he describes it, the closure of the American nest—and the completion of *American Ornithology*—would coincide with the domestication of the entire North American continent:

> A time is approaching when obstacles to knowledge of birds will no longer exist, when the population of this immense western Republic will have diffused itself over every acre of ground fit for the comfortable habitation of man—when farms, villages, towns and glittering cities, thick as the stars in a winter evening, overspread the face of our beloved country, and every hill, valley and stream has its favorite name, its native flocks and rural inhabitants; then, not a warbler shall flit through our thickets but its name, its notes and habits will be familiar to all, repeated in their sayings and celebrated in their village songs. At that point if you think of me remember that when three-fourths of these birds were unknown . . . without patron, fortune or recompense, he brought the greater part of these from the obscurity of the ages.[78]

This passage summarizes the Jeffersonian aim of making nature human and historical in every detail. Like Jefferson (and Peale), Wilson saw the nation as "nest"—and identified that nest with the entire continent, if not with the entire world. As a Scots immigrant, former artisan, and impoverished worker, however, Wilson also identified his own social obscurity with the namelessness of unidentified bird "people," projecting a world in which—he hoped—nothing would finally be left obscure. Frozen and rather horrifying in its finality, Wilson's global village is quaintly homogeneous, even while his futuristic fantasy of "glittering cities" is incommensu-rate with "village sayings" and "village songs."[79]

Wilson's projection of a continental, if not global, village was, however, a direct extension of the sentimental Scots dialect tradition of his youth. The topics of village life, its songs, and its dialect were central to the "rural genius" of the Scots vernacular revival, a literary phenomenon that was itself to some degree an early-industrial pursuit of solacing cultural "sur-plus."[80] In 1802, Wilson was employed as a schoolteacher outside Philadel-phia when he wrote to fellow Scotsman Charles Orr that he had decided again "to attempt some Scots pastorals descriptive of the customs and rural manners of our native country, interspersed with scenes of humour, love, and tenderness." His harp "new strung" and his soul glowing with "ardor to emulate those immortal bards, who have gone before me," Wilson waxes rhapsodic:

> Thomson and Burns, Ramsay and Ferguson, with all who have yet followed them, have left a thousand themes unsung, equally interesting with the best of their descriptions, a thousand pictures of rustic felicity that will yet be pourtrayed by the striking pencil of some future genius. My heart swells, my soul rises to an elevation I cannot express, to think I may yet produce some of these glowing wilds of rural scenery—some new Paties, Rogers, Glauds, and Simons, that will rank with these favourites of my country when their author has mixed with his kindred clay. . . . I believe a Scotsman better fitted for descriptions of rural scenes than those of any other nation on earth. His country offers the most picturesque and striking scenery; his heart and imagination warm and animated, strong and rapid in its conceptions, its attachments, and even prejudices. . . . Where is the country that has ever equalled Scotland in the genuine effusions of the pastoral muse, or where so many tears of joy, sympathy, and admiration have been shed by the humblest peasants . . . ?[81]

Within six months after writing this letter, however, Wilson was studying drawing and natural history with William Bartram and had resolved to "make a collection of all our finest birds."[82] In the form of *American Orni-thology*, the rustic felicities of the Scots village and its "glowing wilds" were clearly transferred to the North American interior. But the crucial connec-tion here—between the "pastoral muse" of the Scots nationalist revival and the making of the Jeffersonian collection—is the forging of industrial empire in both Britain and the United States at the dynamic intersection of regional "affect" with international market expansion.

In the 1790s, in fact, Wilson had written a number of dialect poems that were not in the service of rustic felicity. These were, instead, a direct attack on the industrialization of textile manufacturing in Scotland. It was be-cause of these dialect poems that Wilson had been forced to emigrate in

1794. Many years later, in 1811, he was in Philadelphia, working on volume 3 of his *Ornithology* when his half-brother David arrived from Scotland, bringing with him copies of the political poems that Wilson had written in Paisley in the early 1790s. Wilson reportedly "threw them in the fire, unread, saying that if he had followed his worthy father's counsels they never should have seen the light."[83] In Jeffersonian North America, Wilson (like Peale) repeatedly claimed that he had "long quitted the turbulent field of politics" for "the arts of peace" ("calculated to improve the taste, to enlarge the understanding and better the heart, [books of natural history] are friends to the whole human race, are generally welcomed by people of all parties").[84] As the first American ornithologist, he came to represent his early participation in radical politics as an aberration: after 1801, apart from delivering a speech or two on behalf of presidential candidate Jefferson, he turned single-mindedly to his pursuit of literary celebrity.

Nevertheless, Wilson had participated fully in the Scots struggle against British industrial expansion in Paisley and in that struggle had been charged with sedition. His crime was the writing and circulating of a dialect poem inciting his fellow weavers to revolt against local mill owners. Wilson had been imprisoned once before in the previous year, for libeling a Paisley mill owner in a poem titled "The Hollander, or Light-Weight Detected." This poem satirized a Dutch silk manufacturer ("Willie") who cheated his Scottish weavers by scrutinizing their work for holes and weighing it for stolen thread:

> Attend a'ye, wha on the loom,
>   Survey the shuttle jinking,
> Whase purse has aft been sucket toom,
>   While Willie's scales war clinkin'. . .
>
>   . . . .
>
> See! cross his nose he lays the Spec's,
>   And owre the claith he glimmers
> Ilk wee bit triflin' fau't detects,
>   And cheeps, and doleful yaummers,
> "Dear man!—that wark 'ill never do;
>   See that: ye'll no tak' tellin';"
> Syne knavish chirts his fingers through,
>   And libels down a shilling
>   For holes that day.[85]

The black market in stolen thread was, in fact, an important industry for Paisley weavers: like manufactory workers in nearby Glasgow, weavers in Paisley had felt the brunt of social and economic changes introduced by foreign investment and the gradual mechanization of textile manufacturing at the end of the eighteenth century.[86] In the midst of the growing British reaction to the revolution in France, Wilson combined weaving, dialect poetry, and chronic poverty with radical politics—specifically, involvement in a Painite Jacobin organization called "The Friends of Liberty and Reform."[87] Jacobin organizations such as this in industrial west Scotland had begun to connect the ideals and events of the French Revolution with Scots artisan resistance to British industrial development, combining an artisan-based Scots nationalism with resistance to Britain's commercial and manufacturing expansion. It was not in the crafts and guilds of Edinburgh but in the mills and manufactories of Glasgow and Paisley that Wolfe Tone's Society of United Irishmen found counterpart Societies of United Scotsmen—united against a double "tyranny" of industry and empire.[88]

This was the larger occasion, then, of Wilson's emigration to Philadelphia. The poem that directly occasioned his flight was "The Shark, or Lang Mills Detected." "The Shark" described the fantasy beating of a Paisley mill owner ("Lang Willy Shark") and, by comparison with "The Hollander," was a more explicit incitement to violence:

> Whiles, in my sleep, methinks I see
>   Thee marching throught the city,
> And Hangman Jock, wi' girnan glee,
>   Proceeding to his duty.
> I see thy dismal phiz and back,
>   While Jock, his stroke to strengthen,
> Brings down his brows at every swack,
>   "I'll learn your frien' to lengthen,
>   Your mills the day."
>
> Poor wretch! in sic a dreadfu' hour
>   O' blude and dirt and hurry,
> What wad thy saftest luke or sour
>   Avail to stap their fury?
> Lang Mills, was rise around thy lugs
>   In mony a horrid volley;
> And thou be kicket to the dugs,
>   To think upo' thy folly
>   Ilk after day.[89]

In its failure to convert aggression into industrious consent, a dialect poem like "The Shark" did not lead to celebrity in the British literary market. For this reason, among others, Wilson was never successful at commodifying himself as a Scots bard. Not only his political poems, but also his published *Poems* were almost completely ignored by British reviewers and the subscribing public, not even attracting the kind of condescending praise that George Logan bestowed upon Burns of being "a natural but not Legitimate son of the muses."[90] Wilson nevertheless clearly recognized the manufactory requirement, so perfectly exemplified by Burns, that demanded a balanced—and carefully cultivated—mixture of legitimacy and illegitimacy. Edwin Muir describes Burns's poetry as a protean collection of voices, observing that any reader might find the Robert Burns he or she wished to find in his work: the many voices of his dialect poetry and the errant ("Shandean") style of his letters were politically and socially inclusive to the point of embracing revolutionary Jacobin and Whig politicians, the Jacobite radical and the universal "man of feeling," the licentious sexual "libertine" and the virtuous republican.[91] Burns succeeded in crisscrossing the borders of Scots/British literary culture, but when Wilson attempted to bridge the same borders of industry and empire (production and its circulation), he displayed contradiction more often than (protean) synthesis. As the pedlar-poet of Paisley, Wilson repeatedly aimed, but failed, to seduce.

On the one hand, Wilson recognized that a successful bard must display not only his wares but also himself as a desirable and curious commodity. Where Burns embraced the persona of the "Heaven-born ploughman," Wilson assumed the character of a pedlar, shouldering a pack of cloth and setting off across Scotland in search of customers as well as of adventures that could be made into more dialect poetry. The pedlar was a socially marginal figure but also a recognized literary and cultural type, a curious, even "impudent" character that, Wilson hoped, would prove both conventional and transgressive enough to float him in the British market.[92] Both the English-language preface to Wilson's *Poems* and many of the poems themselves are spoken, therefore, by the character of a pedlar-poet, wandering through rural Scotland. Instead of appealing to "sportsmen" and "professional gentlemen" (as he would in *American Ornithology*), Wilson's dialect *Poems* of 1790 addressed an imaginary collectivity of fellow weavers and pedlars: "Ye weaver blades! ye noble chiels!"; "O Ye, my poor sca't [scattered] brethren."[93] At the same time, however, the preface includes a copy of a handbill that, Wilson claims, he carried with him and distributed while peddling his textiles and his text. Titled "Advertisement Extraordinary," this English-language poem addresses a female audience as collective consumers of fashion.

> Fair ladies, I pray for one moment to stay,
> Until with submission, I tell you,
> What muslins so curious, for uses so various,
> A Poet has here brought to sell you.
>
> Here's handkerchiefs charming, book-muslin like ermine,
> Brocaded, strip'd, corded, and check'd;

Sweet Venus they say, on Cupid's birth-day,
In British-made muslins was deck'd.

. . . .

Now, ye Fair, if ye choose any piece to peruse,
With pleasure I'll instantly show it;
If the pedlar should fail to be favour'd with sale,
Then I hope you'll encourage the Poet.[94]

Crucially, the pedlar-poet's "Advertisement" is couched in English, the language of industry and empire, rather than in dialect. To reach and integrate both sides of a mixed or Scots/British audience, Wilson relies here—as Burns did—upon a "British-made" machinery of literary/textile production: "Sweet Venus they say. . . . In British-made muslins was deck'd. . . ." The market for British goods imagined by Wilson's "Advertisement" did not require that its poets actually *be* pedlars, threshers, or ploughmen—although they might have been. It simply demanded that they perform their relation to production, labor, and the soil. Where industry and empire came together, the market for British-made products demanded that a cultural worker produce, divide, and display himself as a fascinatingly mixed or marginal person—both the performer and distributor of origins, and originality—who had somehow managed to make the disjunction between labor and its representation, between his own locale and its mechanical reproduction, the (raised) center of "himself."

In *American Ornithology*, it is the Mocking Bird who is defined by this distinction between originality and its reproduction, legitimacy and illegitimacy, elevated versus debased genres. Wilson's Mocking Bird represents the project of *American Ornithology* itself, insofar as he is the bird who can represent all other birds: "he can adopt the songs of any and all birds," Wilson writes, and "would even bark like a dog":

His elevated imitations of the brown thrush are frequently interrupted by the crowing of the cocks; and the warblings of the Blue Bird, which he exquisitely manages, are mingled with the screaming of swallows or the cackling of hens; amidst the simple melody of the Robin, we are suddenly surprised by the shrill reiterations of the Whip-poor-will; while the notes of the Killdeer, Blue Jay, Martin, Baltimore and twenty others, succeed, with such imposing reality, that we look round for the originals, and discover, with astonishment, that the sole performer in this singular concert is the admirable bird now before us.[95]

Some naturalists believe that this mixture "injures" the quality of his song. Wilson points out that the Mocking Bird possesses "native notes of his own," though these are "generally interspersed with imitations." But in fact what is most remarkable about the Mocker's song, what makes it "rise preeminent over every competition," is its combination of original and imitated notes, in a mixture "varied seemingly beyond all limits."[96] The Swedish traveler Peter Kalm believed that the song of the Mocking Bird surpassed the European Nightingale, except that "from the attention which the mocker pays to any other sort of disagreeable noise, these capital notes would be always debased by a bad mixture."[97] On the contrary, Wilson argues, "the introduction of extraneous sounds, and unexpected imitations . . . give a perpetual novelty to his strain": "In short, if we believe in the truth of that mathematical axiom, that the whole is greater than a part, all that is excellent or delightful, amusing or striking, in the music of birds, must belong to that admirable songster whose vocal powers are equal to the whole compass of their whole strains."[98] In this passage, the Mocking Bird epitomizes the federalizing strategy of *American Ornithology* wherever linguistic, ethnic, and economic differences are reproduced, displayed, and consumed as novelties. In instances when song or sound is imported into the ornithological text, the tension between local or regional vernaculars and a collective national character corresponds with the distinction between dialect and English—the national language, or genuine "note," which circulated in print.[99] The bird languages transcribed in *American Ornithology* distantly resemble not only lines of dialect but also the phonetic transcriptions of Indian-language words. Transcribed bird dialects also recall lines of poetry, with meters and accents marked. For example, the song of the Red-Winged Starling is "conk-quer-ree"; of the Maryland Yellow Throat, "whìtititee, whìtititee"; of the Yellow-Throated Flycatcher, "preeò preeà; of the Redstart, "weése, weése, weése"; and, of the Wood Peewit Flycatcher, "peto wāy, peto wāy, pee way."[100] In addition, natural bird languages are imported into the texts in exactly the same way in which human and native dialect is introduced. For example, Wilson reports that "the [Algonquian] natives of Hudson's Bay" call the Gold-Winged Woodpecker "Ou-thee-quan-nor-ow," from the golden color of the shafts and lower side of the wings. In some cases, *American Ornithology* gives English-language dialect variations on the official identification: local, as opposed to national or "American," communities call the Gold-Winged Woodpecker by a variety of names, some of which are onomatopoetic variations on the species' own dialect: "The Gold-Winged Woodpecker," Wilson reports, "has numerous provincial appellations in the different States of the Union, such as 'Hittock,' 'Yucker,' 'Piut,' 'Flicker,' by which last it is usually known in Pennsylvania." These varieties, Wilson writes, "have probably originated from a fancied resemblance of the bird's notes to the sound of the words . . . which, by the help of the hearer's imagination, may easily be made to resemble any or all of them."[101] As an exhibition of transcribed sounds—epitomized by the Mocking Bird—the all-incorporative structure of *American Ornithology* lies in its trompe l'oeil capacity for representing (without assimilating) the whole songs of whole tribes. But, as an extension of the Linnaean fantasy of actual, or transparent, representation, in *American Ornithology* the representational strategies of domestic expansion do not hold, and the Jeffersonian nest is far from seamless.

Wilson concludes his account of the Mocking Bird by describing attempts in Philadelphia and elsewhere to domesticate the species. Mr. Klein of North Seventh Street, for example, tried to raise a family of mockingbirds in the upper floor of his house. Near a wire-grated window, he planted a cedar bush in a box, and scattered materials "suitable for building." There he placed "a male and female Mocking Bird," and they began to build: "The female laid five eggs, all of which she hatched, and fed the young with great affection until they were nearly able to fly." Mr. Klein's Mocking Bird experiment recalls the principle of transparency that structured Peale's museum of art and nature, wherein the interior space of the world in miniature was "fully and faithfully" identified with the natural world outside its walls. (As a museumizing project, the Mocking Bird's room also recalls the rooms in Huttig's house encountered by John Quincy Adams during his tour of Silesia and described for the *Port Folio*.) Mocking Bird–like, the Jeffersonian museum held out the possibility of an identity between words and things on the grounds of labor performed and disseminated. In the case of Mr. Klein's Mocking Birds, however, when "the proprieter" was away on business, his birds were neglected ("by his domestics") and, after two weeks, the young ones perished. Wilson asserts, nevertheless, that, in a quiet interior, fitted up "with various kinds of shrubbery," a mockingbird can be domesticated and "by proper management, may be made sufficiently tame to sing." The bird will lose "little of its power and energy by confinement," Wilson declares, and will ventriloquize, by turn, "the mewing of the cat, the creaking of a passing wheelbarrow . . . the quiverings of the Canary, . . . or the tune taught him by his master."[102]

The history of United States expansion into the continental interior is often still understood developmentally, as a progressive sequence in which the initial appropriation of western territories and settlement by scouts and traders leads (naturally) to the general emigration of families, the establishment of towns, and "domestication." According to this narrative, the continental interior was first penetrated by "white savages" (Natty Bumpo, Daniel Boone, Davy Crockett), who fought, traded, and often intermarried with Native Americans, only to be followed by families of homesteaders and finally by the institutions and artifacts of the national culture of the United States: towns, laws, churches, commerce, and consumer goods.[103] What Wilson's *Ornithology* makes clear is that these processes were, in fact, never narratively or temporally sequential. Nor (despite attempts to represent it otherwise) did they ever celebrate masculine productivity apart from a domestic ideology that also made women and children, as well as plants and animals, the subjects and objects of natural history. Federalist-era expansion was always inseparable from the circulation of American manufactures: from shoes, clothing, hats, and guns to the illustrated books, magazines, pictures—and the celebrated authors—of early industrial culture. These American subjects and objects constituted a "New World" of representative consumers as well as producers, projecting a furnished interior of texts and textiles, fabrics and frames, via multiple structures of representation that, on the grounds of "fidelity," tried to marry words to images, and to things.

The failures of *American Ornithology* to "fly"—its unwieldiness and its inability, in the end, to "raise" its maker into the light of fame he craved—are summarized by an anecdote from one of Wilson's travel letters from Kentucky. In 1810 Wilson went bird hunting at the Big Bone Lick, where an "enormous congregation" of mammoth skeletons were known to be sunk or buried beneath the mud. Having propelled his "batteau" into the Big Bone Creek, Wilson "amuses" himself for a time "shooting ducks and paroquets" at "that great antediluvian rendezvous of the American elephants." While pursuing a bird across the Lick, Wilson feels himself beginning to sink: "In pursuing a wounded duck across this quagmire, I had nearly deposited my carcass among the grand congregation of mammoths below, having sunk up to the middle, and had a hard struggling to get out."[104] This anecdote summarizes the kind of border-life Wilson led as an immigrant poet in pursuit of literary independence. It also encodes the ambivalent, ultimately tenuous position Wilson sustained on the expanding ground of the federal state he served. Caught curiously between union and specificity, between resistance to and deployment of the representational practices that produced him together with his collection, Wilson is caught, so to speak, between the mammoth and the bird. Contrary to the situation of Peale, who was similarly positioned between mammoth and birds (the one and the many) in *The Artist in His Museum* (fig. 7), Wilson finds the ground (of self-assembly) giving way beneath his feet. As an objectified and buoyant "work," manufactured by a market that assembled, displayed, and sent him forth as an exemplary producer, this American manufacturer feels himself drawn into a swampy burial ground of "grand" (republican and federalist) carcasses—the remains of the great works and workers that have gone before him.

CHAPTER SIX

Picture-Nation: *Pat Lyon at the Forge,* 1798–1829

I**N THE** fall of 1798, Patrick Lyon spent three months in the Philadelphia jail without trial, accused of robbing the Bank of Pennsylvania, whose doors and locks he had installed. Lyon was a Philadelphia locksmith, a recent Scots immigrant, and a solitary man, whose wife and child had recently died of yellow fever. Unlike fellow Scotsman Alexander Wilson, Lyon had never openly participated in the radical Painite politics of the 1790s; when he was imprisoned in the Walnut Street Gaol, however, he carried with him a Bible and a copy of "Robert Burns's Scotch *Poems.*"[1] Lyon prided himself on what he termed the "natural character" of his rank; like Burns, the poetical "ploughman of Ayrshire," the locksmith of Philadelphia believed that the workingmen of the world came closer to the social and moral truth of things. Farmers and mechanics, Lyon believed, had access to the moral and economic virtue masked by the countless false aristocrats—bankers, lawyers, priests, mill owners—of the New World as well as the Old. And a plain-speaking mechanical artist could see even more deeply into the mechanical structure of nature's truth: like the steamboat inventor John Fitch, Lyon had a literal-minded faith in what Fitch termed "the laws of God in Mechanism."

Lyon was not only a proud mechanic, however; he was also a writer, although the only book he ever produced, it seems, was a pamphlet published in 1799 titled *The Narrative of Patrick Lyon[,] who suffered three months severe imprisonment in Philadelphia gaol; on merely a vague suspicion, of being concerned in the Robbery of the Bank of Pennsylvania* (Philadelphia: Robert & Francis Bailey, 1799). In keeping with his (virtually Linnaean) faith in the possibility of actual representation, Lyon confidently believed that his pamphlet would serve as a kind of key, freeing him from all false representations. The honest locksmith would ultimately bring into view—and into being—the true order of things, and only bankers, forgers of counterfeit money, and other such "paper aristocrats" would see it otherwise.

Some twenty-five years after his arrest for bank robbery, Lyon also became the subject of a famous portrait: *Pat Lyon at the Forge* (1826, 1829) (fig. 12). In 1825 John Quincy Adams was president of the United States, and Lyon was an old—and now wealthy—man when he commissioned his portrait from an ambitious young painter named John Neagle. Neagle's

Figure 12. John Neagle, *Pat Lyon at the Forge* (1829).
(Courtesy of the Pennsylvania Academy of the Fine Arts.)

portrait of Lyon remains among the most often reproduced early American paintings, and in the late 1820s it helped to make Neagle's fortune.[2]
Frequently reproduced but less often analyzed, *Pat Lyon at the Forge* is typically viewed as a straightforward celebration of the American workingman,
a populist portrait of Jacksonian democracy in the figure of a forger and
founder, in whose fiery—yet pragmatic and empirical—craft the mechanical arts are linked with the literary and visual ones in an emerging national
culture. But in fact its iconic fusion of the federalist-era artisan with the
Jacksonian workingman, and the federal mechanic with the Romantic visual artist, is far from neat or successful. Upon scrutiny, the junctures of

words and things, "narrative" and image, are full of puzzling gaps, ironies, and unintended revelations.

Both the original 1826 and the slightly altered 1829 versions of Neagle's portrait are deeply engaged with the events of the 1790s. As William Dunlap put it in his description of the portrait in 1834: "[I]n the background at a distance, is seen the Philadelphia prison, and thereby 'hangs a tale.'"[3] Indeed, in both copies of the painting, it is the roof, cupola, and weather vane in the window of the painting's background that articulate the complex connection between the hardworking mechanic of 1798 and the successful, legally vindicated Patrick Lyon of 1825. The weather vane and cupola belong to the roof of the Walnut Street Gaol, a landmark in the city and a tourist attraction, as demonstrated by its inclusion in William R. Birch's collection of engravings *Philadelphia in 1800*. Located directly across the street from the garden behind Independence Hall (the Pennsylvania State House), the jail was easily identified by its emblematic weather vane: two keys crossed.[4] In Lyon's case this weather vane is also an ironic emblem. Lyon had been working in Philadelphia only five years when the Bank of Pennsylvania accused him of having forged duplicate keys that had allowed him to steal more than $160,000 in bank notes and Spanish gold from the bank's vault. When Lyon commissioned Neagle to paint his portrait some twenty-five years later, however, he was no longer a working blacksmith but a mechanical engineer, a reputable manufacturer of fire engines, and a man of considerable property in Philadelphia. Nevertheless, he asked Neagle to represent him as he would have appeared in 1798, in the costume of what Lyon considered to be his essential or true character: an honest, straight-talking blacksmith rather than a wealthy or false "gentleman." "I wish you to understand," Lyon reportedly told Neagle, "that I do not desire to be represented in the picture as a gentleman—to which character I have no pretension. I want you to paint me at work at my anvil, with my sleeves rolled up and a leather apron on."[5] In Neagle's portrait, then, the fifty-seven-year-old machinist poses at his anvil with a single apprentice, as he had worked more than a quarter of a century before.

However, the gaps between the two Patrick Lyons—between the blacksmith and locksmith of 1798 and the hydraulic engineer of 1825, and between the blacksmith's genuine versus his artful, or artfully constructed, character—remain far from resolved by the painting. Most commentators on *Pat Lyon at the Forge* have noted several anachronisms: Lyon wears a clean white shirt and silver shoe buckles that seem out of place in the smithy, while his relaxed pose, hammer resting on the anvil, bespeaks the nonchalance of "privilege" and "freedom from manual tasks." The "anti-gentleman" is, vaguely, a gentleman; the workman is at rest.[6] But what is most disruptive of easy faith in the smith's character is the prison in the background, the narrative to which it refers, and the activity of reading that it demands. Neagle's portrait is obviously engaged with the story of Pat Lyon's unjust imprisonment and eventual vindication, a story told and retold in Philadelphia, in legal transcripts, in newspaper reports, and in Pat Lyon's own *Narrative* of 1799. Eventually, with the help of Philadelphia's most skillful lawyers, Lyon would win a countersuit against the Bank of Pennsylvania for malicious prosecution and false imprisonment. His case was something of a landmark in American legal history, resulting in precedent-setting revisions of the common law on the questions of malice and probable cause.[7] Finally vindicated in 1805, Lyon went on to success as owner of an engine manufactory and designer of the most powerful and efficient fire engine of its time, called "the Diligent."[8] Retold many times, the story of the innocent locksmith of Philadelphia became something of a local legend; it was performed as a play by James Rees in the 1840s and republished as late as 1854 in the form of a children's book titled *The Locksmith of Philadelphia*.[9]

Clearly, then, the jail in the background of *Pat Lyon at the Forge* references "the good old bad days" of the late 1790s, which—via the figure of the apprentice at the bellows—are funneled allegorically into the workshop of the present. William Dunlap classified *Pat Lyon at the Forge* as an "historical portrait" on account of the view of the jail behind Lyon and the relationship between past and present, suffering and success, that it implies.[10] Fanning his master's fire, the apprentice behind the smith allegorizes the way the sufferings of the 1790s inspire the present: in the figure of Pat Lyon, the portrait argues, the emerging class division, social conflict, and political struggles of the 1790s (epitomized, among other things, by the Alien and Sedition Act of 1798) are summarized, contained, and overcome in this Vulcan of industry, this mechanic of 1825. On the other hand, the juncture between past and present represented by *Pat Lyon* is actually far more troubled than it seems, precisely because the past is represented by a prison. If the Walnut Street Gaol of the federal period figures a past that has been survived—like some unenlightened American Bastille—by the industry and honesty of the man in the foreground, then that prison is not only overcome but also restored, or resurrected, in the industrious workshop of the present. The artisan-made-good too, therefore, is a much more ambiguous figure of founding when he is viewed as the forger or framer of the locks and walls of a prison as well as of mansions, vaults, and security boxes.

The historical transformation of artisans into workers implied by the disjunction between Lyon the engine manufacturer and Lyon the artisan, and by the relationship of the prison to the workshop, disrupts the portrait's message of continuity and union through industry. Far from celebrating the social solidarity or class consciousness of urban artisans (or of artist with artisan), *Pat Lyon at the Forge* in fact figures the civic solidarity of a managerial and professional elite of engineers, bankers, lawyers, and manufacturers against labor. Neagle's portrait registers the successful emergence of a middle-class cohort of forgers and founders—the steam-boat, turnpike, and railroad entrepreneurs—of early American industrial development. And, ultimately, the painting figures the success of the pyra-midal representational structure of American manufacturing that had been in the making since the Grand Federal Procession of 1788.

Certainly, merchants and manufacturers in Philadelphia had always identified themselves as workingmen or (like Benjamin Franklin) as arti-sans-made-good who had learned the craft secrets of labor's constitution and containment through (the frames and fabric of) republican represen-tation. Neagle himself was a professional painter who made his career painting the portraits of Philadelphia lawyers, ministers, and statesmen—not blacksmiths. Although *Pat Lyon* is one of Neagle's most popular and famous portraits, it remains relatively anomalous among his other por-traits of the 1820s, 30s, and 40s, precisely because it seems to take as its subject a member of the mechanic class rather than an urban professional or political leader. When *Pat Lyon* first hung in the art academies of New York and Philadelphia, it was characterized by at least one reviewer as "looking delightfully cheek by jowl" with the portraits of professional gen-tlemen hung around it.[11]

By 1825, the constitution of national collectivity celebrated in 1788 as a union among "federal mechanics" had come, quite clearly, to mean the civic solidarity of an industrial leadership of engineers, bankers, manufac-turers, and learned professionals (including literary and visual artists) over and against a growing class of unskilled laborers and working poor. Neagle's *Pat Lyon* is an icon of this consolidation of an urban manufactur-ing elite. But because that consolidation was inseparable from the transfor-mation of artisans into wage laborers between 1783 and 1830, that history as well is recapitulated by *Pat Lyon*. The gaps and contradictions in Neagle's portrait between the Lyon of 1798 and the Lyon of 1825 articu-late the uneven, multilevel transformation of artisans into workers be-tween 1788 and 1825—a transformation that by 1825 was well beyond the capacity of any single artist (or mechanic) to represent in the seamless form of unity, or continuity.

Pat Lyon had attained the rank of master smith in Edinburgh, after fourteen years as an apprentice and journeyman. He then emigrated to Philadelphia in 1793, at the age of twenty-five: "When I arrived in America," Lyon wrote in his *Narrative* of 1799, "little did I think that I was to become an author; and as little did I think that ingenious men were ever liable to suffer . . . prejudice, malice and injustice."[12] In eighteenth-century fashion, Lyon classified himself by "station" or "rank" rather than "class," comparing the mechanic virtue and fixity of his character to the confusing doubleness of the so-called gentlemen around him, from the gentlemanly forgers imprisoned with him at the Walnut Street Gaol to the bank directors and magistrats who tried him for bank robbery: "[I]t has been my chief study," he declares, "to fulfill the station which I believe nature intended me for."[13] Despite assertions of fixed and natural rank, however, Lyon's social station was far from clear or self-identical, even in 1799. Certainly, in the United States the process of industrialization took rather different paths than in Britain. Compared with the more rapid development of factory towns in England and Scotland at the end of the eighteenth century, industrial capitalism in North America proceeded along a network of disjunct, but intersecting, routes: the "diffusion of knowledge," technological experimentation, the engineering of public works, and the gradual implementation of manufactory production. It was also encouraged, as historian Thomas Cochran has argued, by increased "liquidity," the creation of innovative and flexible financial institutions, such as banks, insurance companies, and stock and bill exchanges, in the Delaware Valley.[14] However, as the Grand Federal Procession demonstrated, early American manufacturers were equally fascinated by and invested in new technology: in the United States, as well as in Britain, new modes of production were simultaneously attributed to and extracted from the person and knowledge of the artisan.

Pat Lyon, himself, for example, was not only a blacksmith; he was also an innovative metalworker—at once blacksmith, whitesmith, locksmith, engineer, and inventor. After emigrating to the United States in 1793, he would introduce more than ten new kinds of iron manufacturing to Philadelphia.[15] By his own account, he possessed "[a] shop full of tools, that I do not believe there is such in America; I am certain there is not such a collection in Philadelphia."[16] He also instructed his apprentice Jamie McGinley in "the useful problems of Euclid's Elements," until, through education in the principles of geometry, Jamie "began to see into the stupidity of the old mode of working which gave him an enthusiastic spirit of enquiry."[17] And, when the Bank of Pennsylvania brought its iron doors to his shop in a cart, Lyon was busy devising a hydraulic engine for a merchant named Cramond.[18]

As a skilled mechanic and a literate inventor, therefore, an aura of mingled awe and suspicion surrounded Lyon, resembling that which (as Julia Wrigley argues) structured contemporary expressions of ambivalence toward skilled craftsmen in early industrial Britain.[19] Consider, for example, Charles Buck's anecdote of an encounter with Lyon in Philadelphia in 1806. Buck wanted Lyon to open a chest to which Buck had lost the key. Lyon reportedly told Buck that he could open the lock, but the chest must be brought to his shop, with which I had to comply, and to my astonishment, what no one else could undertake was performed in a few minutes. He bored a small hole, gave a slight touch, and the lock sprang open. It was an old-fashioned German lock with 6 or 8 bolts to spring up and down, right and left, and proved to me that to a skillful hand, no lock of any kind can be of much security.[20]

In this instance, Lyon is both an ingenious mechanic and a threat to property and its "security." Furthermore, Lyon forces compliance from Buck by demanding that the chest be brought to the shop, a detail that suggests that what was equally outrageous about Lyon was the way he worked. As an independent smith of considerable skill, Lyon was able to rest or work, labor or read, as he wished; he could stop to buy peaches at the docks, tinker with hydraulic engines, or leave Philadelphia at will. Lyon was not only an ingenious "old countryman"; he was also slow and independent. His work habits were out of the control of his employers, and this forced them to feel their dependence upon him. In his itinerance and independence, which were connected to the privileges of leisure and literacy, the Patrick Lyon of 1798 (like the steamboat inventor John Fitch, ten years earlier) already articulated the lines of a shifting social hierarchy where class difference was slowly and often painfully emerging.

It was precisely his independence and the ambivalence inspired by his skills that made Lyon a suspect in a crime he did not commit. The officers of the Bank of Pennsylvania stated that they were first convinced that Lyon had robbed the vault because he had taken such a long time refitting their doors and locks. On 11 August 1798, the bank was in the midst of moving from Philadelphia's Masonic Hall to Carpenters' Hall (next to the State House) when the doors were hauled to Lyon's shop for refitting. They remained at his smithy for almost three days.[21] According to trial transcripts, the bank's emissary, a man named Robinson, "went several times to Lyon's shop to get the work expedited but contrary to their wishes the doors was detained all Friday and not put up till Saturday Afternoon."[22] On one occasion, when Robinson came to hurry him along, Lyon reportedly replied, "[D]amn your work[,] take it away."[23] When the doors were done, the bank was forced to hire another smith to help with installing them, because Lyon had worked so slowly. When Lyon later asked, "why not suspect the other smith: They answered me he did his work in half the time."[24]

As late as 1829, William Dunlap would recount another anecdote of Lyon that linked his mechanical skills with the control he exerted over his time and wages:

Being sent for to open an iron chest made by himself, lock and all, whose owner had lost the key, Pat dexterously performed the operation, and hold-

ing the lid with one hand, presented the other, with a demand for ten dollars. It was refused. Pat let fall the lid, the spring lock took its former hold,
and the blacksmith walked off, leaving the treasure as fast sealed as before.
There was not remedy, and reluctantly the owner of the strong box, again
sent for Pat. He promptly appeared, and the box was as quickly opened. The
first demand of ten dollars was instantly offered; but no, 'I must have twenty
now,' says the operator: and twenty was paid without demur, for the lid and
the lock were still in the iron grasp of the maker.[25]

Anecdotes such as this demonstrate that Lyon was an ambiguous figure,
viewed with ambivalence because he was both a mere mechanic and a
"man of science," a "rough smith" and a literate immigrant who fashioned
hydraulic engines and was conversant with Euclid. The word "ingenuity,"
which was used repeatedly to describe Lyon during his trials, neatly focuses
the social tensions he evoked as a mirror of the American manufactory.
Suggesting (without meaning) "genius," the word "ingenuity" denotes the
emerging, or manufactory, intersection of print literacy and mechanical
inventiveness, by implicitly identifying writing with the machinery of industrial production. This identification of texts with ingenious mechanical
devices was made in and between multiple media. As a quality associated
with Benjamin Franklin, as well as with Pat Lyon, "ingenuity" was a door
through which a mechanical artist entered the collective rhetorical projec-
t(ion) of the federal state—a door that was opening at the nation-making
juncture of word with image, language with graphic design.

    In Lyon's trial of 1805, "ingenuity" unmistakably implied the particular
danger presented by an innovative metalworker who fashioned and fixed
not only commodities but language as well on the pattern and "principles"
of craft production. In fact, it was the "straightness," the mechanical logic,
of Lyon's alibi that further implicated him in the robbery of the Bank of
Pennsylvania. Even as late as the twentieth century, Lyon's mechanical
logic is the most memorable aspect of "the greatest robbery in early Philadelphia history": "Lyon was put on trial and the Mayor [Wharton] in testi-
fying said that 'Mr. Lyon gave a history of where he had been, but he told
such a straight and well-connected story that I was sure he was guilty!' "[26]
From the moment of his arrest, Lyon was able to provide overwhelming
(and overwhelmingly detailed) evidence that he had been in Lewistown,
Delaware, at the time of the robbery, accompanied by his nineteen-year-
old apprentice, who died of yellow fever during the trip. Lyon and Jamie
had left Philadelphia in flight from the yellow fever, but while sailing for
Delaware on the Broadkill Creek in an old scallop, Jamie became ill ("stag-
gering . . . like a man in a state of intoxication . . . his head was like a ship's
mast having lost all her braces").[27] A few days later, Jamie died at an inn
near Lewistown. Lyon buried his apprentice and moved on to do various

odd jobs in the area, involving himself briefly off the coast on board a British ship, helping to fashion and launch a "diving bell" for use in raising wrecks.[28] After three weeks (from 28 August to 21 September) spent at a distance of 150 miles from Philadelphia, Lyon learned from a friend that he was suspected in the robbery of the Bank of Pennsylvania and returned at once to Philadelphia. It was the detailed particularity and precision of the narrative of his journey to and from Lewistown that worked against him as proof of ingenuity: "[A]fter all my trouble in relating every point, which I thought would have so operated, as to cause my discharge—I found myself disappointed."[29]

In the course of his initial trial, the bank's own lawyer William Rawle admitted, "[H]e was at Lewistown the time the robbery was committed . . . and the account of his travail throughout we are in possession of which is allowed to be true and just, but still he is an ingenious man."[30] In tracing Lyon's guilt to his ingenuity, not only the bank, but Lyon himself, assumed a powerful correspondence between a craftsman's use of language and the forged or tinkered objects of his craft. For example, Lyon asked the bank to declare it publicly "if the language they have made use of respecting me is not of their manufacture."[31] The blacksmith even praised his prosecutor, Rawle, declaring, "I dearly love to see a good and ingenious workman in any profession."[32] And when Lyon's own lawyers initially failed to free him, he complained that had they handled the evidence "in a true workman like manner, [it] might have completely operated for my discharge."[33]

It was at the country estate of city magistrate and bank director John C. Stocker that Lyon first delivered his alibi, when he arrived there on 21 September 1798 after walking all the way from Lewistown. Exhausted and pale, he recounted his journey to and from Delaware, while Stocker and others "took down in writing all my travels from the time that I left Philadelphia."[34] (Later, Lyon's lawyers would point out that this initial hearing resulted in a mere half-page of writing, so convinced was Stocker that Lyon was guilty.)[35] Lyon himself turned to writing soon after his arrest, in the conviction that it was the only device that might effectively "operate for [his] discharge." Composed in the Walnut Street Gaol, Lyon's *Narrative* and its circulation were so critical to the locksmith's hope for freedom that he became deeply identified with them as the key to vindication, refusing to leave the prison without his "writings."[36]

Lyon would not be legally vindicated until 1805, six years later, when his lawyers argued that it had been the negligence of the bank's cashier, Jonathan Smith, that put the vault keys into the hands of the bank's porter, a man named Cunningham. The bank's obsession with Lyon was a "screen," they argued, distracting the gaze of the public from the true criminals. In fact, the robbery had been committed "from the inside," by the bank's own guard and his accomplice, "one Isaac Davis," a "bank lounger" and the "amiable" son of a local judge.[37] Porter Cunningham—who would himself be dead of yellow fever five days after the robbery—had slept that night inside the bank. When he was awakened on the morning after the robbery, Cunningham "tore his hair" and "appeared mad or insane."[38] In fact, he had simply admitted Davis during the night and then used the bank's own keys to open the cash vault. "[M]ust a man's life and liberty be sported with," Lyon's lawyers demanded, "because he tells a straight story?" The bank had maliciously pursued Lyon, they argued, solely from a desire "to screen" themselves "from the [charge] of gross negligence of duty, which furnished the porter and his friend Davis with the opportunity of committing the robbery."[39]

Remarkably, while Lyon was imprisoned for three months, alone in a jail storeroom with little food or water, Isaac Davis was allowed to go free, after he had handed over the state's money and delivered a full confession. Even after Davis confessed, the bank kept Lyon in prison for a full month, accusing him of having abetted Davis and Cunningham by forging the keys that, they claimed, were necessary to open the bank's vault. Rather than implicate themselves, the bank's cashier and directors had instead looked resolutely "outside," incriminating not only Lyon but two watchmen patrolling in the street that night with their dogs. His lawyers declared: "[Porter] Cunningham was not examined at all! . . . yet it was evident the robbery was committed from the inside, and he alone lodged inside. —[Even] [t]he watchmen were suspected who were on the outside. —What, a shameful and base mode of selecting victims!" The bank's directors and cashier "saw what was done, they heard what was said, but they neither heard nor saw what was evidently upon the surface, the magic jingle of false keys and Patrick Lyon operate even at this day . . . !"[40]

The defense argued, further, that the locksmith was selected as a "false key" because he too was an outsider, not only an ingenious mechanic but a recent British immigrant or, as Lyon put it, "an old countryman likewise."[41] Lyon had left London in 1793, a year of increasingly intense political repression in Britain, when large numbers of Scots, Irish, and English republicans were emigrating to the United States. This group included such "Friends of Liberty and Reform" as Thomas Callender, William Duane, Thomas Cooper, Denis Drisol, Matthew Lyon, and John Daly Burke. Virtually all these men had been imprisoned or had fled sentencing in Europe, and many were Irish.[42] The Alien and Sedition Act of 1798 would be aimed at precisely this group of highly literate and politically engaged immigrants, many of them experienced journalists sympathetic to France and hostile to John Adams's administration.

Ultimately, however, the interlocking tensions articulated by Lyon's story—between insider and outsider, immigrant locksmith and legitimate gentleman, rhetorical performances and empirical proof—should focus our attention not only on the "malice" of the bank directors but upon the making of a newly federalized viewing public. This public found itself reconstituted in spectatorship by the "jingle" of dynamic binaries that rang in the federalist order of things: of false versus true keys, corruption versus production, the rhetorical versus the real, foreigners versus true Americans. When, in July of 1805, a verdict was finally delivered in favor of Lyon for twelve thousand dollars in damages, the court reporter Thomas Lloyd noted the crowd's response: "an universal clamor of exultation took place among the audience, the most numerous the reporter remembers ever to have assembled in that court room. Justice Yates ordered silence, and told the citizens applauding, that they were not in a play house, but in a court of justice."[43]

The enthusiasm over Lyon's vindication in 1805 can be explained in part by the fact that, for Philadelphia's Jeffersonian-Republicans who had survived both recurrent yellow fever epidemics and the politics of the 1790s (and lived to see Thomas Jefferson elected president in 1801), Lyon epitomized their collective suffering and ultimate vindication. The 1790s had witnessed vociferous political divisions and striking instability in some of the key iconographic structures of the federal state. Between 1794 and 1796, George Washington himself was pilloried in the American press as a common thief, while France, the colonies' former ally, was represented in the Federalist-party press as an enemy or, at best, a dangerous friend. In 1794, Tom Paine was arrested in Paris by the Jacobins and held for ten months in the Luxembourg prison, while President Washington did nothing to obtain the release of the author of *Common Sense*.[44] In 1796, Paine infamously accused Washington himself of treason and imposture: "As to you, sir, treacherous in private friendship, and a hypocrite in public life; the world would be puzzled to decide, whether you are an apostate or an imposter; whether you have abandoned good principles, or whether you ever had any."[45]

Among the most charged political issues in the struggles between Federalist and Jeffersonian partisans was the institution of a commercial banking system and the distinction between "specie" versus printed or paper money. Not only did the financial speculation of urban banks and stock exchanges revolve around this distinction, but party differences were constellated by it, whenever the distinction between specie versus paper overlapped with dichotomies such as authentic versus artificial "character," the productive versus the idle classes, or Jeffersonian-Republicans versus the Federalist party of Hamilton and Adams.[46] In the course of extended debates over the operation of the state's banks, antifederalism reemerged in western Pennsylvania over the question of paper money. In the late 1780s, as rural settlers were advocating the printing of money, Philadelphia's artisans found themselves in a swing position on the question of national banks, caught between the (solid gold) interests of (national) specie and national banking interests versus the supposedly insolvent localism of paper. Instead of allying themselves with the state's unskilled and itinerant laborers (as they had in the early years of the Revolution), many artisan republicans—such as Charles Willson Peale and Tom Paine himself— identified artisan economic interests with those of urban nationalists, merchants, and the banks that made capital available for commerce and manufactures. Eric Foner traces the slow fading of Tom Paine's popularity after the American Revolution to his siding with nationalist financiers such as Robert Morris in support of the national Bank of North America, over and against economic localists and the city's working poor, many of whom were allied with the paper money interests of the west.[47]

What Neagle's *Pat Lyon at the Forge* recapitulates, then, is the struggle to remove social control from the hands of unskilled labor by a representational strongbox of merchant and manufacturing capital. What particularly marks *Pat Lyon* from this point of view is the complete absence of multiple and "journeyman" workers from the shop in the painting. As recounted by most social histories of artisan life after the Revolution, it was the journeyman artisan (the shop worker positioned in between the apprentice and master craftsman) who was the most likely to fall out of the class of artisan and into the ranks of itinerant wage laborers in the course of the long reorganization of craft production into mass production. By 1805, journeyman artisans were increasingly itinerant and temporary employees, connected to master craftsmen (now their employers) primarily by a wage relationship. Just one year after Lyon's trial of 1805, for example, Philadelphia witnessed one of the most significant events in early American labor history: the 1806 conspiracy trial of the journeyman cordwainers (or shoemakers) for combining against their masters to close shops and raise wages.

This early labor trial signaled both changes in the crafts and journeyman resistance to their (loss of) status as they became, increasingly, wage laborers without hope of becoming master craftsmen in their own right. It also gave evidence of journeyman efforts to organize some resistance to the economic instability and social disorganization arising from decades of market expansion and multiform reorganizations of production. Accused of illegally "combining," the cordwainers were defended (as Lyon had been) by powerful Philadelphia lawyers. Unlike Lyon, however, the journeymen cordwainers lost—but not without receiving a spectacular defense from their lawyer, Caesar Rodney (who, ironically, quoted copiously from Adam Smith throughout his argument). During his defense, Rodney employed the myth of Daedalus and Icarus as a way of undermining an assumption that journeyman cordwainers were itinerant or unstable compared with their supposedly settled and substantial masters. In the course of his peroration, he compared the journeymen's supposed itinerance (as "birds of passage") to the Icarian flight of their masters' capital from banks—on "wings of paper." The prosecution had represented the journeymen, Rodney argued,

> as mere birds of passage, who can at any moment flock and depart in a body. [But] [s]o can the masters if it suits their interest. . . . It is true, [the masters] own houses and possess a large capital. Of the former they can conveniently dispose, and though their capital may now lay deposited in bars of silver or wedges of gold, in the cells of the different banks of this city, secured by iron doors and bolts, nothing can more readily escape, or is of more easy transportation. With wings of paper, more faithful than those of the son of D[a]edalus, [the masters' capital] can fly across a sea, wider than the Icarian, or alight on some eligible spot in the United States, where it will be the most productive.[48]

In this passage the journeyman is a man of journeys, an itinerant, masterless man, dangerously unconfined in his search for work. But his itinerance is also refigured and reorganized by the (Icarian) figure of capital—bank notes, currency, specie versus paper—which "flies" from the locked vaults, treasure boxes, and "cells of different banks of this city." Here, the flight of capital accompanies the early industrial transformation of craft production—and the transformation of journeymen into workers. Ultimately, the allusion to Icarus argues that the exhibitionary reproduction of production is the central mythic structure of nation building in the United States and that the commodity form is the longest-lived representational projection of the American Enlightenment. Insofar as the federalist manufactory was an artifact of visual and verbal arts—and of the (forging of) connection between them—it was a form of assembly raised on the backs of journeymen mechanics, as well as of unskilled, unnamed, enslaved, and non-English-speaking immigrant workers, whose livelihoods were under assault, not simply by masters become employers, but by a federalizing order of things that extracted from the figure of the republican artisan two other figures: the party-identified bourgeois employer on the one hand (identified with the aestheticisms of "taste") and the class-identified worker on the other (associated, in turn, with the functional mechanics of mass culture).

NEAGLE'S *PAT LYON AT THE FORGE* (1826/1829)

In the place of the missing journeyman worker, then, Neagle's portrait substitutes the representational strongbox of federalist self-making familiar since the Grand Federal Procession of 1788, when the American workplace was moved center stage for an endless performance of American manufacturing. As a theater or playhouse of production, the edifice of the federal state had, by the 1820s, proliferated numerous professions, fields, and institutions within itself as epitomes of *E pluribus unum* in miniature. As Neagle's *Pat Lyon* demonstrates, such self-making/self-legitimating professions included portrait painting, which, like literature and painting generally, was emerging as a profession precisely by virtue of its opposition to, and difference from, the crafts or mechanical arts.[49] Even while it celebrates "the innocent locksmith," then, Neagle's *Pat Lyon* articulates the historical triumph of the fine artist—together with the lawyer, engineer, and banker—as an urban professional over and against the mechanical artist as a mere maker of commodities.

Lyon is pictured alone in Neagle's portrait with the exception of his single apprentice—despite the fact that, except for the brief period in 1798 when he had only one apprentice (Jamie), the smith was always assisted in his shop by at least two or three journeymen and apprentices, and usually more. While the boy at the bellows is in part a memorial to Lyon's long-dead apprentice, he also serves as an allegory of the relationship of the mechanical arts to the fine arts. Here, the relationship of the apprentice to his master translates into an allegory of inspiration. As a kind of mechanic's muse, the boy keeps the older man's fire going, his bellows funneling a picture of the past (the gaol) into the painting (and workshop) of the present. As a figure for inspiration, the apprentice also, however, represents the ambivalent relationship of the visual or literary artist to the mechanical artist—that is, a productive tension between the (inspiration of) the fine arts and (the economics and instrumentality of) the mechanical arts upon which they depend.

This ambiguous triumph of the artist over the mechanic is articulated by the painting's celebration of the power of creation writ large, or applied to all media. In *Pat Lyon at the Forge*, the elimination of multiple and journeyman workers from the worksite is an effect of a representational apparatus that assumes a correspondence between visual and linguistic structures on the grounds of production. This union of words and things through representation is summarized by the sketch of the Pythagorean theorem in the bottom right-hand corner of the 1829 copy of the painting. In addition, however, the Pythagorean sketch indicates that the painting's pyramidal composition is one with the blacksmith's own plan of work, through the universal principles (or mysteries) of design articulated by Euclidean geometry. Dated and signed by Neagle, the sketch of the Pythagorean theorem rests beside Lyon's anvil as if it were an architectural design from which the smith has been working. In its appropriation of, and identification with, the universal principles of construction—or geometry as natural law—the 1829 version of *Pat Lyon* marks not only the emergence of the portrait painter as professional but also the erasure of the journeyman mechanic from the workshop.[50] In Neagle's portrait, the journeyman craftsman is missing, but his place is taken by the abstract, inspirational machinery of republican viewership: with the display of the Pythagorean triangle, the triadic organization of the classic workshop sequence (from apprentice through journeyman to master) is hypostatized as a principle of construction and as the triangle of visual perspective—a triangle that is opposed to (even while, as a phenomenon of empiricism, it is supposedly rooted in) the material or everyday relations of things to things.

As Bruce Chambers observes, the Pythagorean theorem was also a commonplace of Masonic iconography. It could be found wherever the Masons met; it was embroidered for example, on George Washington's Masonic apron, together with other Masonic icons, including a miniature Noah's Ark and the famous pyramid with a mystical eye at its center, sometimes called the eye of Providence (the same motif that appears on the back of the U.S. dollar bill). As in Enlightenment Europe, the Masonic brotherhood served eighteenth-century North America as an organizational mechanism for empowering and consolidating new economic and social groups. Virtually all interpretive histories of the brotherhood agree that Anglo-European Masonry had helped to constitute a new entrepreneurial and manufacturing class by providing a site where aristocratic, bourgeois, and, eventually, the artisanal classes could mingle and "combine" as brothers, in a space protected from both women and ethnic outsiders.[51] Masonic ritual was patterned upon the semisecret organizational practices of European guilds—specifically, of course, the craft traditions of itinerant stonemasons. The ritual key to the establishment of Masonry as a corporate brotherhood was the hierarchy of secrets revealed to each Mason as a sequence of mystic "degrees" that mimed the artisanal progression from apprentice to journeyman to master of "the craft."[52] In fact, the inclusion of the Masonic emblem in the second copy of *Pat Lyon at the Forge* does not signal the public suppression of Masonry but celebrates (as universal) the principles of construction and production in general, as grounds for corporate unity at any worksite.

Patrick Lyon was a Mason—as was virtually every political leader and visual artist of the Revolutionary generation (including Charles Willson Peale, Benjamin West, Benjamin Franklin, and Washington). Masonry's status as a secret society frequently opened it to accusations of conspiracy, and when Neagle was painting *Pat Lyon at the Forge*, Masonry was coming under sharp and often paranoid political attack. Bruce Chambers argues that Neagle included the Pythagorean triangle in his 1829 copy of the portrait because this was a private version, intended for Lyon's parlor or hallway, rather than for public display.[53] Juxtaposed with Neagle's signature, however, the Masonic triangle was also the painter's way of publicly signing and owning the second version of the portrait, after the public success of the first. In *Pat Lyon at the Forge*, Neagle employs the Pythagorean theorem to signal his identification with the universalist republican and craft principles of Lyon. But he also employs it to mark his own ascension to social power as an entrepreneurial—but also, of course, antimarket—artisan/artist at the forging of another grand federal union of narrative with graphic design, name with icon.

The relationship in the painting between the older smith and the much younger apprentice might also be read, furthermore, as a record of the relationship between Pat Lyon and John Neagle himself. Born in 1798, Neagle was exactly half Lyon's age when he painted *Pat Lyon at the Forge*, but Neagle had his own vexed relationship to the uneven transformations of the American manufactory: in boyhood he had been apprenticed as a coach painter while learning his craft as a painter of portraits. An apprentice to both portrait painting and coach painting, he had carried his brushes and palette back and forth between the shop of the Philadelphia coachmaker and the studio of Bass Otis, where he learned portraiture.[54] Later, Neagle would lead a group of artists in a brief struggle to make the merchant-and lawyer-dominated Pennsylvania Academy of Fine Arts more responsive to the needs of practicing painters and sculptors.[55] His relationship to both the discourses of artisan republicanism and to the market for portraits was, therefore, ambivalent, strategic, and indebted. *Pat Lyon at the Forge*, in turn, represents the portrait painter's relationship to the social and political power of the mechanical artist. By the late 1820s, Neagle, now a full-time portrait painter, refigures mechanical production as mythic forging, or creation, as a way of signaling the legitimacy of his own work as a fine artist.

Many years later, after the Civil War and during the heyday of railroad construction, a Philadelphia machinist named Joseph Harrison, Jr.. made a fortune inventing locomotive devices as a railroad engineer. Harrison was also a Mason, and in the 1870s he published a book of Masonic memoirs, poetry, and essays for which he composed a narrative poem titled "The Blacksmith and King Solomon: A Rabbinical Legend."[56] According to Scripture, no iron was permitted in the building of the Temple of Solomon, because it was a material used for war. But once, according to Harrison, when King Solomon gave a feast in the Temple for all its chief artificers and builders, a man forced his way into the hall. It was the blacksmith—an ironworker. All the craftsmen at the king's table objected immediately to the intrusion, saying that this uncouth man was neither a sculptor nor a carpenter nor a worker in gold and silver. When the blacksmith heard their objections, however, he was not dismayed, but walked up to Solomon's table, and, snatching up a cup of wine, toasted the king, declaring that indeed he was not a craftsman like other craftsmen, that he was in fact superior to them all: " 'Before they lived I was created. I am their master, and they are all my servants.' And he turned him around and said to the chief of the carvers in stone":

> Who made the tools with which you carve?
> And he said: THE BLACKSMITH.
> And he said to the chief of the workers in wood:
> Who made the tools with which you hewed the trees of Lebanon, and formed them into pillars and roof for the Temple?
> And he said: THE BLACKSMITH.
> And he said to the artificer in gold and ivory:
> Who makes your instruments by which you work beautiful things for my Lord the King?
> And he said THE BLACKSMITH.[57]

In this Masonic narrative Harrison's blacksmith represents the founding power of a creator God who, as the Maker of all other makers, encompasses and unites the multiplicity of crafts. Of course, in the 1870s, the early days of railroad travel, Harrison's Vulcan-like blacksmith also ratifies locomotive construction and railroad companies as logical extensions of nature's "Book" read as technographic "scripture."[58] Like Harrison's blacksmith, John Neagle's *Pat Lyon* likewise is a mythic forger and framer, an emblem of the industrial division, rationalization, and management of productive power through the mechanics of collective self-making.

As Charles Buck's anecdote of Lyon and the strongbox had revealed in 1806, the ambivalence that surrounded the changing form and function of the artisan articulated an unresolved tension over who controlled the strongbox—where the strongbox is understood broadly. On the one hand, the strongbox is the actual, literal machinery of commodity production and distribution, and Lyon the actual mechanical producer who threatens to control it.[59] At the same time, however, the box is the representational structure of the arts, or media, of the extended republic, a representational apparatus that one might call a "(bi)camera(l) obscura": a Euclidean box of dynamic binaries allied with, and paralleling, the bank vault itself as a way of producing, circulating, displaying, and preserving "treasure." In fact, of course, as the place where originality and its reproduction were fused, it was the strongbox itself that was the federalist—and republican—treasure, wherever the box figured the representational apparatus of production's reproduction, joining an array of early national architectures, from the changing workshops and machine shops to the courthouse, playhouse, prisonhouse and, of course, the banks of the nation. And this struggle over the architectural space of viewership and readership was a gendered, sexualized, and racialized one: in *Pat Lyon at the Forge,* the pyramidal clarity of the strongbox and its structure emerges only after the white, male worker's workplace has become an isolated, even lonely place—a state of solitude that is underlined by the painting's connection of the smithy to the prison. The pyramidal secret of republican representation, in other words, is communicated only after all other unrepresentative persons (except for the apprenticed boy) and all other possible arrangements of work life, street life, and livelihood have been erased from the scene of production.

VIEWS OF PHILADELPHIA IN 1800 AND 1828

In 1828, the Philadelphia engraver William Russell Birch published his fourth and last edition of *The City of Philadelphia . . . as it appeared in the Year 1800.* But it is the first edition of 1800 that, as a series of twenty-eight paired plates, emerges as most remarkable in composition and complexity, by contrast both with the three later Birch editions and with Cephas G. Childs's similarly conceived *Views of Philadelphia,* also published in 1828. An illustrated text of twenty-five plates, Childs's *Views* are a set of randomly arranged engravings. Highly individuated and monumental in style, his plates represent exemplary architecture (churches, banks, public works, etc.) and are accompanied by detailed descriptive essays.[60] By contrast, the first edition of Birch's *Views* is a series of sequentially arranged plates that constitute a visual tour of the city ordered strategically as a series of legible architectural and social juxtapositions or contrasts. Birch's tour is primarily visual, accomplished without accompanying text except for a short preface, a guide (or key), and a list of 156 subscribers ("Jefferson, Gilbert Stuart, Thomas Mifflin and William Hamilton . . . ").[61] It was this first 1800 edition of Birch's *Views* that Jefferson displayed for years in his "visiting Room" in Washington.

By the late 1820s, there were, certainly, many new sites where one could find the representational architecture of federalism refigured and fulfilled. The new Eastern State Penitentiary was under construction and was a centerpiece of Childs's collection; the old Walnut Street Gaol would be demolished in 1835 and was already referred to as "the old jail." In 1798, when Birch first arrived in Philadelphia from England, the Walnut Street Gaol was a city landmark and a viewing attraction for foreign visitors: in his *Views* of 1800, it is still a "new" jail, juxtaposed with the old wooden structure being hauled off by oxen in the foreground of the plate (fig. 14). In Birch's *Views,* this engraving of the Walnut Street Gaol is paired with plate 23, "The State House Garden," and the two plates together constitute an ironic juxtaposition. The Walnut Street Gaol was literally located directly behind the State House Garden, across Walnut Street from Independence Square.[62] But the link, or interplay, between plates 23 and 24 is made explicit within plate 23, where the huge doors at the rear

STATE-HOUSE GARDEN, PHILADELPHIA.

Figure 13. William Russell Birch, "State-House Garden, Philadelphia,"
in *The City of Philadelphia in the State of Pennsylvania North
America as it appeared in the Year 1800* (Springfield Cot, Pennsylvania:
William Birch, 1800), plate 23. (Courtesy of the Library
Company of Pennsylvania.)

of the garden open directly out onto Walnut Street and the jail. The windows of the jail are, in fact, just visible behind the trees lining the garden
wall to the left of the doors (fig. 13). Here, the garden's opening doors
resonate with the Janus-faced juxtapositions that structure Birch's *Views*
throughout, as in such pairings as "The New Lutheran Church, in Fourth-
street"/"The Old Lutheran Church in Fifth-street" (Birch, plates 5e and
6); "High Street from the Country Market-place"/"High street from Ninth
street" (Birch, plates 11 and 12); "The [finished and empty] House intended for the President of the United States in Ninth-street/An unfinished [and empty] house, in Chestnut street" (Birch, plates 13 and 14).
These paired sequences of the first edition articulate contrasts that seem,
at times, vaguely Hogarth-like. But, thematizing the century's end itself as
a door between the eighteenth and nineteenth centuries, the first edition
of Birch's *Views* do not focus, as Hogarth's engravings often did, primarily
upon human character; they attend instead to contrasts of architecture
and edifice. As views of streets and buildings, Birch's plates muse, some-

Figure 14. William Russell Birch, "Gaol, in Walnut Street
Philadelphia," in *The City of Philadelphia in the State of Pennsylvania
North America as it appeared in the Year 1800* (Springfield Cot,
Pennsylvania: William Birch, 1800), plate 24. (Courtesy of
the Library Company of Philadelphia.)

times ironically and sometimes nostalgically, over the intersections of past
with present, exit with entrance, progress with stasis, and commerce with
virtue in the urban landscape of 1800.

The juxtaposition of the garden with the jail in plates 23 and 24, therefore, constitutes a relatively complex and troubled reflection on the representational mechanics of the extended republic, their "nature" and character. In plate 22, another view of the State House Garden, a sign reading
"MUSEUM" is just barely discernible in the background of the plate, linking
the scene with Peale's natural history museum. Housed at the edge of the
State House Garden, Peale's museum also opened onto the green square
of the State House Garden. The door to the museum was likewise marked
by Peale with a plaque declaring the world of Nature and the world of the
museum to be united on the grounds of natural law ("The book of Nature
open / ——explore the wondrous work / ——an Institute / of Laws eter-
nal, whose unaltered page / No time can change, no copier corrupt"[63]).

Plates 23 and 24 of Birch's *Views*, by contrast, offer a far less cheerful view of the identity of "art" and nature. In Birch's *Views*, the juxtaposition of the (exit from the) garden with the (opaque windows of the) jail constitutes a reflection upon the visual architecture of social discipline: confinement and control lies behind the open viewing space of the parklike garden, where, as in the rooms of the Peale Museum, viewers are viewed in their viewing. As is the case in the crowds and street scenes throughout Birch's *Views*, the assembly of people in the State House Garden is diversified by gender (and, in plate 22, by ethnicity), but that diversity is contained and organized by the grid of republican viewership. The prison windows behind the trees articulate a structure of solitude or isolation behind the mixed crowd, connecting punishment with natural liberty. Birch's conflation of the garden wall with the prison wall at the rear of plate 23 reflects ironically and even humorously upon the representational devices that not only link Nature with Art and garden with museum but which also frame his own *Views*. In plates such as the "State House Garden," Birch's *Views* of 1800 brings the Grand Federal Edifice of 1788 into view once more as a commercial scaffolding raised into view over people who emerge within it as viewing subjects and objects surveyed. By identifying the prisonhouse with the State House, then, views 23 and 24 reflect upon the fact that, as a technographic phenomenon, the "New Roof" of 1788 not only represented but enforced Union.

In 1800, Birch's *Views* constituted a "memorial" to a former capital, since the national capital was moved in that year from Philadelphia to the District of Columbia. In his autobiographical manuscript, Birch writes: "It may be easily conceived what the opinion was of this work with [Jefferson] our late Friend and best wisher to mankind that formed the constitution of the Country, while it is recollected that during the whole of his presidency it layed on the sophia in his visiting Room at Washington till it became ragged and dirty, but was not suffered to be taken away."[64] The narrative and moral interest of the pairing of plates in Birch's *Views* explains why the first edition, placed in Jefferson's reception room in Washington, was well-worn. Since 1800, however, Birch's *Views* have been read and employed in a piecemeal way, reproduced individually as illustrations in historical texts and architectural guidebooks or as nostalgic evidence of growth and change by way of comparison with landmarks of the present. After the printing of the first edition (sold in pairs, by subscription), even Birch himself used the plates in this way. In his second, third, and fourth editions, he increasingly abandoned the sequential coherence of the first edition and issued his plates separately, mixing new plates randomly with the plates that had proved most popular from the first edition. In 1812, as Birch considered issuing his third edition, he noted that complaints had emerged that his *Views* were not sufficiently "elegant." He therefore began to emphasize plates representing monumental architecture or "memorial scenes," subjects that he considered more appealing, anecdotal, or "elegant." In the preface to the final edition of 1828, he describes the change: "[A]s the first edition contained many of minor subjects and inferior Plates, which in this day of a more correct stile of publishing, would not be thought praiseworthy, they have been left out to lessen the price of the work; but every caution has been taken, to retain or add to those old subjects, which in any case might be thought desirable to save, such as by fire or removals deprived the City of anecdote or ornament."[65]

By 1828, in his fourth and final edition, Birch would, in fact, issue only ten of his *Views*, advertising them as a collector's supplement to Childs's *Views*. (Four of the ten plates included in Birch's 1828 edition were representations of the city's banks: the Philadelphia Bank, the Bank of Pennsylvania, Girard's Bank, and the United States Bank.[66]) Prefacing these with an elaborate apology, Birch characterized his first edition of 1800 negatively, as belonging to the domain of the mechanical—as opposed to the truly fine—arts:

> [I]t can only be said that if the lovers of the arts wish to indulge a gratification in the higher powers of the tool, or polygraphic art, they should seek it as more worthily bestowed upon the fine arts, of which this is not considered a branch—[these plates] are only mechanical, and more labour on such large plates would make them less useful. . . It would be useless for the proprietor to say anything about the historical part or further descriptive of the city, [as] there are other works that have taken that up largely. . . . [T]his is intended as a book of reference, that will stand in future ages as correct.[67]

These words were written in 1828, within the context of intensified efforts to produce and preserve Philadelphia's past: the 1820s and 30s saw a proliferation of Historical Societies and city "annals"; Cephas Childs would dedicate his *Views* of 1827–30 to the Historical Society of Pennsylvania; and, just thirteen years earlier, the Pennsylvania State House itself was purchased by the city and became a designated landmark: Independence Hall.

By comparison with Birch's first edition of *Views*, Childs's *Views* of 1827–30 do not reflect ironically or critically (by way of juxtaposition and contrast within and between plates) upon their relationship to the architecture of a "mechanical" past embedded in and engaged with the living, commercial, and exhibitionary present. Childs's *Views* display, instead, a series of isolated and monumental examples of architectural "taste," as represented by the city's banks and other state institutions. Held up for particularly lavish description in Childs's *Views* are "The Bank of the United States" (designed by William Strickland) and "The Eastern Penitentiary of Pennsylvania" (designed by John Haviland). Such plates do not reflect upon the city nostalgically or ironically as the former capital, but as an "elegant" urban center of financial, social, and technological innovation. In Childs's collection, monumental buildings utterly dominate street life, whereas in Birch's first edition of *Views*, diverse and active groups of people fill the streets. In Birch's street scenes, porters, idle soldiers, and African-American children mix with tourists, viewers, walkers, and hawkers, and wooden market stalls and blacksmith shops are juxtaposed with the facades of churches and public buildings. In Childs's description of the Bank of the United States, by contrast, he compares the bank to the Parthenon, praising its architecture as an attempt "to preserve the purity of the public taste—to wean it from the admiration of gaudy and showy exhibitions, and to fix its choice on those pure and simple forms, such as are embodied in this building, which so harmoniously associate the beautiful and the useful, and which have not rival, and can have no superior, in the deep and enduring impressions they stamp on the mind."[68] It is in the interest of humanitarian reform, then, as well as elegance, that the multiplicity and ironic opacities of Birch's *Views* and viewers are excised from Childs's project of centering and "purifying the public taste" through the clean lines of Greek architecture. Fireproof, healthful, humane, and enlightened, the architectural character of the Bank of the United States, Childs writes, "cannot [be] too often or too anxiously recommended to the study and imitation of our countrymen."

In his description of the new Eastern State Penitentiary, Childs similarly celebrates the monumentality of Gothic designs ("calculated to convey to our citizens the external appearance of those magnificent and picturesque castles of the middle ages, which contribute so eminently to embellish the scenery of Europe").[69] The Gothic spatial architecture of the new penitentiary is deemed even more republican—because more open, airy, and well-ventilated—than the crowded apartments occupied by the city's "industrious mechanics":

> We . . . have never seen a building so admirably adapted to the purposes of security, seclusion, health and convenience, as this Penitentiary. The rooms are larger, viz. containing more cubic feet of air, or space, than a great number of the apartments occupied by industrious mechanics in our city; and if we consider that two or more of the latter frequently work or sleep in the same chamber, they have much less room than will be allotted to the convicts; whose cells moreover, will be more perfectly ventilated.[70]

In this passage, the huge and healthful architecture of the penitentiary has superseded the "crowded apartments" of the city's "industrious mechanics." The new penitentiary, furthermore, never employs labor as punishment (in public works, highway repair, or ditch digging); instead, labor is an instrument of reform, embraced by prisoners as a "relief" from the idleness and tedium of confinement in the eight long corridors of solitary cells radiating from a central observatory.[71] In Childs's "Eastern State Penitentiary," the mechanical artist has been left behind—or has disappeared into—the architecture of the state. Whereas the Grand Federal Procession of 1788 had celebrated the "federal mechanics" of the city as the authors and viewers of the "New Roof," here they are missing from—because absorbed by—a framework that erases labor entirely from the scene of its division, mechanization, and employment. This negation of "the industrious mechanics in our city" by the cells of Childs's penitentiary parallels the erasure of market scenes and "inelegant" street life from Birch's *Views* of 1828, reiterating Birch's denigration and negation of his own art of engraving as a degraded form of "mechanical" rather than "fine" art.

Graphic memory marks the differences. In its erasure of the journeyman from the scene, Neagle's *Pat Lyon at the Forge* likewise figured the migration of the manufactory-era mechanical artist and his (changing and intermediate) shop world away from representational centrality. The difference, however, is that while Neagle's Lyon is an icon of industry, the portrait's reference to "the old gaol" and to Lyon's "tale" does indeed reference a more "mechanical" past. But, as the Pythagorean triangle suggests, by connecting the Pat Lyon of 1828 to the decade of the 1790s, Neagle also aimed to accomplish a seamless (rather than critical or ironic) incarnation and celebration of the federalist-era mechanical artist in the industrial present. In the case of *Pat Lyon*, the texts, narratives, and transcripts that surround and exceed the painting accomplish a disruption of its iconic attempt to fuse past and present. Like the tidy cells of the penitentiary, Neagle's *Lyon* represents the absorption of the artisan/mechanic by, and his disappearance into, the arts of a grand federal republic constituted (in 1828 as in 1788) by the division of labor's powers and the creation(ism) of an elevated—or architectural—class. When the former locksmith donned the costume of a blacksmith for his portrait of 1826, Philadelphia's mechanics were, in fact, no longer wearing craft costumes or performing their crafts in Philadelphia parades as they had in 1788. The city's first Workingman's Party was formed in 1829, and, as Susan Davis recounts, the costume worn by its members during street demonstrations and parades of the 1830s was an almost uniform-like black suit.[72]

Neagle's *Pat Lyon*, then, at rest at his forge, wearing sheepskin apron and silver-buckled shoes, is a museum piece, while his blacksmith's shop is, in effect, a craft museum. Neagle's portrait of 1829 constitutes a doorway leading out of the era of the manufactory in Philadelphia and, presumably, into the era of the factory proper, away from the world of apprentices and masters and into the world of employers and employees. But, as is the case with doorways (to factories, mansions, museums, theaters, and prisons), this one too is both entrance and exit. From one point of view, *Pat Lyon at the Forge* opens out onto a nineteenth-century world in which the ("old") technographies of representative self-production only more fully dominate the scene: well forged, intact, monumentalized, miniaturized, and prolific. At the same time, though, the portrait's reference to the old roof of the Walnut Street Gaol reminds us that these structures of representative self-production were never unitary or solitary, always multiple, disjunctive, and incommensurate. Multidimensional, disproportionate in form and format, the artifacts of the American manufactory exceed their own taxonomies. Not only do they indicate, without rooting themselves in, the material that falls outside their interaction; they utterly fail to constitute a coherently progressive line or single point of origin from which to raise— or to view—an unmediated history of the world.

Introduction. The Extended Republic in the Age of Manufactures

1. St. John de Crèvecoeur, *Letters from an American Farmer* (Harmondsworth, England: Penguin, 1985), 194–95.

2. The historical John Bartram took up botany in the early 1720s, a full ten years before the first edition of *Systema Naturae* in 1735; Bartram wrote to Sir Hans Sloane, "The first authors I read were [William] Salmon, [Nicholas] Culpeper and [William] Turner." Quoted in Ernest Earnest, *John and William Bartram, Botanists and Explorers* (Philadelphia: University of Pennsylvania Press, 1940), 22.

3. Crèvecoeur, *Letters*, 195.

4. My discussion of Linnaeus here extends to British North America Mary Louise Pratt's discussion of the opening of continental interiors through the global project of Linnaean science in "Science, Planetary Consciousness, Interiors," chap. 2 of *Imperial Eyes: Travel Writing and Transculturation* (London: Routlege, 1992), 15–37.

5. Michel Foucault, *The Order of Things: An Archaeology of the Human Sciences* (New York: Random House, Vintage Books, 1973), 135; originally published as *Les Mots et les choses* (Paris: Gallimard, 1966). By way of the living stamp of its organic structure, "the visibility of the animal or plant" is permitted "to pass over in its entirety into the discourse that receives it" and, ultimately, "may manage to reconstitute itself in visible form by means of words." Conversely, the printed text, "in its variables of form, arrangement, and quantity, should have a vegetable structure: . . . the Adumbration would exactly contain the whole history of the plant, such as its names, its structure, its external assemblage, its nature, its use. The plant is thus engraved in the material of the language into which it has been transposed and recomposes its pure form before the reader's very eyes. The book becomes the herbarium of living structures" (135).

6. "The great Book of Nature must be opened and studied leaf by leaf." "Introduction to a Course of Lectures," in *The Selected Papers of Charles Willson Peale and His Family*, ed. Lillian B. Miller (New Haven, Conn.: Yale University Press, 1988), vol. 2 (pt.1), 268.

7. The term "field of visibility" is Foucault's: "In fact, it was not an age-old inattentiveness being suddenly dissipated, but a new field of visibility being constituted in all its density." *The Order of Things*, 132. Linnaean science extended the longstanding empirical and rhetorical ideal of an unadorned "plain style" to a graphic and mechanistic extreme. For a discussion of the plain style in science, see Barbara Stafford, *Voyage into Substance: Art, Science, Nature, and the Illustrated Travel Account, 1760–1840* (Cambridge, Mass.: MIT Press, 1984); Geoff Bennington, "That Perfect Cheat: Locke and Empiricism's Rhetoric," in *The Figural and the Literal: Problems of Language in the History of Science and Philosophy*, ed. Andrew E. Benjamin, Geoffrey N. Cantor, and John R. R. Christie (Manchester: Manchester University Press, 1987), 103–23.

8. Crèvecoeur, *Letters*, 39–50. The parody of the farmer James in "Letter I" sets the

precedent for the parodic tone that runs through many of the *Letters*. Myra Jehlen, "J. Hector St. John de Crèvecoeur: A Monarcho-Anarchist in Revolutionary America," *American Quarterly* 31 (Summer 1979): 204–22.

9. Crèvecoeur tells us, furthermore, that this egalitarian, Pennsylvania Quaker, Bartram, has freed his African-American slaves, who now, however, work alongside of him on his farm "by their own choice," as employees, for wages. "We gave them freedom and yet few have quitted their ancient masters." Crèvecoeur, *Letters*, 195–97.

10. Thomas Childs Cochran, "Cotton Textiles and Industrialism," in *Science and Society in Early America: Essays in Honor of Whitfield J. Bell, Jr.*, ed. Randolph Klein (Philadelphia: American Philosophical Society, 1986), 251–71; idem, *Frontiers of Change: Early Industrialism in America* (New York: Oxford University Press, 1981), 3–77; Thomas Doerflinger, *A Vigorous Spirit of Enterprise: Merchants and Economic Development in Revolutionary Philadelphia* (Chapel Hill: University of North Carolina Press, 1986), 134–64. Cochran argues, further, that the technological origins of industrialism must be traced not merely to the textile mills of Lowell, Massachusetts, or Manayunk, Pennsylvania, but, more importantly, to the hundreds of "blacksmith shops" in late-eighteenth-century Philadelphia (such as those run by artisan-engineers like Oliver Evans, Nathan Sellers, and Patrick Lyon). These shops innovated the innumerable improvements in "machines for making machines," the devices for boring, milling, planing, and cutting metal and wood that were responsible for meeting the demands of territorial and market expansion—demands for new housing and durable goods, farm equipment, improved transportation, and the production of heavy machinery, particularly steam-driven ferryboats, pumps, dredges, fire engines and, eventually, locomotives. Here, the technological changes indicated by the term "manufactory" are inseparable from Euro-American emigration into the continental interior, from Ohio and Kentucky to Tennessee, Alabama, and Louisiana.

11. Marquis de Chastellux, *Travels in North America in the Years 1780, 1781, and 1782*, trans. Howard Rice (Chapel Hill: University of North Carolina Press, 1963), 1:181, quoted by Doerflinger, *A Vigorous Spirit of Enterprise*, 63.

12. John F. Kasson, *Civilizing the Machine: Technology and Republican Values in America, 1776–1900* (New York: Grossman Publishers, 1976), 53–107.

13. Richard S. Dunn, "Servants and Slaves: The Recruitment and Employment of Labor," in *Colonial British America: Essays in the New History of the Early Modern Era*, ed. Jack P. Greene and J. R. Pole (Baltimore, Md.: Johns Hopkins University Press, 1984), 188; Sharon V. Salinger, *"To Serve Well and Faithfully": Labor and Indentured Servants in Pennsylvania, 1682–1800* (New York: Cambridge University Press, 1987).

14. John R. Commons et al., *History of Labour in the United States* (New York: Macmillan Co., 1918); *Documentary History of American Industrial Society*, vol. 3, *Labor Conspiracy Cases, 1806–1842*, ed. John R. Commons et al. (Cleveland, Ohio: Arthur H. Clark Co., 1910), 61–248; Mark A. Lause, *Some Degree of Power: From Hired Hand to Union Craftsman in the Preindustrial American Printing Trades, 1778–1815* (Fayetteville: University of Arkansas Press, 1991); Eric Foner, *Tom Paine and Revolutionary America* (New York: Oxford University Press, 1976); Sean Wilentz, *Chants Democratic: New York City and the Rise of the American Working Class, 1788–1850* (New York: Oxford University Press, 1984); David Montgomery, *Citizen Worker: The Experience of Workers in the United States with Democracy and the Free Market during the Nineteenth Century* (Cambridge, Mass.: Cambridge University Press, 1993); Gary Nash, *The Urban Crucible: Social Change, Politi-*

cal Consciousness, and the Origins of the American Revolution (Cambridge, Mass.: Harvard University Press, 1979); Howard B. Rock, *Artisans of the New Republic: the Tradesmen of New York City in the Age of Jefferson* (New York: New York University Press, 1979); Bruce Laurie, *Artisans into Workers: Labor in Nineteenth-Century America* (New York: Hill and Wang, 1989); Billy Gordon Smith, *The "Lower Sort": Philadelphia's Labouring People, 1750–1800*, (Ithaca, N.Y.: Cornell University Press, 1990); Stephen Rosswurm, *Arms, Country and Class: The Philadelphia Militia and the "Lower Sort" during the American Revolution, 1775–1783*, (New Brunswick, N.J.: Rutgers University Press, 1987); Cynthia J. Shelton, *The Mills of Manayunk: Industrialization and Social Conflict in the Philadelphia Region, 1787–1837* (Baltimore, Md.: Johns Hopkins University Press, 1987); Ronald Schultz, *The Republic of Labor: Philadelphia Artisans and the Politics of Class, 1720–1830* (New York: Oxford University Press, 1993); Alfred Young, *Beyond the American Revolution: Explorations in the History of American Radicalism* (Dekalb: Northern Illinois University Press, 1993). Often thought of as a Marxist, Charles Beard, in fact, insisted upon a "hard," or economic and statistical, as opposed to either a strictly Marxist or a culturally mediated interpretation of the Constitution. In arguing that the Constitution served the interests of agrarian gentlemen, urban merchants and bankers, and investors in public securities, Beard foregrounded class formation as "economic investedness"—although he never really used the word "class." His argument was iconoclastic rather than Marxist. Beard made his shattering argument, however, at the expense of reducing the investments of federalism not only to the economic investments of the federalists themselves but to the written Constitution, which he viewed as the repository of federalism and its economic interests. In fact, then, the work of American social and labor historians has been inspired less by Beard than by E. P. Thompson's *The Making of the English Working Class* (1963; New York: Pantheon, 1964). In sometimes helpful, sometimes limiting ways, however, the American variations on this English Marxist tradition force attention to economic and power differentials—but tend, in the process, to forget federalism. See Forrest McDonald, "A New Introduction," in Charles Beard, *An Economic Interpretation of the Constitution* (New York: Free Press, 1986), vii–xl.

15. David R. Brigham's study of Peale's museum is something of an exception: *Public Culture in the Early Republic: Peale's Museum and Its Audience* (Washington, D.C.: Smithsonian Institution Press, 1995).

16. Wilentz, *Chants Democratic*, 10–19; Herbert G. Gutman, *Power and Culture: Essays on the American Working Class*, ed. Ira Berlin (New York: Pantheon, 1987).

17. Herbert F. May, *The Enlightenment in America* (Cambridge, Mass.: Harvard University Press, 1976); Robert A. Ferguson, *The American Enlightenment, 1750–1820* (Cambridge, Mass.: Harvard University Press, 1997).

18. Text-centered interpretation takes many forms. In *The Letters of the Republic*, Michael Warner speaks of "the cultural mediation of the print medium" and substitutes a comparatively immanent way of understanding print for the fallacies of historians of the book who adhere to a naive technological determinism, viewing "the printing press" as somehow causing or producing civic virtue, representative government, and even democracy itself. But the notion of "the cultural mediation of the print medium" itself limits, and even insists on limiting, cultural mediation to linguistic forms (writing, text and textuality, discursive enterprise). His recourse to "cultural mediation" is itself finally a discursive mediation—a return to textual rather than

"cultural" mediation. Warner's history of the cultural mediation of print is an analysis of turning points in the elaboration of "print discourse"—meaning a second-order, or meta-, discourse that mediates the medium of print. Here, though, the "mediation of the print medium" is linguistic or discursive rather than "cultural" and, thereby, systematically avoids the question of labor and class formation. Perhaps most telling is Warner's failure to criticize Benjamin Franklin: Franklin's representative life in letters is a monument to the entrepreneurial power of print's universalizing presumption that it can circulate safely above "culture" or above the many—potentially counterlinguistic, unpublishable—forms that a "cultural mediation of the print medium" might include. Michael Warner, *The Letters of the Republic: Publication and the Public Sphere in Eighteenth-Century America* (Cambridge, Mass.: Harvard University Press, 1990).

19. It is also necessary to avoid limiting one's analysis of federalism as technology to the comparison often made between the structure of the government described by the Constitution and the efficient workings of a "machine."

20. The best known of these political taxonomies is *The Spirit of Laws by Montesquieu: A Compendium of the First English Edition*, ed. David Wallace Carrithers (Berkeley: University of California Press, 1977).

21. Tony Bennett, "The Exhibitionary Complex," *New Formations* 4 (Spring 1988): 76–80; repr. in *The British Museum: History, Theory, Politics* (London: Routledge, 1995), 59–86. "Even a cursory glance through Richard Altick's *The Shows of London* [Cambridge, Mass.: Belknap Press of Harvard University Press, 1987]," Bennett writes, "convinces that the nineteenth century was quite unprecedented in the social effort it devoted to the organization of spectacles" (78).

22. I owe this application of "abstract concrete labor" to Jonathan Magidoff, who discussed this project with me at length in 1995. See also Richard Handler's definition of the "collective individual" in "On Having a Culture: Nationalism and the Preservation of Quebec's Patrimoine," in *Objects and Others: Essays on Museums and Material Culture*, ed. George W. Stocking, History of Anthropology, no. 3 (Madison: University of Wisconsin Press, 1985), 210–11.

23. See Carl Bridenbaugh, *The Colonial Craftsman* (New York: New York University Press, 1950); W. J. Rorabaugh, *The Craft Apprentice: From Franklin to the Machine Age in America* (New York: Oxford University Press, 1986); and Foner, *Tom Paine*.

24. Terry Eagleton, *The Ideology of the Aesthetic* (Oxford: Basil Blackwell, 1990). My argument is compatible with Eagleton's where Eagleton emphasizes that the sense experience inscribed by and as aesthetics—and aesthetic theory per se—not only reinscribed ideologies of the bourgeois subject but also enabled resistance to it.

25. For this definition of "anthropology"—meaning those ways in which capitalism makes and reproduces (the maker) "Man"—see Martin Jay, *The Dialectical Imagination: A History of the Frankfurt School and the Institute of Social Research, 1923–50* (Boston: Little, Brown, 1973); and Jean Baudrillard, "Marxist Anthropology and the Domination of Nature," in *The Mirror of Production*, trans. Mark Poster (St. Louis, Mo.: Telos Press, 1975), 53–69.

26. This description of the artisan as a figure encompassing "labor" and "work" draws upon Hannah Arendt's definition of these terms in *The Human Condition* (Chicago: University of Chicago Press, 1958), although Arendt distinguishes very sharply

between labor as the domain of the "household" and its "mere" reproduction of bio-logical life itself versus the "platonic" insights that constitute the knowledge, or plans, of craft work.

27. Julia Wrigley, "The Division between Mental and Manual Labor: Artisan Educa-tion in Science in Nineteenth-Century Britain," in *Marxist Inquiries: Studies of Labor, Class, and States*, ed. Michael Burawoy and Theda Skocpol, American Journal of Sociol-ogy, no. 88, supplement 1982 (Chicago: University of Chicago Press), 36, 40, 48.

28. The myth of a master craftsman's original "autonomy" or independence is itself one of the ideologies of industrial development. Jacques Rancière makes this argu-ment in "The Myth of the Artisan: Critical Reflections on a Category of Social History," in *Work in France: Representations, Meaning, Organization, and Practice*, ed. Steven Lau-rence Kaplan and Cynthia J. Koepp (Ithaca, N.Y.: Cornell University Press, 1986). See also Jacques Ranciere, *The Nights of Labor: The Workers' Dream in Nineteenth-Century France*, trans. John Drury (Philadelphia: Temple University Press, 1981).

29. Wrigley, "The Division between Mental and Manual Labor," 36.

30. Alfred Sohn-Rethel, *Intellectual and Manual Labor: A Critique of Epistemology* (At-lantic Highlands, N.J.: Humanities Press, 1978). The distinction between mental and manual labor was made by Locke in his narrative of property's origin in *both* "labor" and "work"—or "the labor of the body and the work of the hand." John Locke, "Of Property," in "The Second Treatise of Civil Government," in *Two Treatises of Govern-ment*, ed. Peter Laslett (New York: New American Library, 1960), 328–29: "Though the Earth, and all inferior Creatures be common to all Men, yet every Man has Prop-erty in his own Person. This no Body has any Right to but himself. The Labour of his Body, and the Work of his Hands, we may say, are properly his. Whatsoever then he removes out of the State that Nature hath provided, and left in it, he hath mixed his Labour with, and joyned to it something that is his own, and thereby makes it his Property." This passage is quoted by Mark Rose in "The Author as Proprietor: *Don-aldson v. Becket* and the Genealogy of Modern Authorship," *Representations* 23 (1988): 70–73. Rose argues that the legal debates over copyright in England constituted prod-ucts of the mind as property by treating the author's mind according to the Lockean narrative of property formation, as if it were an estate cultivated by the author—a something with which he "mixed" his labor, thus creating a property. The circularity of this Lockean model of literary property was a recipe for self-generation, whereby an author "mixed" his labor with his own "person," or self, thereby producing, not only the work but himself as author, in the form of "a work."

31. John Rule, "The Production of Skill in the Period of Manufacture," in *The His-torical Meanings of Work*, ed. Patrick Joyce (Cambridge: Cambridge University Press, 1987), 99–118.

32. *The Philosophy of Manufactures: Early Debates over Industrialism in the United States*, ed. Michael Brewster Folsom and Steven D. Lubar (Cambridge, Mass.: MIT Press, 1982).

33. Historians have argued that this uneven and multilevel transformation was equally evident in Britain. Maxine Berg, *The Age of Manufactures: Industry, Innovation, and Work in Britain, 1700–1820* (New York: Oxford University Press, 1986); May, *En-lightenment in America*. In *The Age of Manufactures*, Berg gives a detailed discussion of the meaning of "manufactory" or the stage of "manufactures" in Marx. Berg is con-cerned to supplement and historicize Marx by specifying the diverse nature and sites

of early, or manufactory-era, industrialization. Manufactories, she argues, included not only the centralized production site but also the rural putting-out system, which she calls the "domestic system": "Now what Marx actually intended to include in manufacture is a matter of some debate. He characterized manufacture as taking two distinct forms: heterogeneous manufacture, or the mechanical assembly of independently made components of the final product, as in the watch manufacture; and organic manufacture, or a series of connected processes, as in the manufacture of needles. . . . Although Marx included rural industry under the manufacturing phase of capitalist production, he gave little consideration to the changes this rural manufacture might have entailed within the production process. He described how capitalist relations entered into rural production, arguing that manufacture seized hold initially, not of the urban trades, but of the rural secondary occupations where mass quantities were produced for export. But he also classified these occupations as examples of the social [organization of labor,] not the technical division of labour. There is some debate over whether Marx meant to include centralized manufacture in his model, and it has recently been pointed out that as a model 'manufactures' has been related only to light industries. The heavy industries such as iron processing do not fit Marx's criteria of handicraft, manual labor and the absence of machinery. Yet, equally, Marx does refer to ironworks, glass factories and paper mills as examples of industries which did fit his other criteria of mass production, marketing, investment and working capital on a large scale. . . . In spite of the allusions to rural industry and centralized production, then, Marx's model of 'manufactures' seems to have been a large workshop in the hands of a capitalist and organized on the basis of wage labor. Though Marx clearly intended it to be an abstract model, he included many historical signposts . . . [I]t seemed so aptly to encapsulate the structures of some of the leading workshops and proto-factories of the day [including] the minute division of labour of the pin factory described in Diderot's *Encyclopedie*." Berg, *Age of Manufactures*, 73–75.

34. See Francis Hopkinson's list of the trades of Philadelphia in "An Account of the Grand Federal Procession," *The American Museum, or Repository of Ancient and Modern Fugitive Pieces, &c.*, July 1788, 67.

35. As Cynthia Shelton writes of the textile industry, between 1787 and 1837 the transition to industrial capitalism in the Delaware Valley advanced "through successive and overlapping stages of handicraft, manufactory, and factory production." Shelton, *Mills of Manayunk*, 26.

36. The phrase "industrious poor" is used by Tench Coxe, in *A Communication from the Pennsylvania Society for the Encouragement of Manufactures and the Useful Arts* (Philadelphia: Samuel Akerman, for PSEMUA, 1804), 4. See also David Montgomery's chapter on the concept of the police in the United States, "Policing People for the Free Market," chap. 2 in *Citizen Worker*; Smith, *"Lower Sort"*; and Bruce Laurie, *The Working People of Philadelphia, 1800–1850* (Philadelphia: Temple University Press, 1980).

37. Schultz, *Republic of Labor*, 169–70, 271 n.

38. Coxe, *A Communication*, 23–24.

39. See, in particular, the emergence of "the language of labor" out of the language and values of the preindustrial craft corporation in William Sewell, *Work and Revolution in France: The Language of Labor from the Old Regime to 1848* (New York: Cambridge University Press, 1980).

40. May, *Enlightenment in America*; Emory Elliott, *Revolutionary Writers: Literature and Authority in the New Republic, 1725–1810* (New York: Oxford University Press, 1982); Ann Douglas, *The Feminization of American Culture* (New York: Knopf, 1977). The word "machinoculture" is derived from "machinofacture," the word used in the early nineteenth century to describe mechanized production in the early textile factory and manufactory. Schultz, *Republic of Labor*, 169–70.

41. For a summary of this debate, see Joyce Appleby, *Liberalism, Republicanism, and the Historical Imagination* (Cambridge, Mass.: Harvard University Press, 1992).

42. W.J.T. Mitchell, "Beyond Comparison: Picture, Text, and Method," in *Picture Theory: Essays in Verbal and Visual Culture* (Chicago: University of Chicago Press, 1994), 88.

43. As Schultz summarizes the slow turn from commerce to manufacturing: "In the final decade of the eighteenth century Philadelphia accounted for nearly a fifth of all U.S. trade, but only two decades later the city's maritime traffic had fallen to little more than a tenth of the national total. By the 1830s Philadelphia exports amounted to a mere 4 percent of America's foreign commerce." *Republic of Labor*, 165, 270 n.

44. Catherine Bowen, *Miracle at Philadelphia: The Story of the Constitutional Convention, May to September 1787* (Boston: Little, Brown, 1968).

45. On Lockean "environmentalism" in Jeffersonian America, see Bernard Sheehan, *Seeds of Extinction: Jeffersonian Philanthropy and the American Indian* (Chapel Hill: University of North Carolina Press, 1973). On influence and Lockean educational projects, see Jay Fliegelman, *Prodigals and Pilgrims: The American Revolution against Patriarchal Authority, 1750–1800* (New York: Cambridge University Press, 1982), 9–35. On the Lockean/Linnaean structure of bureaucracy, see Pratt, *Imperial Eyes*, 15–37.

46. Alan Liu, "Local Transcendence: Cultural Criticism, Postmodernism, and the Romanticism of Detail," *Representations* 32 (1990): 85.

47. Such arguments are offered by, among others, James Flexner, *The Light of Distant Skies, 1760–1835* (New York: Harcourt, Brace, 1954); Neil Harris, *The Artist in American Society: The Formative Years, 1790–1860* (Chicago: University of Chicago Press, 1982); and most recently, Richard Bushman, *The Refinement of America: Persons, Houses, Cities* (New York: Knopf, 1992).

48. John Atlee Kouenhoven, *Made in America: The Arts in Modern Civilization* (Garden City, N.Y.: Doubleday, 1948); Brooke Hindle, *Engines of Change: The American Industrial Revolution, 1790–1860* (Washington, D.C.: Smithsonian Institution Press, 1986); Kasson, *Civilizing the Machine*.

49. Production has often been criticized because of its centrality to Jeffersonian political economy and the fantasies of "American" independence, nation building—and authorship—that political economy has enabled for property-holding white men. Myra Jehlen and Anne Norton, among others, have analyzed the "incarnational" mystique of production and, particularly, the way it binds production to patriarchy. Myra Jehlen, *American Incarnation: The Individual, the Nation, and the Continent* (Cambridge, Mass.: Harvard University Press, 1986); Anne Norton, *Alternative Americas: A Reading of Antebellum Political Culture* (Chicago: University of Chicago Press, 1986), 19–63. Historians of consumption have offered new perspectives on the politics of production through the changes in meanings attributed to commodities, as, for example, in the case of the boycotts of British goods during the American Revolution. See T. H.

Breen, "The Meaning of Things: Interpreting the Consumer Economy in the Eighteenth Century," in *Consumption and the World of Goods*, ed. John Brewer and Roy Porter (London: Routledge, 1993), 249–60; idem, " 'Baubles of Britain': The American Consumer Revolutions of the Eighteenth Century," *Past and Present* 119 (1988): 73–104; idem, "An Empire of Goods: The Anglicanization of Colonial America, 1690–1776," *Journal of British Studies* 25 (1986): 467–99.

CHAPTER ONE. RAISING THE ROOF

1. Whitfield Bell, "The Federal Processions of 1788," *New York Historical Society Quarterly* 46 (1962): 1, 12; John Fitzhugh Millar, "A Parade of Small Ships," *Nautical Research Journal* 35 (1990): 74–80; Richard G. Kalkhoff, "Toasting the Constitution: New Hampshire's Celebrations of 1788," *Historical New Hampshire* 43 (1988): 291–303; Betty Bandel, "Every Eye Sparkled, Every Heart Glowed . . . ," *Maryland Historical Magazine* 83 (1988): 69–73. In "An Independence Day Celebration in Rhode Island, 1788," Irwin H. Polishook describes the failed federal celebration in Rhode Island. After New Hamphire's ratification on 21 June 1788, federalists in Providence had, like federalists in Philadelphia, attempted to schedule a federal feast to coincide with the state's official Fourth of July celebration. Their efforts were thwarted, however, by the arrival of an estimated 1000 armed antifederalists from "the countryside," who feared in particular that the federalists would "thereby take occasion to represent to. the other States, that town and country had joined to celebrate the adoption of said Constitution, and insinuate that the opposition of this state to the Constitution was given up." *Huntington Library Quarterly* 30 (1966): 85–93.

2. Francis Hopkinson, "An Account of the Grand Federal Procession," *American Museum and Repository of Ancient and Modern Fugitive Pieces, &c.*, July 1788, 62–63.

3. Hopkinson, "Account," 63.

4. Ibid., 61–62, 65.

5. Benjamin Rush, "Observations on the Grand Federal Procession by a Gentleman in this City," *American Museum and Repository of Ancient and Modern Fugitive Pieces, &c.*, 77.

6. Hopkinson, "Account," 64–65, 67.

7. Ibid., 63, 67.

8. On the procession as a revival of certain English Lord Mayor's traditions in a very different context, see Alfred F. Young, "English Plebeian Culture and Eighteenth-Century American Radicalism," in *The Origins of Anglo-American Radicalism*, ed. Margaret Jacob and James Jacob (London: George Allen & Unwin, 1983), 185–212. The craft parades in Britain were, in part, attempts to signal craft unity in the face of its actual breakdown in Europe. Americans had not developed active independent ceremonial roles where the import market for European goods in the colonies undermined the development of skills that required long periods of training and were kept alive by tightly organized bodies of men. Many of the skilled craftsmen who migrated to North America after the Revolution did so precisely because skills, techniques, and standards of living were breaking down in their home cities. As Young notes, "For these men public guild and craft traditions were already a fading memory, and their performance in America must have been a conscious act of revival" (116–17). Other discussions of the Grand Federal Procession include Susan Davis, *Parades and Power:*

Street Parades in Nineteenth-Century Philadelphia (Philadelphia: Temple University Press, 1986), 116–25; "Account of Federal Procession," repr. in *Register of Pennsylvania* (Philadelphia) 2 (July 1828): 417–25; Sarah H. J. Simpson, "The Federal Procession of the City of New York," *New York Historical Society Quarterly Bulletin* 9 (1925): 39–58; Sean Wilentz, "Artisan Republican Festivals and the Rise of Class Conflict in New York City, 1788–1837," in *Working-Class America: Essays in Labor, Community, and American Society*, ed. Michael Frisch and Daniel Walkowitz (Urbana: University of Illinois Press, 1983), 37–77. For an extensive bibliography on the early modern spectacle of the "Triumph," see *Triumphal Celebrations and the Rituals of Statecraft*, vol. 1 of *"All the World's a Stage—": Art and Pageantry in the Renaissance and Baroque*, ed. Barbara Wisch and Susan Scott Munshower (University Park: Department of Art History at the Pennsylvania State University, 1990), 370–85; and Robert Withington, *English Pageantry: An Historical Outline*, 2 vols. (New York: Benjamin Blom, 1926). The Lord Mayor's celebrations were, in part, emblematic masques that also drew heavily upon the skills of master artificers and builders of triumphal arches, stages, and stage props. These spectacles were referred to as triumphs during the Elizabethan and Jacobean periods. Royal entries and Lord Mayor's pageants both helped to establish the "body of the civic pageant." London guilds, especially carvers and painters, were deeply involved in mounting such displays but had not become the center of their meaning. These Renaissance processions were rich in emblematic iconology and mechanical wonders, such as "the Chariot of Time with seven wheels symbolizing the seven ages of man; drawn by two lions and two sea horses; with Time the principle figure." David M. Bergeron, *English Civic Pageantry 1558–1642* (Columbia: University of South Carolina Press, 1970), 271, 243–308. For republican festivals during the French Revolution, see Mona Ozouf, *Festivals and the French Revolution*, trans. Alan Sheridan (Cambridge, Mass.: Harvard University Press, 1988).

9. Rush, "Observations on the Procession," 75–76.

10. The famous Philadelphia exhibition of 1876, then, was, in many ways, nothing new as an exhibition of American manufacturing.

11. These included the often discussed "Funerals of Liberty," in which a female figure of Liberty was mourned and carried in procession to a burial ground, where she rose again, restored. Ann Fairfax Withington, *Toward a More Perfect Union: Virtue and the Formation of American Republics* (New York: Oxford University Press, 1991), 145–47. See also Peter Shaw, *American Patriots and the Rituals of Revolution* (Cambridge, Mass.: Harvard University Press, 1981). On the renewed control of the streets at the end of the Revolution, see Steve Rosswurm, *Arms, Country, and Class: The Philadelphia Militia and the "Lower Sort" during the American Revolution* (New Brunswick, N.J.: Rutgers University Press, 1987).

12. Hopkinson, "Account," 63.

13. Rush, "Observations on the Procession," 75.

14. David Walstreicher, "Rites of Rebellion, Rites of Assent: Celebrations, Print Culture, and the Origins of American Nationalism," *Journal of American History* 82 (1995): 37–60. Walstreicher points out the dynamic between street performance and its reporting as a cause of Union, arguing that "American nationalism emerged from the conjunction of local celebrations and their reproduction in the press" (38). "Diffused by print," he writes, "the unruly rites of rebellion could serve as ruling rites of assent" (38). Walstreicher's essay argues that the ultimately consensual character of American

nationalism as a performativity of localism is denied by a print nationalism that "nevertheless relies upon it and its contestatory vigor": "[P]rint and the rituals of revolution fed one another, increasing both the geographical reach of ideology and the opportunities for local practice" (38). What it is necessary to add to Walstreicher's discussion of this "collation" and reproduction of ritual or ad hoc performances in print is the degree to which it was writing, viewing, and *making*—or the visibly legible performances of production—that stamped the federalist-era intersections of print and ritual.

15. Rush, "Observations on the Procession," 76.

16. Hopkinson, "Account," 62.

17. Agriculture consisted of the Agricultural Society and its president, onetime Philadelphia mayor Samuel Powell, carrying a flag that represented "industry in the form of a ploughman . . . followed at a small distance by the goddess of Plenty, bearing a cornucopia . . . [and] in the background a view of an American farm—[its] motto 'venerate the plough.' " The characters on the flag were replicated in the street by seven men dressed as farmers and "driving two ploughs, one drawn by four oxen and directed by Richard Willing, esq [a city merchant] in a farmers dress." Hopkinson, "Account," 60.

18. Ibid.

19. Ibid.

20. Davis, *Parades and Power,* 118.

21. Robert Levare Brunhouse, *Counter-revolution in Pennsylvania, 1776–1790* (Harrisburg, Pa.: Pennsylvania Historical Commission, 1972).

22. *The Records of the Federal Convention of 1787,* ed. Max Farrand (New Haven, Conn.: Yale University Press, 1911), 1:43 (31 May), quoted in Samuel H. Beer, *To Make a Nation: The Rediscovery of American Federalism* (Cambridge, Mass.: Harvard University Press, Belknap Press, 1993), 361.

23. Hopkinson, "Account," 70–71.

24. Ibid., 71.

25. As Samuel Beer argues, "Wilson foresees an attachment of the people to the new republic comparable to that attributed to the citizens of the small state by classical writers. What he says, however, is not an echo of ancient philosophy but an anticipation of modern democratic nationalism." *To Make a Nation,* 368.

26. Ibid., 363–77.

27. *Records of the Federal Convention,* 1:43 (31 May), quoted in Beer, *To Make a Nation,* 361.

28. Jay Fliegelman, *Declaring Independence: Jefferson, Natural Language, and the Culture of Performance* (Stanford, Calif.: Stanford University Press, 1994), 51.

29. Bruce Laurie, *Artisans into Workers: Labor in Nineteenth-Century America* (New York: Hill & Wang, 1989). American republican festivity was always already inseparable from the exhibitionary making and displaying of "celebrities," but perhaps a federalist performer like Wilson would say that the great compensation for the inequalities of elevation is that any American can, theoretically, walk out upon this stage—this visual field. As Wilson wrote, "a citizen and legislator of the free and united states of America will be one of the first characters of the world!" Quoted in Beer, *To Make a Nation,* 362.

30. Francis Hopkinson, "The raising: a song for federal mechanics," *American Museum and Repository of Ancient and Modern Fugitive Pieces, &c.,* July 1788, 95.

31. Gordon Wood, "Interest and Disinterestedness in the Making of the Constitution," in *Beyond Confederation: Origins of the Constitution and American National Identity*, ed. Richard Beeman, Stephen Botein, and Edward Carter II (Chapel Hill: University of North Carolina Press for the Institute of Early American History and Culture, Williamsburg, Virginia, 1987), 69–109.

32. For the concepts of actual and virtual representation, see Bernard Bailyn, *The Ideological Origins of the American Revolution* (Cambridge, Mass.: Harvard University Press, 1967), 162–75.

33. Rousseau addresses spirits rather differently: see, for instance, *Politics and the Arts: Letter to M. D'Alembert on the Theatre*, trans. Allan Bloom (Ithaca, N.Y.: Cornell University Press, 1960). For him, the real danger is feminization: "Never has a people perished from an excess of wine; all perish from the disorder of women" (109). Elsewhere, Rousseau follows Plato's *Laws* in stating that old age, in fact, can benefit from an infusion of "spirits": "But let half-chilled blood seek a support which reanimates it, let a beneficent liquor take the place of the spirits that it has no more" (109).

34. Consider Franklin's refusals to drink and his attack on St. Monday during his sojourn in a London print shop in the *Autobiography*, as well as Gutman's famous analyses of cultural resistance to work discipline. Herbert Gutman, *Work, Culture, and Society in Industrializing America: Essays in American Working Class and Social History* (Oxford: Basil Blackwell, 1977). For episodes of resistance in Philadelphia, see Cynthia Shelton, *The Mills of Manayunk: Industrialization and Social Conflict in the Philadelphia Region, 1787–1837* (Baltimore, Md.: Johns Hopkins University Press, 1986), 7–25, 27–35, 37–46.

35. E. P. Thompson, "The Moral Economy of the English Crowd in the Eighteenth Century," in *Customs in Common: Studies in Tradition and Popular Culture* (New York: New Press, 1993), 185–258.

36. Wilson was one of a number of merchants who had resisted the committee's attempt to regulate the price of salt, flour, and other goods then in short supply. Foner, *Tom Paine and Revolutionary America*, 145–82. The Committee of Trade included forty-seven artisans, among them "seventeen shoemakers." Benjamin Rush believed the militia "were enraged chiefly by liquor," and their objects were "unknown." Quoted in Foner, *Tom Paine and Revolutionary America*, 176.

37. The men who rescued Wilson and the other merchant "Tories" offer a symbolic anticipation of thé more middle-class leaders of the artisan republicans in Philadelphia; the rescuers included portrait painter and militia captain Charles Willson Peale and Timothy Matlack, the son of a Quaker brewer. Foner, *Tom Paine and Revolutionary America*, 108–10.

38. Quoted in Bell, "The Federal Processions of 1788," 38.

39. Rush, "Observations on the Procession," 76.

40. Rousseau, *Letter to D'Alembert*, 133. Rousseau states, "If the Orientals, whose warm climate causes them to sweat a good deal, do little exercise . . . at least they go and sit in the open air . . . while here the women take great pains to suffocate their friends in sound rooms well closed" (102).

41. Rousseau, *Letter to D'Alembert*, 132–34.

42. The irony of Rousseau's fantasy of the republic's face-to-face appearance to itself is that Rousseau himself writes at a great distance from his home city, as part of a Genevan "diaspora." Fully "half" of Geneva's citizens, Rousseau acknowledges, are

"scattered throughout the rest of Europe and the world," either forced abroad in search of "resources" or propelled by "so great an inclination to travel that there is no land where they are not to be found dispersed." *Letter to D'Alembert*, 132.

43. Ibid., 125.

44. Ibid., 126.

45. For an extended discussion of the debate over size, see Rosemarie Zagarri, *The Politics of Size* (Ithaca, N.Y.: Cornell University Press, 1981); *The Anti-Federalist: Writings by the Opponents of the Constitution*, ed. Herbert J. Storing (Chicago: University of Chicago Press, 1985), 92–95, 103, 113–16, 235–36.

46. Montesquieu, *The Spirit of the Laws by Montesquieu: A Compendium of the First English Edition*, ed. David Wallace Carrithers (Berkeley: University of California Press, 1977), 176–77. Beer, *To Make a Nation*, 207–8, 221–22, 233–36.

47. James Madison, *Federalist* no. 10, *The Federalist Papers*, ed. Isaac Kramnick (Harmondsworth, England: Penguin Books, 1987), 127–28.

48. Ibid., 123, 127.

49. For related arguments about the English Constitution, see Philip Richard D. Corrigan and Derek Sayer, *The Great Arch: English State Formation as Cultural Revolution* (Oxford: Basil Blackwell, 1985).

50. Rush, "Observations on the Procession," 76.

51. Ibid.

52. *American Museum*, July 1788, 96. William Dowling, *Poetry and Ideology in Revolutionary Connecticut* (Athens, Ga.: University of Georgia Press, 1990).

53. Rush, "Observations on the Procession," 75.

54. Ibid., 76.

55. Ibid., 77.

56. Ibid., 77.

57. Ibid., 78.

58. Ibid., 78.

59. Hopkinson, "Account," 66.

60. Ibid., 67.

61. Ibid., 66.

62. Ibid., 66.

63. Ronald Schultz, *The Republic of Labor: Philadelphia Artisans and the Politics of Class, 1720–1830* (New York: Oxford University Press, 1993), 69–101.

64. Rush, "Observations on the Procession," 77.

65. Ibid., 75.

66. Terry Eagleton, "Free Particulars," chap. 1 of *The Ideology of the Aesthetic* (Oxford: Basil Blackwell, 1990), 13–30.

67. Hopkinson, "Account," 60.

68. W. Bell, "The Federal Processions of 1788," 16.

69. Rush, "Observations on the Procession," 75.

70. On the paper money debate, see Eric Foner, *Tom Paine and Revolutionary America*, 149–50, 173–74, 197–200.

71. Francis Hopkinson, "The New Roof," *American Museum and Repository of Ancient and Modern Fugitive Pieces &c.*, August 1788, 143.

72. Ibid.

73. Ibid.

74. Sharon V. Salinger, *"To Serve Faithfully and Well": Labor and Indentured Servants in Pennsylvania, 1682–1800* (New York: Cambridge University Press, 1987).

75. Hopkinson, "The New Roof," 143.

76. Samuel Bryan was the son of Judge George Bryan, a Pennsylvania legislator and judge, and a leader of the antifederalists in Pennsylvania. Storing, *Anti-Federalist,* 7–12.

77. Hopkinson, "The New Roof," 143.

78. Ibid., 143–44.

79. Ibid., 145.

80. Ibid. As explained in a footnote to the table of contents in the July issue of *The American Museum,* "The New Roof" was intended for the special July issue on the Federal Procession, though it did not appear until August (104).

81. Paul E. Johnson and Sean Wilentz, *The Kingdom of Matthias: A Story of Sex and Salvation in 19th-Century America* (New York: Oxford University Press, 1994); Ronald Schultz, "The Anglo-American Radical Tradition in the Eighteenth Century," in *The Republic of Labor* (New York: Oxford University Press), 1993), 3–35; E. P. Thompson, "The Liberty Tree," in *The Making of the English Working Class* (New York: Pantheon, 1964), 17–185.

82. Morton J. Horwitz, *The Transformation of American Law, 1780–1860* (Cambridge, Mass.: Harvard University Press, 1977); Christopher L. Tomlins, *Law, Labor, and Ideology in the Early American Republic* (New York: Cambridge University Press, 1993); Brook Thomas, "The Legal Fictions of Lemuel Shaw," in *Cross Examinations of Law and Literature: Cooper, Hawthorne, Stowe, and Melville* (New York: Cambridge University Press, 1987).

83. Hopkinson, "The New Roof," 145.

84. The term exhibitionary complex is taken from Tony Bennett's article "The Exhibitionary Complex," *New Formations* 4 (1988): 73–102.

85. William Russell Birch, *The City of Philadelphia in the State of Pennsylvania North America as it appeared in the Year 1800, Consisting of twenty eight Plates* (Springland, Cot, Pa.: William Birch, 1800), repr. in *Birch's Views of Philadelphia: A Reduced Facsimile of the City of Philadelphia . . . as It Appeared in the Year 1800* (Philadelphia: Free Library of Philadelphia, 1982), plates 5e and 6; 11 and 12; 13 and 14.

86. In 1800, Birch was a recent English immigrant. Before arriving in Philadelphia, he had executed a series of picturesque views of the British countryside and its mansions titled *Délices de la Grande Bretagne.* Like this pictorial tour of British mansions, Birch's Philadelphia *Views* are structured as reflections on contrasts of station and rank. The Philadelphia *Views* are utterly different, however, from *Délices de la Grande Bretagne* in their attention to street and work life and in their focus on public works in a rising city that, by 1800, was the nation's former rather than present capital. *Délices de la Grande Bretagne* is a collection of engravings copied from famous landscape paintings by well-known British painters; there is no guided tour or opening map. Copy consulted at the Huntington Library, San Marino, Calif.

87. Hopkinson, "Account," 61.

88. Ibid., 62.

89. On Philadelphia's "White Oaks," see James H. Huston, "An Investigation of the Inarticulate: Philadelphia's White Oaks," *William and Mary Quarterly* 28.1 (1971): 3–25.

90. Hopkinson, "Account," 61–62.

91. Ibid., 57.

92. Birch, *Views*, plate 29.

93. This is a different way of reading the relationship between theatricality and "absorption"—or silence—than is found in Michael Fried's study of looks and work in French painting in *Absorption and Theatricality: Painting and Beholder in the Age of Diderot* (Chicago: University of Chicago Press, 1980). Despite the fact that the dialectics of absorption and theatricality often center around performances of work or labor (in paintings of people at work), Fried is not interested in the ways in which the interplay of absorption and theatricality constitutes a performance (or "production") of production that is inseparable from a spectatorial, class-constituting, cultural mechanics of early industrialization.

94. Birch, "Preface," in *Views*, n.p..

95. Ibid.

96. The so-called 'Quasi-War' with the French, 1797–1801.

97. *American Museum and Repository of Ancient and Modern Fugitive Pieces, &c.*, July 1788, 51.

98. On the juxtaposition of invention and automata in natural history museums, see Barbara Stafford, *Artful Science: Enlightenment, Entertainment, and the Eclipse of Visual Education* (Cambridge, Mass.: MIT Press, 1994), 217–79.

99. Bruce McConachie, *Melodramatic Formations: American Theater and Society, 1820–1870* (Iowa City: University of Iowa Press, 1992), 161–97.

100. Rather than melodrama, McConachie writes, Peale's Enlightenment Museum "had exhibited few 'human curiosities,' preferring instead to emphasize the rationality of nature." McConachie, *Melodramatic Formations*, 163.

101. David Brigham, *Public Culture in the Early Republic: Peale's Museum and its Audience* (Washington, D.C.: Smithsonian Institution Press, 1995).

102. Hopkinson, "Observations," 59–60.

103. The Carpenters' Company was the most guildlike association in Federal Philadelphia, a city that lacked an embedded guild tradition. Founded in 1712 and patterned on the Worshipful Company of Carpenters in London, the Carpenters' Company was composed of "wealthy builder-architects" and housed itself in Carpenters' Hall, which still stands today on Independence Square, next to the old Pennsylvania State House. Most members of the Carpenters' Company were closely connected with merchant and government power. Foner, *Tom Paine and Revolutionary America*, 39; Roger W. Moss, Jr., "The Carpenters' Company of Philadelphia," *Historic Preservation* 26.3 (1974): 37–41.

Chapter Two. The Mechanic as the Author of His Life

1. In fact, as Christopher Looby argues, the central meaning of Franklin's *Autobiography* seems to lie in the utter absence of the Revolutionary War from (or, one might say, in the Revolution's complete absorption by) the text. Christopher Looby, "'The Affairs of the Revolution Occasion'd the Interruption': Self, Language, and Nation in Franklin's *Autobiography*," in *Voicing America: Language, Literary Form and the Origins of the United States* (Chicago: University of Chicago Press, 1996), 99–144.

2. Mitchell R. Breitweiser, *Cotton Mather and Benjamin Franklin: The Price of Representative Personality* (New York: Cambridge University Press, 1984).

3. See, for example, Fitch's dedication in the "Life": "my life Sir has been filled with such a variety of changes which will afford such useful lessons to mankind I think I should hardly do my duty which I owe my fellow men was I to supress it. John Fitch, "Life," in *The Autobiography of John Fitch*, ed. Frank D. Prager (Philadelphia: American Philosophical Society, 1976), 19.

4. In fact, Fitch represents precisely the category of democratic and revolutionary "licentiousness" against which worthiness was defined. Gordon S. Wood, "The Worthy against the Licentious," in *The Confederation and the Constitution: The Critical Issues*, ed. Gordon S. Wood (Boston: Little, Brown & Co., 1973), 86–113.

5. "To the Librarian," appendix to *The Autobiography of John Fitch*, 207–8.

6. Thomas Boyd, *Poor John Fitch, Inventor of the Steamboat* (New York: G. P. Putnam's Sons, 1935), 138.

7. In the 1780s, it was cheaper for farmers in western Pennsylvania, Ohio, Western Virginia and Kentucky to ship produce (flour, corn, tobacco, hogs, whiskey) down the Mississippi to New Orleans than to transport it over the Allegheny mountains to eastern seaports. Since it was almost impossible to travel upstream, the journey down the Mississippi was one-way, usually made by flatboats whose steersmen returned by land or sea.

8. James Flexner, *Steamboats Come True: American Inventors in Action* (New York: Viking Press, 1944), 66–81: "[I]t was the settling of the west that called imperiously for a steamboat" (66).

9. John Fitch, "Steamboat History," in *The Autobiography of John Fitch*, 113, 148–50.

10. In the introduction to his "Steamboat History," Fitch presents the reader with "a long train of reasoning to prove that I was not a Lunitic": "What I call Lunacy is a train of deranged unconnected Ideas. It is well known that a Steam Engine is a Complicated Machine, and to make that and connect it with the works for propelling a Boat, must take a long train of Ideas and them all connected . . . [although] to reflect on the disproportion of a man of my abilites to such a task, I am apt to charge myself with being deranged. . . . But on examining over my papers, I find that there was 46 . . . principle Characters for Philosophy and machinism, that gave me their opinion that the scheme was rational." Fitch, "Steamboat History" (143–44).

11. Fitch, "Life," 130.

12. Fitch, "Steamboat History," 175.

13. M. M. Bakhtin, *The Dialogic Imagination: Four Essays*, trans. Caryl Emerson and Michael Holquist, ed. Michael Holquist (Austin: University of Texas Press, 1981); M. M. Bakhtin, *Rabelais and His World*, trans. Hélène Iswolsky (Bloomington: Indiana University Press, 1984).

14. By "novelization" I understand Bakhtin to mean writing that disrupts, ventriloquizes, or displays other genres and practices as artifacts of its own power of disruption and recombination. See "Epic and Novel," in *The Dialogic Imagination*, 3–40.

15. Second and Third Letters to the Librarian of the Philadelphia Library Company, in *The Autobiography of John Fitch*, 207–8.

16. Fitch, "Life," 25, 30, 32.

17. Ibid., 37, 38.

18. Ibid., 38.

19. Ibid., 41.

20. Ibid., 36.

21. Richard Sennett makes a related argument in "Paternalism, an Authority of False Love," in *Authority* (New York: Vintage Books, 1980), 76: "the paternalist image was an attempt to bridge a gulf between economic individualism and the desire for community. It is not surprising, therefore, that revolutionary regimes which have expropriated this image can officially declare the conflict between individualism and community to be over . . . [eliminating] 'the tragedy of loneliness from which men of the capitalist world suffer.' "

22. Edmund Morgan, "The People's Choice: Elections and Electioneering," in *Inventing the People: The Rise of Popular Sovereignty in England and America* (New York: Norton, 1988), 174–208.

23. Fitch, "Life," 27, 29.

24. Ibid., 29.

25. Ibid.

26. Ibid.

27. Breitweiser, *Cotton Mather and Benjamin Franklin: The Price of Representative Personality.* On Franklin's career as a teacher of swimming techniques, see *Autobiography*, 53–54; for "swimmingly" used as a metaphor, see *Autobiography*, 73.

28. Fitch, "Steamboat History," 193. "Although he ascribed many of his later troubles to his 'insignificant appearance,' he was to stand more than 6 feet tall and give his contemporaries an impression of great power." See the posthumous woodcut from *Lloyd's Steamboat Directory* (1856) in Flexner, *Steamboats Come True*, 21.

29. Fitch, "Life," 32.

30. The grotesque in Fitch's manuscripts is not, in other words, a version of the transgressive, Bakhtinian carnivalesque traced by Peter Stallybrass and Allon White in *The Politics and Poetics of Transgression* (Ithaca, N.Y.: Cornell University Press, 1986).

31. It is tempting here to apply a psychoanalytic (i.e., object relations) framework to Fitch, particularly when he compares himself or his friends, as he frequently does, to Jesus, Mohammed, Newton, or George Fox. One thinks of Kohut, Klein, and Winnicott, in other words, whenever Fitch voices his grandiose fantasies of world fame or finds himself, painfully or hilariously, unable to achieve a functional balance as an ordinary or integrated self among others. As a technique for analyzing the archaic structure of subject/object dynamics, object relations theory is relevant to Fitch: the analyst would trace the inventor's failures of relatedness and his chronic outrage to archaic experiences of disrupted self-object (caretaker-infant) relations, with a resulting failure of those functions that constitute the self in relation to itself, that is, failures to integrate, soothe, or, interestingly, to bring one's self into view, i.e., as one's own "mirror." But object relations itself is enmeshed in the social constitution of "working," or functional, subjects. Mapping the power circuitry of an introjected struggle between "big" versus "little" selves, an object relations theorist or therapist may or may not reflect upon the theory's role in the making and maintenance of class difference.

32. Fitch, "Life," 59.

33. Ibid., 61.

34. Ibid., 62–114.

35. Ibid., 66–70.

36. The most general principle of inclusion throughout Fitch's "Life" seems to be the category of "interesting matters," as he says (to Rev. Irwin) near the end of the captivity: "Sir as I am sure that the remainder of my life cannot be filled with interesting matters I mean to confine the whole to the 4th Book of the Steam Boat History to which I refer you for the remainder." Ibid., 94.

37. Fitch, "Life," 30.

38. Ibid., 70.

39. Ibid., 71.

40. Ibid., 70.

41. Ibid., 72.

42. Ibid., 76.

43. Ibid., 83.

44. Ibid., 92.

45. Ibid., 78.

46. Ibid., 79.

47. Ibid., 57.

48. Fitch, "Steamboat History," 148–50.

49. Fitch, "Life," 87–94.

50. Ibid., 94.

51. Ibid., 94.

52. Ibid., 103.

53. Brook Hindle, *Emulation and Invention* (New York: New York University Press, 1981), 38.

54. Franklin to Benjamin Vaughan, 14 May 1788; Benjamin Rush to John Coakley Lettsom, 4 May 1788; Thomas J. Pettigrew, *Memoirs of the Life and Writings of the Late John Coakley Lettsom* (London, 1817), 430–31, quoted in Hindle, *Emulation and Invention*, 38–41. Fitch's companies were drawn largely from the middling class of tradesmen but included a few merchants, bankers, and learned gentlemen. His first joint-stock company, organized in 1786, included Thomas Hutchins, geographer-general of the United States; Richard Wells, a member of Tench Coxe's Manufacturing Company and cashier of the Bank of North America; Benjamin Morris, retailer of wines and groceries; Joseph Budd, a hatter; and Magnus Miller, Thomas Palmer, and Gideon Wells, who were all either merchants or tavern keepers. See Boyd, *Poor John Fitch*, 152–53.

55. Fitch, "Steamboat History," 154.

56. Ibid., 156.

57. Ibid., 156–57.

58. "Letter to Thomas Jefferson," in *The Autobiography of John Fitch*, 207.

59. Gordon Wood, "The Worthy against the Licentious," in *The Confederation and the Constitution: The Critical Issues*, ed. Gordon Wood (Boston: Little, Brown & Co., 1973), 87.

60. Wood, "The Worthy against the Licentious," 111.

61. Ibid.

62. Ibid.

63. "[I]t is rather of an entertainment than a Burthen to go to meeting where you are to deliver a discourse even if it is on the most absurd Text that you can pick out of a jargon of Absurdities." Fitch, "Life," 111.

64. Ibid., 111, 113.

65. Fitch, Ibid., 113–14.

66. Ibid., 153–54.

67. Boyd writes, "From their deliberations at Independence Hall, or from their lodgings at the Indian Queen, or the Bunch of Grapes, most of the delegates strolled down to the Front Street wharves to see the strange invention." *Poor John Fitch*, 179–81. The ship is pictured in Hindle, *Emulation and Invention*, 70 (fig. 17).

68. Boyd, *Poor John Fitch*, 179–81.

69. Ibid., 180.

70. Ibid., 231.

71. Ibid., 239–40.

72. *Port Folio*, May 1809, 364.

73. Ibid., 365.

74. Ibid.

75. Richard Dunn, "Servants and Slaves: The Recruitment and Employment of Labor," in *Colonial British America: Essays in the New History of the Early Modern Era*, ed. Jack P. Greene and J. R. Poole (Baltimore: Johns Hopkins University Press, 1984).

76. In query 8, "On Population," Jefferson employs "licentiousness" to describe recent immigrants. Jefferson was deeply concerned about the infusion of large immigrant populations into a new country that, he hoped, would be dominated in representation at least by "husbandmen"—or agricultural, rather than commodity, producers (with the class divisions commodity culture implies). Among the potentially licentious body of immigrants, however, Jefferson exempts the imported artisan, whose potential for Old World licentiousness is counterbalanced by the value of his mechanical art or science: "but I doubt the expediency of inviting [immigration] by extraordinary encouragments. I mean not that these doubts should be extended to the importation of useful artificers. The policy of that measure depends on very different considerations. Spare no expence in obtaining them. They will after a while go to the plough and the hoe; but, in the mean time, they will teach us something we do not know." Jefferson, *Notes*, 85. Jefferson's exemption of the artisan is significant at this juncture. Potentially suspect but potentially valuable, this sketchy figure emerges in the text just long enough to practice or pass on his knowledge (to whom and for what purpose?) before returning to the soil. As an intermediary man, Jefferson's manufactory-era artisan stands between organic and mechanical production, cultivation and manufacturing, linking without fully belonging to either mode of production. Geniuslike, this ambiguously useful figure joins cultivated liberty with uncultivated licentiousness while standing, curiously, outside both categories.

77. "If it be thought unequal to compare Europe with America, which is so much larger, I answer, not more so than to compare America with the whole world." Jefferson, *Notes*, 48–49.

78. Ibid., 47.

79. Ibid., 64.

80. Fitch, Postscript 3, 121.

81. Fitch, Ibid., 120–21; Postscript 5, 132.

82. Postscript 3, 121–22, 124.

83. Fitch, Postscript 5, 130–32.

84. Henry F. May, *The Enlightenment in America* (New York: Oxford University Press, 1976); Margaret Jacob, *The Radical Enlightenment: Pantheists, Freemasons, and Republicans* (London: Allen & Unwin, 1981). Jacob focuses on the distinction between pantheists and the Newtonians in the Royal Society.

85. Fitch, Postscript 3, 122–23.

86. Paul Henry Thiery, baron d'Holbach, *The System of Nature: or, Laws of the Physical and Moral World* (1770; New York: Garland Publishing, 1984); Adolph Koch, *Republican Religion: The American Revolution and the Cult of Reason* (New York: Columbia University Press, 1933), repr. as *Religion of the American Enlightenment* (New York: Thomas Y. Crowell, 1968); Donald H. Yer, *The Democratic Enlightenment* (New York: Capricorn Books, 1975); Richard Twomey, *Jacobins and Jeffersonians: Anglo-American Radicalism in the United States, 1790–1820* (De Kalb: Northern Illinois University, 1974); Pauline Maier, "Reason and Revolution: The Radicalism of Dr. Thomas Young," *American Quarterly* 28 (Summer 1976): 239–49.

87. "[Palmer] both cites and paraphrases frequently from the 1797 London edition of Mirabaud's *System of Nature* and the 1795 New York edition of Boulanger's *Christianity Unveiled*, apparently giving credence to the pseudonymous authorship of both works." Roderick S. French, "Elihu Palmer, Radical Deist, Radical Republican," in *Studies in Eighteenth-Century Culture*, vol. 8, ed. Roseann Runte (Madison: University of Wisconsin Press, for the American Society for Eighteenth-Century Studies, 1979), 100.

88. Fitch, Postscript 7, 138.

89. Ibid., 138–39.

90. Fitch, Postscript 3, 122.

91. Ibid., 121.

92. Ibid., 124.

93. The terms "confessions" or "postscripts" are Frank D. Prager's. Introduction to *The Autobiography of John Fitch*, 11.

94. Fitch, Postscript 2, 115

95. Fitch, Postscript 2, 116; Postscript 3, 123–24.

96. Fitch, Postscript 6, 137–38.

97. Boyd, *Poor John Fitch*, 239–46.

98. Fitch, Postscript 3, 124; Postscript 5, 128.

99. Fitch, Postscript 6, 136–37.

100. Fitch, Postscript 4, 125; see also Postscript 6, 133.

101. Fitch, Postscript 4, 124–25; Postscript 6, 134.

102. Fitch, "Steamboat History," 203.

103. Fitch, Postscript 4, 128.

104. Fitch, Postcript 6, 136–37; "Steamboat History," 144.

105. Fitch, Postcript 6, 137, 136.

106. Ibid., 136.

107. Denise Riley, *Am I That Name?: Feminism and the Category of "Women" in History* (Minneapolis: University of Minnesota Press, 1988).

108. Londa Schiebinger, *The Mind Has No Sex?: Women in the Origins of Modern Science* (Cambridge, Mass.: Harvard University Press, 1989); Laurel Ulrich, *The Midwife's Tale: The Life of Martha Ballard, Based on Her Diary, 1785–1812* (New York: Knopf, 1990).

109. Quoted in Brooke Hindle, *Emulation and Invention*, 19.

110. The medieval craft and guild tradition involved corporate practices of secrecy to which the Enlightenment ideal of the public good was directly opposed. Nevertheless, in England, the Masonic Brotherhood grew up alongside Britain's Royal Society, preserving the mysteries or "secrets" inherited from the guilds while combining them with Enlightenment ideals of universalism, social progress, and social mobility. Margaret C. Jacob, *The Radical Enlightenment*, 50–95.

111. Mark Rose, "The Author as Producer: 'Donaldson v. Becket' and the Genealogy of Modern Authorship," *Representations* 23 (Summer 1988): 51–85.

112. Fitch, "Steamboat History," 151–52.

113. Boyd, *Poor John Fitch*, 254.

114. John Smail, "New Languages for Labour and Capitalism: The Transformation of Discourse in the Early Years of the Industrial Revolution," *Social History* 12 (1987): 71; Christopher Tomlins, *Law, Labor, and Ideology in the Early American Republic* (New York: Cambridge University Press, 1993).

115. Boyd, *Poor John Fitch*, 266–68.

116. Ibid., 267.

117. Ibid.

118. Ibid., 268–69.

CHAPTER THREE. PEALE'S MAMMOTH

1. "I have begun the view of the pit em[p]tied, and which will in a more particular manner shew the immen[s]e labour I had." Charles Willson Peale to Rubens Peale, 10 September 1806, in *The Selected Papers of Charles Willson Peale and His Family*, ed. Lillian B. Miller (New Haven, Conn.: Yale University Press, 1988), vol. 2, part 2, 982.

2. Rembrandt Peale, *An Historical Disquisition on the Mammoth, or great American incognitum, an extinct, immense, carnivorous animal, whose fossil remains have been found in North America*, (London: 1803), in *The Selected Papers*, vol. 2, part 1, 571. The story of the excavation and reconstruction of the mastodon is also recounted in the following sources: Charles Willson Peale's "Autobiography," of which the typewritten transcript by Horace W. Sellers appears in *The Collected Papers of Charles Willson Peale and His Family*, ed. Lillian B. Miller (National Portrait Gallery, Smithsonian Institution, Washington, D.C.; Millwood, N.Y.: Kraus-Thomson Organization, 1980), ser. II-C, microcards 1–21; *The Selected Papers of Charles Willson Peale and his Family*, esp. vol. 2, part 1, 308–592; Charles Coleman Sellers, *Mr. Peale's Museum, Charles Willson Peale and the First Popular Museum of Natural Science and Art* (New York: Norton & Co., 1980); and Charles Coleman Sellers, *Later Life*, vol. 2 of *Charles Willson Peale*, 2 vols. (Philadelphia: American Philosophical Society, 1947).

3. Rembrandt Peale, "An Account of the Mammoth" (London: 1802), 5.

4. Thomas Jefferson to Charles Willson Peale, 5 May 1809, *Pennsylvania Magazine of History and Biography* 28 (1904): 318.

5. Thomas Jefferson, "Manufactures," in *Notes on the State of Virginia*, ed. William Peden (New York: Norton & Co., 1954), 164–65. Peale had read Jefferson's *Notes*, as demonstrated by a debate with an Englishman, recorded in his diary: "John Bull replied, ah we shall see by and by—Roberspere once was thought highly of and we shall see whether the President will have resolution to keep to the Sentiments of his

[inaugural] Speech. I replied that he had before shewed himself to be a man of firm nerves by his writings. He replied that some of his works had been brought forward to his censure. Yes, but by a party that stoped at nothing to obtain their end, making improper implications and misrepresentations[,] and more honor than want of just sentiments [is] manifest to every one who will read the whole of his notes on Virginia." Diary 18, part 1: Philadelphia to New York, 5 June–2 July 1801, in *Selected Papers*, 314; also quoted in Sellers, *Mr. Peale's Museum*, 125.

6. Eric Foner, *Tom Paine and Revolutionary America* (New York: Oxford University Press, 1976), 101–6.

7. Thomas Jefferson, First Inaugural Address, 4 March 1801, in *The Writings of Thomas Jefferson*, ed. Paul Leicester Ford (London G. P. Putnam's, 1897), 2:3.

8. Quoted in Jeffery A. Smith, *Franklin and Bache: Envisioning the Enlightened Republic* (New York: Oxford University Press, 1990), 102. Louis Hartz distinguishes the Federalists from the European reaction in *The Liberal Tradition* (1955; New York: Harcourt Brace Jovanovich, 1983), 80: "There is a feudal bleakness about man which sees him fit only for external domination, and there is a liberal bleakness about man which sees him working autonomously on the basis of his own self-interest; Maistre believed in the one, Adams believed in the other. . . . Everything goes to show that the difference between Federalism and the European reaction is the difference between liberal Whiggery and the European 'ancien régime.' "

9. Drew McCoy, *The Elusive Republic: Political Economy in Jeffersonian America* (Chapel Hill: University of North Carolina Press, 1980), 121–84, 211–59; John Nelson, *Liberty and Property: Political Economy and Policymaking in the New Nation, 1789–1812* (Baltimore: Johns Hopkins University Press, 1987), 22–36.

10. For a description of this transformation in the Delaware Valley, see Cynthia Shelton, *The Mills of Manayunk: Industrialization and Social Conflict in the Philadelphia Region, 1787–1837* (Baltimore: Johns Hopkins University Press, 1986), 7–25, 27–35, 37–46; Ronald Schultz, *The Republic of Labor: Philadelphia Artisans and the Politics of Class, 1720–1830* (New York: Oxford University Press, 1993), 128–34.

11. Joyce Appleby, "Commercial Farming and 'the Agrarian Myth' in the Early Republic," *Journal of American History* 68.4 (1982): 833—49. Sean Wilentz summarizes: "The Progressive's insistence that political parties, in New York and elsewhere, directly embodied class interests—that the Whigs were the party of business, the Democrats the party of farmers and labor, or simply 'the people'—led them in turn to ignore the plain truth that in New York and in the rest of the country, both major parties were led by established and emerging elites and their progressive allies, usually lawyers." "However," he continues, "in refuting the Progressives . . . American historians from the late 1940s through the early 1970s retained some of their elders' assumptions, above all their fixation on party politics and their willingness to understand class as an abstract institution . . . the counter-Progressives discovered a past in which political conflict turned on deep ethnic, religious, and 'status' divisions but in which class and class consciousness were either nonexistent or submerged by an American entrepreneurial consensus." Sean Wilentz, *Chants Democratic, New York City and the Rise of the America Working Class, 1788–1850* (New York: Oxford University Press, 1984), 8.

12. Jefferson's interest in natural history was of long standing and well known: like Peale, he believed that "the very sinews of government are made strong by a diffused

knowledge of this science." Charles Willson Peale, "Introduction to a Course of Lectures on Natural History delivered at the University of Pennsylvania, Nov. 16, 1799," in *Selected Papers*, vol. 2, part 1, 267. While president of the United States Jefferson was also president of the American Philosophical Society (of which Peale was curator) and in 1799 published a paper on the giant sloth, or megalonyx, of Virginia. In May of 1797, soon after his election as president of the American Philosophical Society, Jefferson presided over a meeting in which the society considered "A plan for the collecting of information respecting the Antiquities of North America." The editors of the Peale Papers recount that "A year later a committee was appointed with Jefferson and Charles Willson Peale as members, that drafted a public letter appealing for information concerning the whereabouts of natural and archaeological artifacts. An entire skeleton of the 'mammoth' was singled out as something important to acquire." *Selected Papers*, vol. 2, part 1, 348–49 n.

13. Quoted in a letter from Thomas Jefferson to Dr. Caspar Wistar, Washington, D.C., 3 February 1801; cited in Henry Fairfield Osborn, "Thomas Jefferson as a Paleontologist," *Science*, n.s., 82 (6 December 1935), 535. Jefferson comments: "From this extract, and the circumstance that the bones belong to the town, you will be sensible of the difficulty of obtaining any considerable portion of them. . . . It is not unlikely they would with common consent yield a particular bone or bones, provided they may keep the mass for their own town."

14. Thomas Jefferson to Dr. Caspar Wistar, Washington, 20 March 1808; cited in Osborn, "Thomas Jefferson as a Paleontologist," 536.

15. Linda K. Kerber, *Federalists in Dissent: Imagery and Ideology in Jeffersonian America* (Ithaca, N.Y.: Cornell University Press, 1970), 1–23, 67–95.

16. William Cullen Bryant, "The Embargo" (Boston: printed for the purchasers, 1808); facsimile edition with introduction by Thomas O. Mabbott (Gainesville, Fla.: Scholars' Facsimiles and Reprints, 1955), 22.

17. J. H. Powell, "The Mammoth Cheese," in *General Washington and the Jack Ass and Other American Characters in Portrait* (New York: Thomas Yoseloff, 1969), 261.

18. Ibid., 252–66.

19. See, for example, Samuel Ewing's Federalist "Satire on the Mammoth" in the *Port Folio*, 20 February 1802, published in response to a description in the *Aurora*, 18 February 1802, of a Republican "Mammoth Feast" held at the Peale Museum prior to Rembrandt and Rubens Peale's journey to Britain with the duplicate skeleton. Both are reprinted in Samuel Ewing Esquire, "The Mammoth Feast," in *The Philadelphia Souvenir: A Collection of Fugitive Pieces from the Philadelphia Press* (Philadelphia: Port Folio Office, Wm. Brown, Printer, 1826) and in *Selected Papers*, vol. 2, part 1, 401–7, 408 n.

20. John Wilmerding and Lillian Miller argue that *The Exhumation of the Mastodon* is generically hybrid, a creative (or disastrous) blend of history, genre, and portrait painting. Lillian B. Miller, "Charles Willson Peale as History Painter: *The Exhumation of the Mastodon*," *American Art Journal* 13.1 (1981): 30–51; John Wilmerding, "Peale, Quidor, Eakins: Self-Portraiture as Genre Painting," in *Art Studies for an Editor: Twenty-five Essays in Memory of Milton S. Fox* (New York: Harry Abrams, 1975), 290–305. Miller determines that *The Exhumation of the Mastodon* is a history painting and traces its ancestry through Peale's earlier work; however, due to Peale's failure "to generalize" adequately, it is not so much "a history painting" as "an assemblage of portraits." Conversely, John Wilmerding praises as typically American Peale's eccentric and creative blending of portraiture, history, and genre painting in *The Exhumation of the*

Mastodon. Abraham Davidson interprets the painting in light of eighteenth-century theories of catastrophism: "Charles Willson Peale's 'Exhuming the First American Mastodon': An Interpretation," in *Art Studies for an Editor,* 61–71. Also published in *American Quarterly* 21 (1969): 620–29.

21. Charles Willson Peale, *Guide to the Philadelphia Museum* (Philadelphia: Museum Press, 1804), in *Selected Papers,* vol., 2, part 2, 764. Likewise, in his "Autobiography" (1822), Peale claimed that the idea of founding a museum had come to him at the end of the American Revolution with a small pile of mammoth bones, uncovered during the war. Charles Willson Peale, "Autobiography," in *Collected Papers,* ser. II-C, microcards 1–21, 107–8.

22. *An Historical Disquisition on the Mammoth,* in *Selected Papers,* vol. 2, part 1, 554.

23. Peale was appointed a commissioner of forfeited estates on 6 May 1778. Charles Coleman Sellers, *Early Life,* vol. 1 of *Charles Willson Peale,* 2 vols. (Philadelphia: American Philosophical Society, 1947), 185.

24. Ibid., 12, 151–214.

25. Ibid., 215–17.

26. Ibid., 220–22.

27. "Discourse Introductory to a Course of Lectures on the Science of Nature; with original music, composed for and sung on the occasion," delivered in the Hall of the University of Pennsylvania, 8 November 1800 (Philadelphia: printed by Zachariah Poulson, Jr.), 41.

28. Charles Willson Peale, 12 January 1802, in *Selected Papers,* vol. 2, part 1, 386.

29. Charles Willson Peale, "Address to the Public," *Aurora,* 27 January 1800, in *Selected Papers,* vol. 2, part 1, 274.

30. Peale, "Introduction to a Course of Lectures," 19.

31. Charles Willson Peale, "A Walk Through the Philadelphia Museum" (unpublished MS, 1805), in *Collected Papers,* n.p. Never completed, this description of the museum was written in imitation of "A Walk" through the Paris museum by J. B. Pujoulx: *Promenades au Jardin des Plantes, à la Ménagerie et dans les galeries du Musée d'Histoire Naturelle* (Paris, 1803). Sellers, *Mr. Peale's Museum,* 199.

32. Sellers, *Mr. Peale's Museum,* 218.

33. "Introduction to a Course of Lectures," in *Selected Papers,* vol. 2, part 1, 268.

34. *Guide to the Philadelphia Museum* (Philadelphia: Museum Press, first printing 1804), in *Selected Papers,* vol. 2, part 2, 761.

35. Ibid., 759–66.

36. Philadelphians were proverbial for punning. In Washington Irving's mock travel account of a trip to Philadelphia in *Salmagundi,* he writes that "The amusements of the philadelphians are dancing, punning, tea-parties and theatrical exhibitions." Upon arriving in the city, Jeremy Cockloft, the narrator, is immediately confined to his bed "with a violent fit of the pun mania—strangers always experience an attack of the kind on their first arrival." "The Stranger in Pennsylvania, By Jeremy Cockloft the Younger," in *Salmagundi; or, the Whim-whams and Opinions of Launcelot Langstaff, Esqu. and Others,* ed. Bruce I. Granger and Martha Hartzog, in *The Complete Works of Washington Irving,* ed. Henry A. Pochmann et al. (Boston: Twayne Publishers, 1977), 185, 188.

37. *Guide to the Museum,* 764.

38. Charles Willson Peale, "Autobiography," quoted in Charles Coleman Sellers, "A Supplement to 'Portraits and Miniatures by Charles Willson Peale,'" *Transactions of the American Philosophical Society,* n.s., 59.3 (1969): 36.

39. Charles Willson Peale to Thomas Jefferson, 10 January 1803, in *Selected Papers,* vol. 2, part 1, 480. See also Charles Willson Peale to Rubens Peale, 10 September 1806: "I have begun a view of the pit emtied . . . the figures in this piece will be large enough for me to introduce some portraits, I have prepared the Canvis of it 22 Inches wider than that which Rembrandt began." *Selected Papers,* vol. 2, part 2, 982.

40. Charles Willson Peale to Elizabeth DePeyster Peale, 28 June 1801, in *Selected Papers,* vol. 2, part 1, 336; R. Peale, *Historical Disquisition,* 552.

41. These supplies included pumps and military tents (such as the one pictured in the background of *The Exhumation of the Mastodon*), provided by Jefferson through the War Office of the secretary of the navy. Thomas Jefferson to Charles Willson Peale, 29 July 1801, *Pennsylvania Magazine of History and Biography* 28 (1904): 137.

42. "For several weeks no exertions were spared, and the most unremitting were required to insure success: bank after bank fell in; the increase of water was a constant impediment, the extreme coldness of which benumbed the workmen. Each day required some new expedient, and the carpenter was always making additions to the machinery: every day bones and pieces of bones were found between six and seven feet deep. . . . Twenty-five hands at high wages were almost constantly employed at work." R. Peale, *Historical Disquisition,* 553–54.

43. Charles Willson Peale to Angelica Peale Robinson, 13 September 1806, in *Collected Papers* (Millwood, N.Y.: Kraus Microform, 1980), ser. II-A, microcard 39.

44. *Historical Disquisition,* 553.

45. In the best recent study of the museum, David R. Brigham documents the many ways in which it relied upon—and constituted—an audience deeply divided by class, race, and gender. *Public Culture in the Early Republic: Peale's Museum and Its Audience* (Washington: Smithsonian Insitution Press, 1995).

46. *Historical Disquisition,* 543–44, 550.

47. Charles Willson Peale, Diary 19, in *Selected Papers,* vol. 2, part 1, 361 n.

48. *Historical Disquisition,* 551–52.

49. Ibid., 552.

50. Ibid., 553.

51. Ibid., 543–44, 550.

52. Ibid., 552.

53. Ibid.

54. "Intent upon manuring his lands to increase its production (always laudable) he felt no interest in the fossil shells contained in his morass." Ibid., 552.

55. Bryan J. Wolf, *Romantic Revision* (Chicago: University of Chicago Press, 1982), 123–26.

56. In his autobiography, Peale identifies the family members and friends represented in *The Exhumation of the Mastodon.* The information is reproduced in Sellers, *Later Life,* 205; Charles Coleman Sellers, "Portraits and Miniatures by Charles Willson Peale," *Transactions of the American Philosophical Society,* n.s., 42 (1952): 75; and Edgar P. Richardson, Brooke Hindle, and Lillian B. Miller, *Charles Willson Peale and His World* (New York: Harry N. Abrams, 1982), 85.

57. This is not as farfetched as it may seem: in the foreground of an earlier family portrait, *The Peale Family* of 1773, a half-peeled apple and apple peel punningly represent "the Peales."

58. "Autobiography," in *Collected Papers,* ser. II-C, 331–34.

59. The first Titian Ramsay Peale was Rachel Brewer's son. He died of yellow fever in 1798 at the age of eighteen. When Elizabeth Peale gave birth to a son a year later, Peale named him Titian Ramsay Peale II. The "second birth" of Titian Peale formed a tenuous link between the two halves of Peale's family, which were otherwise quite divided by age, jealousies, and temperament. By 1806, when Peale was painting *The Exhumation of the Mastodon*, both sets of children had lost their mothers; the presence of Elizabeth DePeyster in the painting suggests that Peale made the fact of shared loss a source of family unity.

60. This is a wedding portrait of Sophonisba and Coleman Sellers. Coleman Sellers was a member of the Sellers family of Philadelphia engineers and manfucturers. Sellers, *Later Life*, 205; "Portraits and Miniatures," 75.

61. Charles Willson Peale to Angelica Peale Robinson, September 13, 1806, in *Collected Papers*, ser. II-A, microcard 39.

62. Sellers, *Mr. Peale's Museum*, 171–87.

63. Jefferson, First Inaugural Address, 3.

64. See n. 56 above.

65. "Since many of my audience may not know under what difficulties I have formed a Museum permit me here to give a concise account of its rise and progress." "Introduction to a Course of Lectures," 21–22.

66. "Having made some progress in [a collection of the portraits of characters distinguished in the American Revolution]—my friend Col. Ramsey suggested the idea of amusing the public curiosity by putting into one corner of my picture-gallery some bones of the mammoth, the enormous non-descript of America. Mr. Patterson (Professor of Mathematics in our University) encouraged the plan, and presented me with the first article, a curious fish of our western waters, with which to begin my Museum. From so small a beginning, arose a fabrick, which in some future day may be an honor to America." "Introduction to a Course of Lectures," 21–22.

67. Luce Irigaray, *The Speculum of the Other Woman*, trans. Gillian C. Gill (Ithaca, N.Y.: Cornell University Press, 1985), 21.

68. Charles Willson Peale, "A Walk Through the Philadelphia Museum" (unpublished MS, 1805), quoted in *Mr. Peale's Museum*, 199.

69. Roger B. Stein, "Charles Willson Peale's Expressive Design: The Artist in His Museum," *Prospects* 6 (1981), ed. Jack Salzman (New York: Burt Franklin & Co., 1981), 157.

70. Charles Willson Peale, "An Epistle to a Friend on the Means of Preserving Health, Promoting Happiness, and Prolonging the Life of Man to its Natural Period" (Philadelphia: from the press of the late R. Aitken, by Jane Aitken, 1803), in *Selected Papers*, vol. 2, part 1, 504–5.

71. "Epistle to a Friend," 505.

Chapter Four. The American Lounger

1. Charles Willson Peale, "A Walk Through the Philadelphia Museum" (unpublished MS, 1805), in the microfilm edition of *The Collected Papers of Charles Willson Peale and His Family*, ed. Lillian B. Miller (Millwood, N.Y.: Kraus Microform, 1980), n.p.

2. Ibid.

3. As Charles Coleman Sellers reports, between 1827 and 1838 Peale's mammoth skeleton was housed in an upper floor of the Philadelphia arcade. *Mr Peale's Museum*, 258–59. Susan Buck-Morss, *Dialectics of Seeing: Walter Benjamin and the Arcades Project* (Cambridge, Mass.: MIT Press, 1989); John Brewer and Roy Porter, eds., *Consumption and the World of Goods* (London: Routledge, 1993); T. H. Breen, " 'Baubles of Britain': The American Consumer Revolutions of the Eighteenth Century," *Past and Present* 119 (1988): 73–104.

4. *Cincinnati Literary Gazette* 1.72 (1824), quoted in Frank Luther Mott, *A History of American Magazines*, 5 vols. (Cambridge, Mass.: Harvard University Press, 1938), 1:126.

5. Peter J. Parker, "Asbury Dickins, Bookseller, 1798–1801, or, The Brief Career of a Careless Youth," *Pennsylvania Magazine of History and Biography* 94.4 (1970): 476.

6. The twenty-five-cent entrance fee was not particularly low. As David Brigham has demonstrated, Peale's museum was far from being a particularly democratic institution. *Public Culture in the Early Republic: Peale's Museum and Its Audience* (Washington, D.C.: Smithsonian Institution Press, 1995). Dennie's "Prospectus" of 1801 appeals specifically to "the clergy" (who "from their literary leisure" were particularly suited to contribute and subscribe); to "gentlemen of the bar" (on whom Dennie claims to depend for the circulation of his weekly); and to "men of letters," by which he means men of "*belles lettres*." This last category refers to those "in the habit of writing," who, "from early youth . . . Together mus'd . . . O'er learned sage, or bard sublime." Joseph Dennie, "Prospectus to the *Port Folio* by Oliver Oldschool Esq" (Philadelphia, Hugh Maxwell, 1801), 3, col. 3. The *Port Folio* also addressed a more interested and narrow category of reader: "the liberal merchant, the inquisitive manufacturer, and the country gentleman" were all invited "to inspect" the *Port Folio* for specific essays on topics of commerce and the useful arts, "if they find leisure, in the intervals of business" (Ibid.). Peter J. Parker attributes the *Port Folio*'s success to the fact that, at the time, it had no competition in Philadelphia—and the city was still the publishing center of the country. With the *Port Folio*, its first publisher, Asbury Dickins, "could hope for the national reputation so necessary for his continued success as a bookseller." Parker, "Asbury Dickins, Bookseller," 476. After Dennie retired in January 1809, the magazine continued under various other editors and publishers until 1824.

7. *Port Folio*, 25 April 1801, quoted in Mott, *American Magazines*, 1:199. In the 1790s a subscription rate of $2.50 would have been prohibitive for most families. Wages for a mechanic were less than a dollar a day; a clergyman received about five hundred dollars a year. Mott, *American Magazines*, 1:33–34.

8. "Prospectus," 3, col. 3.

9. Ibid., cols. 2 and 3.

10. Lewis Simpson, introdcution to *The Federalist Literary Mind: Selections from the Monthly Anthology and Boston Review, 1803–1811* (Baton Rouge: Louisiana State University Press, 1963), 10–31; Harold Ellis, *Joseph Dennie and His Circle: A Study in American Literature from 1792–1812, Bulletin of the University of Texas* 40 (1915): 102.

11. "Prospectus," 1, col. 3.

12. "To Readers and Correspondents," *Port Folio* 1.6 (1801): 46.

13. If the character of the early national museum proprietor was, as William Duer wrote, that of "an enthusiast" who ostentatiously "ruined himself for the benefit of his successors and the public"—the Federalist editor presented himself as a lounger

who never worked. William A. Duer, *Reminiscences of an Old New Yorker* (1867), quoted in Robert M. McClung and Gale S. McClung, "Tammany's Remarkable Gardiner Baker," *New York Historical Society Quarterly* 42 (1958): 145; Ellis, *Joseph Dennie*, 102; Simpson, introduction to *The Federalist Literary Mind*, 10–31.

14. "Prospectus" 3, col. 3.

15. Linda K. Kerber, *Federalists in Dissent: Imagery and Ideology in Jeffersonian America* (Ithaca, N.Y.: Cornell University Press, 1970), 1–22; Linda Kerber and Walter Morris, "Politics and Literature: The Adams Family and *The Port Folio*," *William and Mary Quarterly*, ser. 3, 23 (1966): 351–76; Ellis, *Joseph Dennie and His Circle*.

16. Lewis Leary, "The Literary Opinions of Joseph Dennie," in *Soundings: Some Early American Writers* (Athens, Ga.: University of Georgia Press, 1975), 253–71. Carole Smith-Rosenberg's discussion of the magazines of 1787, and particularly of Matthew Carey's Philadelphia *Museum*, is an exception. See "The Subject of the 'Great Constitutional Debate,'" in *Discovering America: Essays on the Search for an Identity*, ed. David Thelen and Frederick E. Hoxie (Urbana: University of Illinois Press, 1994).

17. "Lessons for Loungers," *Port Folio* 1.3 (1801): 22.

18. On contemporary market regulation and reform in England and Philadelphia, see Peter Stallybrass and Allon White, *The Politics and Poetics of Transgression* (Ithaca, N.Y.: Cornell University Press, 1986), 80–148; Margaret B. Tinkcom, "The New Market in Second Street," *Pennsylvania Magazine of History and Biography*, October 1958, 379–96; Agnes Addison Gilchrist, "Market Houses in High Street," in *Historic Philadelphia from the Founding until the Early Nineteenth Century: Papers Dealing with Its People and Buildings*, ed. Luther P. Eisenhart, *Transactions of the American Philosophical Society* 43.1 (1953): 304–13.

19. J.G.A. Pocock, *The Machiavellian Moment: Florentine Political Thought and the Atlantic Republican Tradition* (Princeton: Princeton University Press, 1975); Richard Sennet, *The Fall of Public Man: The Forces Eroding Public Life and Burdening the Modern Psyche with Roles It Cannot Perform* (New York: Knopf, 1972); Bernard Bailyn, *The Ideological Origins of the American Revolution* (Cambridge, Mass.: Harvard University Press, Belknap Press, 1967); Hannah Arendt, *On Revolution* (New York: Viking Press, 1965); Gordon S. Wood, *The Creation of the American Republic, 1776–1787* (New York: Norton, 1972); William Dowling, *Poetry and Ideology in Revolutionary Connecticut* (Athens, Ga.: University of Georgia Press, 1990). The history of challenges to the republican tradition of historiography is well summarized by Joyce Appleby's collection of essays *Liberalism and Republicanism in the Historical Imagination* (Cambridge, Mass.: Harvard University Press, 1992).

20. This series was reportedly coauthored by Dennie and Charles Brockden Brown. Bruce Granger, ed., *The Farrago by Joseph Dennie* (Delmar, N.Y.: Scholars' Facsimiles & Reprints, 1985), 26.

21. "Prospectus," 3.

22. Granger, *The Farrago by Joseph Dennie*, 17; "Literary Intelligence," *Gazette of the United States* 16 (October 1800), quoted in Ellis, *Joseph Dennie*, 134.

23. Nathan Drake, *Essays Biographical, Critical and Historical, Illustrative of the Rambler, Adventurer and Idler* (London, 1805), quoted in Mott, *A History of American Magazines*, 41 n.

24. Dana Brand, *The Spectator and the City in Nineteenth-Century American Literature* (New York: Cambridge University Press, 1991), 33; John Barrell, *English Literature in History, 1730–1780: An Equal and Wide Survey* (London: Hutchinson, 1983), 176–209.

25. "Criticism," *Port Folio* 1.9 (1801): 67.

26. "Criticism," *Port Folio* 1.8 (1801): 59.

27. "An Author's Evening," *Port Folio* 1.1 (1801): 4.

28. "Prospectus of *The Port Folio*, A Monthly Miscellany" (Philadelphia: Bradford and Inskeep, 1809), 6.

29. "[I]n the Areopagus of Athens or before the judgment seat of Agrippa, [Paul] is equally the courtier, willing to comply with the modes of fashion, willing to yield to trivial prejudices for the sake of reconciling obstinacy and incredulity to his momentous schemes." Dennie, "On Versatility,"in *The Lay Preacher*, ed. Milton Ellis (New York: Scholars Facsimiles and Reprints, 1943), 132. The biblical quotation that opens "The Story of Moses" is Exodus 2:17: "the shepherds came and drove [the seven daughters of the priest of Midian] away: but Moses stood up, and helped them, and watered their flock." *The Lay Preacher*, ed. Ellis, 123.

30. Joseph Dennie, "The Lay Preacher," *Port Folio* 1.3 (1801): 21–22.

31. Joseph Dennie, "On the Sabbath," in *The Lay Preacher*, ed. Ellis, 159–61.

32. "The Lounger's Diary," *Port Folio* 1.3 (1801): 22.

33. Barbara Maria Stafford, *Artful Science: Enlightenment, Entertainment, and the Eclipse of Visual Education* (Cambridge, Mass.: MIT Press, 1994), 67; Richard Altick, *The Shows of London* (Cambridge, Mass.: Harvard University Press, Belknap Press, 1987), 60–62.

34. This is also true of Washington Irving's and James Kirke Paulding's New York series *Salmagundi; or, The Whim-Whams and Opinions of Launcelot Langstaff, Esq & Others*, ed. Bruce I. Granger and Martha Hartzog (Boston: Twayne Publishers, 1977), esp. no. 4, 103–16.

35. Robert A. Ferguson, *Law and Letters in American Culture* (Cambridge, Mass.: Harvard University Press, 1984), 66–95.

36. *Port Folio* 1.4 (1801): 30. This is a reprint of Joseph Dennie's and Royall Tyler's "The Farrago," *Morning Ray* (Windsor, Vt.) 3 (6 March 1792) repr. in Granger, *The Farrago*, 17–21.

37. *Port Folio* 1.4 (1801): 31.

38. Ibid.

39. Michael T. Gilmore, "Magazines, Criticism, and Essays," in *The Cambridge History of American Literature*, ed. Sacvan Bercovitch, (Cambridge: Cambridge University Press, 1994), 1: 558. "During the years of his editorship, Dennie created his persona of the Lay Preacher, a self-description that links him to the [Boston] Athenaeum group [of Joseph Stevens Buckminster, William Emerson, and John T. Kirkland] and palpably conveys the clerical tenor of the emergent genteel tradition." Ibid., 568.

40. Brand, *The Spectator and the City*, 74–78. Without mentioning "loungers," Brand argues that dandies and flaneurs are profoundly different, even opposite, types but that they can always be found together: "It is only when a city can produce a fashionable spectacle in which dandies can participate that it is capable of producing a spectacle of sufficient richness for a flaneur to observe."

41. Charles Baudelaire, "The Eyes of the Poor," in *Paris Spleen* (1869), trans. Louise Varese (New York: New Directions, 1970), 52.

42. Bailyn, *The Ideological Origins of the American Revolution*, 39–42.

43. Dowling, *Poetry and Ideology*, 22–31, 95–126.

44. John Quincy Adams to Thomas Boyston Adams, Berlin, 21 March 1801, in *The Writings of John Quincy Adams*, ed. Worthington Chauncey Ford, 3 vols. (New York: Macmillan Co., 1913), 2:525.

45. D. Simpson, *The Politics of American English*, 63–90.

46. John Quincy Adams to Thomas Boyston Adams, Berlin, 21 March 1801, in *The Writings of John Quincy Adams*, 2:524.

47. Ibid., 2:522.

48. Parker, "Asbury Dickins, Bookseller," 477.

49. John Quincy Adams, "Journal of a Tour," *Port Folio* 1.10 (1801): 73.

50. John Quincy Adams to William Vans Murray, Dresden, 15 September 1800, in *The Writings of John Quincy Adams*, 2:469.

51. "Journal of a Tour Through Silesia," *Port Folio* 1.2 (1801): 9.

52. John Nelson, *Liberty and Property: Political Economy and Policymaking in the New Nation, 1789–1812* (Baltimore: Johns Hopkins University Press, 1987); Joyce Appleby, *Capitalism and a New Social Order: The Republican Vision of the 1790s* (New York: New York University Press, 1984); idem, "Commercial Farming and the 'Agrarian Myth' in the Early Republic," *Journal of American History* 68.4 (1982): 833–49; Steven Watts, *The Republic Reborn: War and the Making of Liberal America, 1790–1820* (Baltimore: Johns Hopkins University Press, 1987).

53. Alexander Saxton, *The Rise and Fall of the White Republic* (London: Verso, 1990), 23–95.

54. Eric Foner, *Free Soil, Free Labor, Free Men* (New York: Oxford University Press, 1971); Appleby, *Capitalism and a New Social Order*, 42–44; Saxton, *The Rise and Fall of the White Republic*.

55. John Quincy Adams to Thomas Boylston Adams, Berlin, 21 March 1801, in *The Writings of John Quincy Adams*, 2:523.

56. John Quincy Adams to William Vans Murray, Berlin, 30 October 1800, in *The Writings of John Quincy Adams*, 472.

57. "Journal," *Port Folio* 1.7 (1801): 49.

58. Ibid., *Port Folio* 1.8 (1801): 57.

59. Ibid., *Port Folio* 1.2 (1801): 9. See also *Port Folio* 1.14 (1801): 105.

60. "Journal," *Port Folio* 1.3 (1801): 17–18.

61. Ibid.

62. Thomas Jefferson, "Productions Animal Vegetable and Mineral," in *Notes on the State of Virginia*, ed. William Peden (New York: Norton, 1954), 64.

63. "Journal," *Port Folio* 1.3 (1801): 18.

64. "Politics. . . . Reflections on the Peace," *Port Folio* 1.50 (1801): 393–94.

65. John Quincy Adams to Abigail Adams, Berlin, 10 March 1801, in *The Writings of John Quincy Adams*, 2:514–15.

66. John Quincy Adams to William Vans Murray, Berlin, 30 October, 1800, in *The Writings of John Quincy Adams*, 472–73.

67. Garry Wills, *Cincinnatus: George Washington and the Enlightenment* (Garden City, N.Y.: Doubleday, 1984); Jay Fliegelman, *Declaring Independence: Jefferson, Natural Language, and the Culture of Performance* (Stanford, Calif.: Stanford University Press, 1994); Ferguson, *Law and Letters*.

68. "The Farrago, No. III," *Port Folio* 1.4 (1801): 30.

69. Sennet, *The Fall of Public Man*, quoted in Brand, *The Spectator and the City*, 19.

CHAPTER FIVE. FEATHERED FEDERALISM

1. Alexander Wilson, *American Ornithology* (Philadelphia: Bradford and Inskeep, 1808–14), preface to vol. 5 (1812), x. All references to Wilson's prefaces will be to this nine-volume first edition of *American Ornithology*. All other references will be to Jardine's three-volume, "unabridged" edition (which omits Wilson's prefaces): Alexander Wilson and Prince Charles Lucien Bonaparte, *American Ornithology; or, The Natural History of the Birds of the United States*, ed. Sir William Jardine, 3 vol. (London: Chatto and Windus, 1876).

2. Thomas Jefferson, "On Manufactures," in *Notes on the State of Virginia*, ed. William Peden (New York: Norton & Co., 1954), 165.

3. Jeanne Boydston, "The Pastoralization of Housework," in *Home and Work: Housework, Wages, and the Ideology of Labor in the Early Republic* (Oxford: Oxford University Press, 1990), 142–63; Freidrich A. Kittler, "The Mother's Mouth," in *Discourse Networks 1800/1900*, trans. Michael Metteer (Stanford, Calif.: Stanford University Press, 1990), 25–69. Kittler is one of the best guides to the late-Enlightenment technologies that accomplished this interiorization of (to use Peale's term) "nature's book": "Nature, in the discourse network of 1800, is [The] Woman. . . . Her function consists in getting people—that is, men—to speak. . . . Maternal instruction . . . was the input component of elementary acculturation techniques. . . . The whole of primary eduation circa 1800, however, attempted the impossible proof for which the writer Carl Philipp Moritz was known . . . 'that letters are not arbitrary, but grounded in human nature and native to all the distinct regions of inner consciousness' " 25–29.

4. Cathy N. Davidson, *Revolution and the Word: The Rise of the Novel in America* (New York: Oxford University Press, 1986), 110–50; Julia A. Stern, *The Plight of Feeling: Sympathy and Dissent in the Early American Novel* (Chicago: University of Chicago Press, 1993); Laurel Thatcher Ulrich, *The Midwife's Tale: The Life of Martha Ballard, Based on Her Diary, 1785–1812* (New York: Random House, 1990), esp. 134–61. Ulrich observes the striking *disjunction* between the sentimental plots of the early American novel and the realities of both premarital pregnancy and women's legal recourse in matters of sexuality in late-eighteenth-century Maine.

5. Charles Willson Peale, Lecture on Natural History no. 18., 1799–1800, 12; quoted in Charles Coleman Sellers, *Mr. Peale's Museum: Charles Willson Peale and the First Popular Museum of Natural Science and Art* (New York: Norton & Co., 1980), 109.

6. Peale, "Discourse Introductory to a Course of Lectures on the Science of Nature," 8 November 1800, delivered at the Hall of the University of Pennsylvania (Philadelphia: Zachariah Poulson, Jr., 1800), 10.

7. "Peale reflect[ed] on the waste he had made of the feathered tribe in order to furnish his Museum." Charles Willson Peale, "Autobiography," typewritten transcript by Horace W. Sellers, in *The Collected Papers of Charles Willson Peale and His Family*, ed. Lillian B. Miller (National Portrait Gallery, Smithsonian Institution, Washington, D.C.; Millwood, N.Y.: Kraus-Thomson Organization, 1950), microfiche, ser. II-C, 202, 205, 244.

8. There is, however, an overall division into Land Birds (vols. 1–6) and Water Birds (vols. 7–9), which deserves attention but is still very secondary. Introduction to *American Ornithology*, vol. 1 (1808), vi.

9. Thomas Jefferson to Archibald Stuart, 25 January 1786, in *The Papers of Thomas Jefferson*, ed. Julian P. Boyd (Princeton: Princeton University Press, 1954), vol. 9, 217–18.

10. Jefferson, "On Manufacturing," in *Notes on the State of Virginia*, 164.

11. Introduction to *American Ornithology*, 1: 1–2; Alexander Wilson to Daniel Miller, 26 October 1808, in *The Life and Letters of Alexander Wilson*, ed. Clark Hunter (Philadelphia: American Philosophical Society, 1983), 286; Alexander Wilson to Daniel Miller, Charleston, 2 February 1809, in *Letters*, 301.

12. Henry Adams, *History of the United States of America during the First Administration of Thomas Jefferson to the Second Administration of James Madison*, 9 vols. (New York: C. Scribner, 1889–91).

13. Henry Adams, *The United States in 1800* (Ithaca, N.Y.: Cornell University Press, 1979), 13.

14. Alexander Wilson to Thomas Jefferson, 6 February 1806, in *Letters*, 249.

15. See Hunter, "Wilson's Principal Ornithological Travels," in *Letters*, 213–14.

16. The subscribers were listed according to state or territory at the end of volume 9 in the first edition of the *Ornithology*. Individual subscribers are listed in letters from Wilson to Daniel Miller from Washington, 24 December 1808, and to Samuel Bradford from Savannah, 8 March 1809. *Letters*, 296, 312. A list of the Virginia subscribers is included in Robert Cantwell, *Alexander Wilson: Naturalist and Pioneer* (Philadelphia: J. B. Lippincott Co., 1961), 277, 305.

17. William Charvat, *Literary Publishing in America, 1790–1850* (Philadelphia: University of Pennsylvania Press, 1959), 23–24, 26. After 1790 and prior to the building of the railroads in the 1830s and 40s, Philadelphia and New York established, and came to dominate, the book trade in the southern and western interior: "Philadelphia publishers began to control the southern book-buying market, and New York the territory west of the Hudson, both cities sharing the trade of the Ohio valley." It was the leading publishers of Philadelphia and New York, rather than landlocked Boston, who, in the age of steamboats and canals, sought "the trade not only of the coast but of the interior"—and who, as Charvat argues, thereby "discovered (in a sense, established) the common denominator in the literary taste of the whole country." Charvat summarizes the transformation from diffuse to centralized and nationalized literary publishing with figures from fiction sales: "In the first decade of the nineteenth century, almost fifty per cent of our native fiction was published outside of New York, Boston, and Philadelphia—in the 1840s, only eight per cent." Nationwide, prior to the War of 1812, printing was local and decentralized, limited—particularly in New England—by the absence of roads and water routes. Even before the War of 1812, however, New York and Philadelphia, linked by turnpike, bridge, and water, had become a publishing axis with an increasingly national rather than local distribution. As Charvat puts it, "up to about 1820, literary publishing was local and decentralized—except in the Philadelphia area." *Literary Publishing*, 25–26.

18. Joseph Hopkinson, *First Annual Discourse to the Pennsylvania Academy of Fine Arts* (Philadelphia, 1810), 15–16. The Academy of Fine Arts would serve as both a school and a professional organization for American engravers. Most Philadelphia engravers became members of the Pennsylvania Academy, where some, such as the silver engraver/trompe l'oeil painter William Harnett (1848–92), would also find training in other arts. By contrast with the Pennsylvania Academy, the British Royal

Society established itself as an academy of fine arts by virtue of its exclusion of (mechanical) engravers. Alfred Frankenstein, *After the Hunt: William Harnett and Other American Still Life Painters, 1870–1900* (Berkeley: University of California Press, 1953), 29–33.

19. In his survey of the history of American engraving, David Stauffer writes that Thomas Dobson's *Encyclopedia* and Bradford's *Cyclopedia* "had so many plates that the names signed to them include about all the active engravers then actually employed in the United States." David McNeely Stauffer, *American Engravers upon Copper and Steel* (New York: Grolier Club of the City of New York, 1907), xxvii. See also Mantle Fielding's *Supplement to Stauffer's American Engravers* (Philadelphia, 1917); Ellis Paxson Oberholtzer, *The Literary History of Philadelphia* (Philadelphia: George W. Jacobs & Co., 1906), 149; John Tebbel, *A History of Publishing in the United States: The Creation of an Industry* vol. 1, (New York: R. R. Bowker, 1972), 174.

20. Trish Loughran, "Virtual Nation: Problems of Representation in the Extended Republic," unpublished manuscript, 1998.

21. Five of these subscriptions were for two or three copies; twenty-one were for institutions: city or college libraries, athenaeums, learned or medical societies, and, in the case of Pennsylvania, the Pennsylvania legislatures (3 copies) and the Pennsylvania Hospital (2 copies).

22. Alexander Wilson to David Wilson, 6 June 1811, in *Letters*, 386–87.

23. Alexander Wilson to Alexander Lawson, Natchez, Mississippi Territory, 18 May 1810, in *Letters*, 358–73.

24. Alexander Wilson to David Wilson, Philadelphia, 6 July 1813, in *Letters*, 406.

25. Preface to *American Ornithology*, vol. 1:i–ii.

26. *American Ornithology*, ed. Jardine, 1:1, 5.

27. Ibid., 6.

28. Ibid., 7.

29. Ibid., 9.

30. Preface to *American Ornithology*, vol. 3 (1811), v. See also Alexander Wilson, "Proposals for Publishing by Subscription . . . *American Ornithology*," in *Letters*, 269.

31. Preface to *American Ornithology*, 5:x.

32. Preface to *American Ornithology*, vol. 2 (1810), vi.

33. *American Ornithology*, ed. Jardine, 1:360.

34. Ibid., 43–44.

35. "Purple Grackle," in *American Ornithology*, ed. Jardine, 1: 337; *American Ornithology*, ed. Jardine, 1:46.

36. *American Ornithology*, ed. Jardine, 1:50–51.

37. "Proposals," in *Letters*, 269.

38. Elizabeth McKinsey offers an overview of the iconography of the viewer within the view in seventeenth-and eighteenth-century engravings of Niagara Falls in chapters 1 and 2 of *Niagara Falls, Icon of the American Sublime* (Cambridge: Cambridge University Press, 1985).

39. *American Ornithology*, ed. Jardine, 1:46.

40. For a discussion of ornithological discourse prior to its twentieth-century professionalization, see Kevin R. McNamara, "The Feathered Scribe: The Discourses of American Ornithology before 1800," *William and Mary Quarterly* 47 (April 1990): 210–34.

41. By the end of the century the bee-eating behavior of the King Bird was nearly as commonplace an anecdote of American nature as rattlesnake fascination. In his *Letters* of 1784, for example, Crèvecoeur treats the King Bird in some detail, narrating the story of an attack on the hive—and the bees' miraculous escape from the King Bird's craw—in an odd allegory of rebirth in the New World. J. Hector St. John de Crèvecoeur, *Letters from an American Farmer and Sketches of Eighteenth-Century America* (New York: Penguin Classics, 1988), 55–57.

42. *American Ornithology*, ed. Jardine, 1:222

43. Ibid.

44. Ibid., 222–23.

45. Ibid., 223.

46. Harriet Ritvo's important work on the economics and semiotics of domesticated quadrupeds in Victorian England is useful here primarily by way of contrast to the "ornithological state" of Jeffersonian America. *The Animal Estate: The English and Other Creatures in the Victorian Age* (Cambridge, Mass.: Harvard University Press, 1985).

47. *American Ornithology*, ed. Jardine, 1:261.

48. Introduction to *American Ornithology*.

49. "The southern Indians" are said to believe that feathered ornaments, used as "amulets or charms," "confer on the wearer all the virtues or excellences of those birds." *American Ornithology*, ed. Jardine, 2:14.

50. Ibid., 13.

51. Ibid., 14.

52. Ibid.

53. Joel W. Martin, *Sacred Revolt: The Muskogees' Struggle for a New World* (Boston: Beacon Press, 1991), 114–86; Bernard Sheehan, *Seeds of Extinction; Jeffersonian Philanthropy and the American Indian* (Chapel Hill: University of North Carolina Press, 1973).

54. Martin, *Sacred Revolt*, 87–116.

55. See, for example, the policy of negotiation and the rituals that shaped the encounters of Lewis and Clark's Corps of Discovery with the Otos and Yanktons, among others. Stephen E. Ambrose, *Undaunted Courage: Meriwether Lewis, Thomas Jefferson, and the Opening of the American West* (New York: Simon & Schuster, 1996), 155–64.

56. *American Ornithology*, ed. Jardine, 1:378.

57. Ibid., 384.

58. Ibid., 385.

59. Ibid.

60. Ibid., 380.

61. Ibid., 386.

62. Ibid.

63. For the best discussion of the contradictions that made Robert Burns a British literary celebrity, see Carol McGuirk, *Robert Burns and the Sentimental Era* (Athens, Ga.: University of Georgia Press, 1985), esp. 103–19.

64. Hunter, "Life," in *Letters*, 30–31.

65. Alexander Wilson, *Poems* (Paisley, Scotland: J. Neilson, 1790); *Poems, Humorous, Satirical and Serious*, 2d ed. (Edinburgh: P. Hill, 1791).

66. Thomas Moore, Letter from Niagara, 24 July 1804, quoted in McKinsey, *Niagara Falls*, 41.

67. McKinsey, *Niagara Falls*, 38.

68. Seeing "by the papers," Wilson wrote Bartram in 1806, "that Mr. Jefferson designs to employ persons to explore the shores of the Mississippi," Wilson's first plan was to travel from Wheeling to New Orleans as the "companion and assistant" of Bartram himself. In January of 1806, he asked Bartram what he would think "of laying our design before Mr. Jefferson with a view to procure his advice and recommendation to influential characters in the route. Could we procure his approbation and patronage, they would secure our success." Alexander Wilson to William Bartram, 27 January 1806, in *Letters*, 247. When Bartram refused, Wilson turned to Jefferson in the hope of being appointed to the projected government expedition "up the Red River." To Wilson's disappointment, Jefferson never responded to his letters, and the expedition was canceled. Wilson's letters to Bartram and Jefferson show that his efforts to be appointed to an expedition were tied to the task of gathering specimens for his *Ornithology.* Alexander Wilson to Thomas Jefferson, 6 February 1806, in *Letters*, 249–50.

69. Alexander Wilson to William Bartram, 27 January 1806, in *Letters*, 247.

70. Alexander Wilson, "The Foresters: A Poem Descriptive of a Pedestrian Journey to the Falls of Niagara in the Autumn of 1804" (Newtown, Pa.: Seigfried and J. Wilson, 1818), 63.

71. Joseph Kastner, *A Species of Eternity* (New York: Alfred A. Knopf, 1977), 223.

72. Writing in his journal in Liverpool, thirteen years after Alexander Wilson's death, John James Audubon described the British naturalist Thomas Bewick as "the Wilson of England." Bewick was a naturalist and engraver whose remarkably popular *History of Quadrupeds* had been published in 1790. This was followed by his two-volume *History of British Birds* (1797–1804), with its famous series of wood engravings. Audubon's comparison of Bewick to Wilson is significant because, like Wilson, Bewick had worked self-consciously to make his *History of British Birds* "a great national work." In his *Memoirs* Bewick writes of his respect not only for John Ray (a British taxonomist who "led the way to truth and to British Ornithology") but for the ornithological works of Gilbert White, Thomas Pennant, and Edward Latham. Latham, whose system of classification would be adopted by Wilson, seemed particularly to Bewick to "have wound up the whole." At the same time, however, Bewick "often lamented" that Latham's work was not—"by being embellished with correct figures—made a great national work, like the Count de Buffon's." Bewick sought to amend this defect with his own British ornithology. Numerous editions of Buffon's forty-four-volume *Histoire Naturelle* of 1749, as well as translations and adaptations from it (such as Oliver Goldsmith's eight-volume *History of the Earth and Animated Nature* [1774]), had initiated a growing popular interest in natural history that Bewick, Wilson, and later, Audubon would exploit and extend. With his nine-volume *American Ornithology*, Wilson likewise aspired to produce a great national work. As Audubon writes in 1833 to his wife, Lucy, "I did not like the work I saw on birds. I prefer Thomas Bewick greatly. Bewick, Lucy, is the [Alexander] Wilson of England." The "work" Audubon refers to is Selby's *Illustrations of British Ornithology* (1833). John James Audubon to Lucy Audubon, Liverpool, 4 August 1826, in *The 1826 Journal of John James Audubon*, ed. Alice Ford Norman (University of Oklahoma Press, 1967), 79; Dr. John Latham, *A General Synopsis of Birds*, 3 vols. and supp. (London, 1781–85); Thomas Bewick, *Memoir of Thomas Bewick, 1822–1828* (London:

John Lane and the Bodley Head Ltd., 1924), 131–32; S. Roscoe, *Thomas Bewick: A Bibliography Raisonné of Editions of the "General History of Quadrupeds," the "History of British Birds" and the "Fables of Aesop" Issued in His Lifetime* (London: Oxford University Press, 1953).

73. "Baltimore Oriole," "Great-Crested Flycatcher," and "White-Eyed Flycatcher," in *American Ornithology*, ed. Jardine, 1:20, 225, 306.

74. On this phrase and its meaning, see Alexander Wilson (no relation), *The Culture of Nature: North American Landscape from Disney to the Exxon Valdez* (Cambridge, Mass.: Blackwell, 1992).

75. Felton Gibbons and Deborah Strom, *Neighbors to the Birds: A History of Birdwatching in America* (New York: W. W. Norton & Co., 1988), 175–89.

76. Mabel Osgood Wright and Elliot Coues, *Citizen Bird: Scenes from Bird-life in Plain English for Beginners* (New York: Macmillan Co., 1897), 61–62.

77. Donna Haraway uses this term in "Teddy Bear Patriarchy: Taxidermy in the Garden of Eden, New York City, 1908–1936," *Social Text*, Winter 1985, 20–63, repr. in Haraway, *Simians, Cyborgs and Women: The Reinvention of Nature* (New York: Routledge, 1991).

78. Preface to *American Ornithology*, 5:vi–vii.

79. On the impossibility and persistence of redemptive self-creation and preservation through ethnographic collecting, see James Clifford, "On Collecting," in *The Predicament of Culture: Twentieth-Century Ethnography, Literature, and Art* (Cambridge, Mass.: Harvard University Press, 1988), 187–253.

80. On the role of pastoral "surplus" under conditions of industrial transformation, see Patrick Wright, *On Living in an Old Country* (London: Verso, 1985).

81. Alexander Wilson to Charles Orr, 15 July 1802, in *Letters*, 193–94.

82. Alexander Wilson to William Bartram, 4 March 1803, and to a friend in Paisley, 1 June 1803, in *Letters*, 202–3.

83. Rev. Alexander B. Grosart, "Memorial-introduction," in *The Poems and Literary Prose of Alexander Wilson*, ed. Alexander B. Grosart, 2 vols. (Paisley, Scotland: Alexander Gardner, 1876), 1:xxxviii; Alexander Wilson to Duncan Wright, Philadelphia, 20 October 1811, in *Letters*, 391.

84. Preface to *American Ornithology*, 3: v.

85. *The Poems and Literary Prose of Alexander Wilson*, 2: 62–63; *Letters*, 413–16.

86. Norman Murray, *The Scottish Hand Loom Weavers, 1790–1850: A Social History* (Edinburgh: John Donald Publishers, 1978), 168–72; Thomas Crawford, "Political and Protest Songs in Eighteenth-Century Scotland II, Songs of the Left," *Scottish Studies* 14 (1970): 105–31; Murray, *The Scottish Hand Loom Weavers*, 40–50, 134. The hand-loom industry in west Scotland saw severe slumps (following cyclical booms) and its first strikes in 1787 and 1793.

87. Hunter, "The Friend of Liberty," in *Letters*, 45–57.

88. William Law Mathieson, *The Awakening of Scotland: A History from 1747–1797* (Glasgow: J. Maclehose, 1910); William Donaldson, *Popular Literature in Victorian Scotland: Language, Fiction and the Press* (Aberdeen: Aberdeen University Press, 1986), ix–35; Brian Maidment, "Essayists and Artisans—The Making of Nineteenth-Century Self-Taught Poets," *Literature and History* 9.1 (1983): 74–91.

89. *The Poems and Literary Prose of Alexander Wilson*, 2: 61.

90. George Logan, review of Burns's *Poems* in the *English Review* (1787), quoted in McGuirk, *Robert Burns and the Sentimental Era*, 68.

91. Quoted in Kenneth Simpson, *The Protean Scot: The Crisis of Identity in 18th Century Scottish Literature* (Aberdeen: Aberdeen University Press, 1988), 235.

92. Grosart, "Memorial-introduction," in *The Poems and Literary Prose of Alexander Wilson*, 1: xxx; Richardson Little Wright, *Hawkers and Walkers in Early America* (Philadelphia: J. Lippincott, 1927).

93. "The Shark," in *Poems*, 2: 35.

94. Alexander Wilson, "Journal," in *Poems*; repr. in *Letters*, 33–34.

95. *American Ornithology*, ed. Jardine, 1:164, 169.

96. Ibid., 168.

97. Ibid., 171.

98. Ibid., 172.

99. Benedict Anderson, *Imagined Communities* (London: Verso, 1983).

100. *American Ornithology*, ed. Jardine, 1:89, 97, 100, 117, 232; 2:29.

101. Ibid., 1:53.

102. Ibid., 169,173–74.

103. For the tradition of this developmental plot, see George Dekker, *The American Historical Romance* (Cambridge: Cambridge University Press, 1987), 73–98.

104. Wilson to Alexander Lawson, Lexington, 4 April 1810, in *Letters*, 335.

CHAPTER SIX. PICTURE-NATION

1. Patrick Lyon, *The Narrative of Patrick Lyon who suffered three months severe imprisonment in Philadelphia gaol; on merely a vague suspicion, of being concerned in the Robbery of the Bank of Pennsylvania* (Philadelphia: Robert & Francis Bailey, 1799), 25.

2. Even today the painting serves as an emblem of early industrial America: in 1989 it illustrated the cover of volume 1 of the McMichael *Anthology of American Literature: Colonial to Romantic*, ed. George McMichael et al., 4th ed. (New York: Macmillan Publishing Co., 1989).

3. William Dunlap, *History of the Rise and Progress of the Arts of Design in the United States* (1834; New York: Dover, 1969), 2:375–76, quoted in Lois Dinnerstein, "The Iron Worker and King Solomon: Some Images of Labor in American Art," *Arts Magazine* 44 (1979): 113–14.

4. R. R. Patrick, "John Neagle, Portrait Painter, and Pat Lyon, Blacksmith," *Art Bulletin* 33 (1951): 190.

5. Dunlap, *Arts of Design*, 2 (part 2), 375, quoted in Bruce W. Chambers, "The Pythagorean Puzzle of Patrick Lyon," *Art Bulletin* 58 (1976): 225.

6. Chambers, "Pythagorean Puzzle," 228; J. H. Powell, "The Case of the Innocent Blacksmith," in *General Washington and the Jack Ass and other American Characters, in Portrait* (South Brunswick, N.J.: Thomas Yosloff, 1969), 215, 337 n. The portrait differs, in particular, from contemporary representations of smithies by Neagle's teacher Bass Otis in that the focus is not primarily on the processes and relations of production but on the figure of the producer.

7. Powell, "Innocent Blacksmith," 330–34 n.

8. For an engraving of the the *Diligent*, see Powell, "Innocent Blacksmith," 128ff.

9. Powell, "Innocent Blacksmith," 336 n.

10. William Dunlap, *A History of the Rise and Progress of the Arts of Design in the United States* (Boston: C. E. Goodspeed & Co., 1918), 3:169.

11. From an unidentified review in the Historical Society of Pennsylvania, quoted in Robert W. Torchia, *John Neagle, Philadelphia Portrait Painter* (Philadelphia: Historical Society of Pennsylvania, 1989), 83, 91 n. "[R]ecollections of the equality of mankind in everything but mind [are stimulated by the portrait] since wealth and power and fashion cannot save their owner from standing in the pictured hall looking delightfully cheek by jowl with the labourer at his forge, when genius gives the word." Scrapbook I, HSP.

12. Lyon, *Narrative*, 6.

13. Ibid., 75.

14. Richard Brown, *Knowledge Is Power: The Diffusion of Information in Early America, 1700–1865* (New York: Oxford University Press, 1989); *America's Wooden Age: Aspects of Its Early Technology*, ed. Brook Hindle (Tarrytown, N.Y.: Sleepy Hollow Restorations, 1975); Hindle, *Engines of Change: The American Industrial Revolution, 1790–1860* (Washington, D.C.: Smithsonian Institution Press, 1986); Leo Marx, *The Machine in the Garden: Technology and the Pastoral Ideal in America* (New York: Oxford University Press, 1964); John F. Kasson, *Civilizing the Machine: Technology and Republican Values in America, 1776–1900* (New York: Grossman Publishers, 1976).

15. Powell, "Innocent Blacksmith," 221.

16. Lyon, *Narrative*, 35.

17. Ibid., 14.

18. Powell, "Innocent Blacksmith," 226.

19. Julia Wrigley, "The Division between Mental and Manual Labor: Artisan Education in Science in Nineteenth-Century Britain," in *Marxist Inquiries: Studies of Labor, Class, and States*, ed. Michael Burawoy and Theda Skocpol (*American Journal of Sociology* 88, supp. [1982]; Chicago: University of Chicago Press, 1982), 36, 40, 48.

20. Charles N. Buck, *Memoirs (1791–1841)* (Philadelphia, 1941), 106, quoted in Chambers, "Pythagorean Puzzle," 232.

21. Thomas Lloyd, *Robbery of the Bank of Pennsylvania in 1798: The Trial in the Supreme Court of the State of Pennsylvania, reported from notes by Thomas Lloyd* (Philadelphia, 1808), 34; Powell, "Innocent Blacksmith," 225–26.

22. *Robbery of the Bank of Pennsylvania*, 34.

23. As Hopkinson argued in 1805: "[T]hey say he kept the doors an unreasonable length of time. . . . Robinson tells you Owen worked on Sunday, but Owen had less to do to the doors than Lyon had. Why was not Owen prosecuted for robbing the Bank as well as Lyon? The Plaintiff did not seek this work, and when he was told the business was urgent he did not court it; on the contrary, he says to Robinson: damn your work take it away—if he was preparing false keys as they would insinuate, he would have spoken more mildly and offered some excuse." *Robbery of the Bank of Pennsylvania*, 80–81.

24. Lyon, *Narrative*, 22.

25. Dunlap, *Arts of Design*, 3:170.

26. John Thom Holdsworth, *Financing an Empire: History of Banking in Pennsylvania* (Chicago: S. J. Clarke Publishing Co., 1928), 1:141.

27. Lyon, *Narrative*, 12, 13.

28. Powell, "Innocent Blacksmith," 231.

29. Lyon, *Narrative*, 31.

30. "I told them (that as a professional man), I knew more about such work, than

the whole of them combined, and put together. Mr. Rawle replied; from that very cause we have got hold of you; as you are from every report . . . an ingenious workman." Lyon, *Narrative*, 33, 34.

31. Ibid., 62.

32. Ibid., 31–32.

33. Ibid., 33.

34. Ibid., 19

35. *Robbery of the Bank of Pennsylvania*, 154.

36. When he tried to send the *Narrative* to his lawyer, Lyon recounts that "[his] writings were debarred going beyond the confines of the prison door." Earlier, when his manuscript had been taken from him prior to his first hearing, he refused to leave his cell, declaring, "I would not go over the prison door, until my writings were restored to me." Lyon, *Narrative*, 49–50.

37. *Robbery of the Bank of Pennsylvania*, 145, 165–66.

38. Quoted in Powell, "Innocent Blacksmith," 224.

39. "To me it is clear as noon-day, that Cunningham was the proper person to be first looked to, and none but those who are wilfully blind, can deny it, unless it be in order to screen themselves from the charge of neglect." Ibid., 77. In defending Lyon in 1805, his lawyers, Joseph Hopkinson and Alexander Dallas, attacked the bank's reading of Lyon: "They may say that a man may have some design in being so particular. . . . [But] must a man's life and liberty be sported with because he tells a straight story . . . [?]" Ibid., 83.

40. Ibid., 147–48.

41. As Adams would write: " 'Foreign meddlers'. . . have a strange, a mysterious influence in this country. Is there no pride in American bosoms? Can their hearts endure that Callender, Duane, Cooper, and [Matthew] Lyon, should be the most influential men in the country, all foreigners and all degraded characters[?]" John Adams, *Works* (Boston, 1850–56), 9:582, quoted in D. H. Gilpatrick, "Nativism in American Journalism 1784–1814," *Proceedings of the South Carolina Historical Association*, 1948, 5; Richard J. Twomey, "Jacobins and Jeffersonians: Anglo-American Radical Ideology, 1790–1810," in *The Origins of Anglo-American Radicalism*, ed. Margaret Jacob and James Jacob (Boston: Allen & Unwin, 1984), 284–99.

42. E. P. Thompson, *The Making of the English Working Class* (1963; New York: Pantheon, 1964), 102–85.

43. *Robbery of the Bank of Pennsylvania*, 183.

44. Eric Foner, *Tom Paine and Revolutionary America* (New York: Oxford University Press, 1976), 241–45.

45. Thomas Paine to George Washington, 30 July 1796, in *The Writings of Thomas Paine*, ed. Moncure D. Conway (New York: G. P. Putnam & Sons, 1894–1908), 3: 213–52.

46. In the press, the Bank of Pennsylvania was regarded as a Jeffersonian-Republican institution, since leading Republicans were in control of it. First chartered in 1793, it ran into debt to the Bank of North America in 1802. At that time, President Jefferson again took (an equally Republican) stand against the Bank of Pennsylvania and banking in general. In response to pleas for assistance, Jefferson refused radical intervention in the affairs of Philadelphia's banks. In his letter, he employed the distinction between specie and paper to complain of the banks' failures to ground them-

selves on the "the precious metals," linking the contagion of paper with the contagious proliferation of banks themselves: "The monopoly of a single bank is certainly an evil. The multiplication of them was intended to cure it, but it multiplied an influence of the same character with the first, and completed the supplanting of the precious metals by a paper circulation. Between such parties the less we meddle the better." Thomas Jefferson to Albert Gallatin, 19 June 1802, in *Works*, 4:439, quoted in Holdsworth, *Financing an Empire*, 142.

47. Foner, *Tom Paine and Revolutionary America*, 183–92.

48. Caesar Rodney, *The Trial of the Boot and Shoemakers of Philadelphia, on an Indictment for a Combination and Conspiracy to Raise their Wages*, taken in shorthand by Thomas Lloyd (Philadelphia: B. Graves, for T. LLoyd and B. Graves, 1806), repr. in *A Documentary History of American Industrial Society*, ed. John R. Commons et al. (Cleveland, Ohio: Arthur H. Clark Co., 1910), 3:197–98.

49. Eighteenth-century English painting legitimated its highest genre, history painting, by virtue of its distance from the mechanical arts and the genres associated with them (such as still life). Under federalism, however, virtually any art could become simultaneously professional and federal by at once distancing itself from and displaying its dependence upon the (disinterested) mechanics of an expanding commodity market, its reproductive technologies, and its displays of those technologies. M. S. Larson points out how the modern nation-state promotes laissez-faire while simultaneously trying to exert control over the market (upon which the existence of the state depends) and how this dual policy mirrors the structure and dynamic of "professions." See Magali Sarfatti Larson, *The Rise of Professionalism: A Sociological Analysis* (Berkeley: University of California Press, 1977).

50. In a second copy, Neagle included a sketch of the theorem, conspicuously signed and dated: "John Neagle, pinx*t.* Philad*a.*, 1829." Lyon had requested the second version of his portrait after the 1826 version of *Pat Lyon at the Forge* was purchased by the Boston Athenaeum.

51. Mary Ann Clawson, *Constructing Brotherhood: Class, Gender, and Fraternalism* (Princeton, N.J.: Princeton University Press, 1989); Margaret Jacob, *The Radical Enlightenment: Pantheists, Freemasons, and Republicans* (Boston: Allen & Unwin, 1981); Dorothy Ann Lipson, *Freemasonry in Federalist Connecticut* (Princeton, N.J.: Princeton Univeristy Press, 1977).

52. Lipson, *Freemasonry in Federalist Connecticut*, 33–34.

53. Chambers, "Pythagorean Puzzle," 228–30.

54. Bass Otis is said (by John Sartain) to have competed with his former apprentice for Lyon's commission; Otis reportedly suggested to Lyon that Neagle was too young for the job, and that Otis would produce a more fitting picture, since he too "came from a smithing family." In 1815, Bass Otis had exhibited the first American painting of an industrial interior, titled "Interior of a Smithy," a firelit scene representing the forging of scythe blades on the floor of a huge beamed room, whose ceiling dwarfs the multiple figures at work below. Neagle's painting obviously eliminates the multiple anonymous figures in the interest of a different representational logic. John Sartain, *Reminiscences of a Very Old Man, John Sartain 1808–1847* (New York: Appleton, 1899), 191–93, quoted in Patrick, "Neagle and Lyon," 188; Gordon Hendricks, "A Wish to Please and a Willingness to Be Pleased," *American Art Journal* 1 (1970): 16–18.

55. Torchia, *John Neagle*, 35–42.

56. Quoted in Dinnerstein, "The Iron Worker and King Solomon," 114–15.

57. Ibid., 114.

58. While Linnaean science was not a Masonic concern, the stamp or living structure of species identity also pointed to the "machine-tool shop" of the Creation, the site where not only all things but the machines for making all things were forged. In Masonic lore, as in other forms of Neoplatonic and Pythagorean mysticism, geometric equations such as the mathematical and musical ratios represented by the Pythagorean theorem were evidence of a Maker's design.

59. Mircea Eliade, *The Forge and the Crucible*, 2d ed., trans. Stephen Corrin (Chicago: University of Chicago Press, 1978).

60. Childs's collection reproduced drawings by well-known artists, including Birch's son Thomas. In 1812, Thomas Birch was just beginning to make a name for himself as a painter of seascapes and naval engagements of the War of 1812. These were painted in a dramatic historical style quite different from his father's line-and-stipple engraving. Thomas Birch's contribution to Childs's collection was "Philadelphia from Kensington." It exactly reproduced the angle of vision of the frontispiece to William Birch's *Views* of 1800, which was, likewise, a view across the Delaware from Kensington. In acknowledgment of his father's precedent, Thomas Birch's view from Kensington opens Childs's *Views* of 1827–30. A quick comparison of William Birch's view from Kensington in 1800 with Childs's engraving of Thomas Birch's view of 1827 reveals many changes, however. The most obvious of these is the elimination of the elm tree that fills the foreground of the earlier work. Known as "Penn's Tree," this elm was popularly believed to mark the site of Penn's treaty with the Indians. It blew down in 1810. In Thomas Birch's painting, instead of Penn's Tree, the ship's mast rises to the right of a rather ominous rock (toward which the foreground rowboat is headed). And instead of the various workmen that people the foreground of his father's picture (boatbuilders, caulkers, dockworkers, and men fishing in the calm water or lounging in the grass), both docks and land have been replaced by rolling water: the city in 1827 seems comparatively afloat, virtually made of masts, boats, and men on shipboard. In the far left, a steamboat makes its way toward the shore, marking a flat and even line across the river (in contrast to the oblique lines of the rowboat and sailing ships). But despite the differences, there are noteworthy parallels: the horizontal lines of the docks, built over the placid river in William Birch's frontispiece are paralleled by the horizontal steamboat in Thomas Birch's painting. And the curves and irregularities of the great elm are replaced by the rolling water and tilting masts, which contrast with the straight line of the steamboat's course as the elm's shape had contrasted with the horizontal and vertical lines of the ships and docks behind it. Here, instead of the elm, the sailing ships seem potentially archaic and at risk. C. G. Childs, *Views of Philadelphia and its Environs from original drawings taken in 1827–30* (Philadelphia: C. G. Childs, 1830). William Russell Birch, *The City of Philadelphia in the State of Pennsylvania North America as it appeared in the Year 1800, Consisting of twenty eight Plates* (Pennsylvania: William Birch, 1800), repr. as *Birch's Views of Philadelphia: A Reduced Facsimile of the City of Philadelphia . . . as it appeared in the Year 1800* (Philadelphia: Free Library of Philadelphia, 1982).

61. Martin P. Snyder, "William Birch: His Philadelphia Views," *Pennsylvania Magazine of History and Biography* 73 (1949): 279; Birch, *The City of Philadelphia* (1800), preface and plate 2, which displays the list of subscribers.

62. Patrick, "Neagle and Lyon," fig. 7, 188–89. Built by Robert Smith in 1774–75, the Walnut Street Gaol was "the largest building in the colonies when erected" (190).

63. Charles Willson Peale, "A Walk Through the Philadelphia Museum," first page of unpublished manuscript (1805), in *The Collected Papers of Charles Willson Peale and His Family*, ed. Lillian B. Miller (Millwood, N.Y.: Kraus Microform, 1980), n.p.

64. William Russell Birch, Autobiography (n.d.), MS, Library Company of Philadelphia, quoted in Snyder, "William Birch: His Philadelphia Views," 281.

65. Birch, introduction to the 1828 edition of *Views* of Philadelphia, quoted in Snyder, "William Birch: His Philadelphia Views," 291–92.

66. Snyder, "William Birch: His Philadelphia Views," 310–11. The list reads: Penns Tree; Second Street; Philadelphia Bank; Pennsylvania Bank; Girard's Bank; United States Bank; State House (Back of the State House); The Late Theater (Chestnut Street); Presbyterian Church no. 10, Taken down in 1820; Water Works in Centre Square Taken Down in 1827; Plate of Four Subjects.

67. Snyder, "William Birch: His Philadelphia Views," 309–10.

68. Childs, *Views of Philadelphia*, plate 11, fifth and sixth pages.

69. Ibid., 3.

70. Ibid., 5.

71. Ibid., 4.

72. Shultz, *The Republic of Labor,* 229–33; Susan G. Davis *Parades and Power: Street Theatre in Nineteenth-Century Philadelphia* (Philadelphia: Temple University Press, 1986), 113–16, 132, 147, 160. Davis writes that there "were no patriotic, multicraft spectacles after the 1830s, although employers continued to use the corporate imagery of labor for their own purposes. Eventually, the enactment of work processes was located in industrious exibitions and museums"(132).

ABOUT THE AUTHOR

Laura Rigal is Associate Professor of English and American Studies
at the University of Iowa.